The Himalayas

The Himalayas
Playground of the Gods

TREKKING, CLIMBING, ADVENTURE

Capt. M S Kohli

VIKAS PUBLISHING HOUSE PVT LTD

VIKAS PUBLISHING HOUSE PVT LTD
Regd. Office: 5 Ansari Road, New Delhi 110002
H.O. Vikas House, 20/4 Industrial Area, Sahibabad 201010
Distt. Ghaziabad, U.P. (India)

1V2K7812

ISBN 0-7069-2387-1

Printed at Jupiter Offset Press, Shahdara, Delhi (India)

ACKNOWLEDGEMENTS

I am grateful to Chris Bonington, Leo Lebon, Guntur Stem, Rommel Verma, Pitts-Tucker, Begum Noon, Frank Hoppe, Harish Kapadia, Romesh Bhattacharji, Air-India, India Tourism Development Corporation/R. Bali, Department of Tourism, Indian Airlines, and Jyoti Khanna who have helped in supplying some photographs and material for the book.

PREFACE

On February 1, 1971, I was deputed by the Indian Navy to serve with Air-India. On joining the airline's Commercial Department in Bombay, I discovered that it had no precise plans with regard to my assignment and responsibility.

After several weeks of briefing and familiarisation with various divisions of the Commercial Department I was still in a quandary — till one fine morning an important development took place. I was invited to address the International Tourism Council. The President of the Council, Mr Homi Taleyarkhan, left the choice of the subject to me but stressed that it have some relevance to tourism.

During the past few years, and especially after our ascent of Everest in 1965, I had given several talks on Everest and other mountaineering and Himalayan subjects, but never on tourism. I was in a fix! Can there be any common ground between the Himalayas and tourism? And then an exciting idea began to evolve — why not promote tourism to the Himalayas? The more I thought of this, the more convinced I became of the tourism potential of the Himalayas. I titled my talk "Operation Himalayas" and spelled out a plan of action to market trekking-tours in the Himalayas. The idea received immediate response and there was wide coverage in the press.

I was now fully convinced of the vast scope and potential of the Himalayas for tourism. And for me this also clinched the issue of my assignment. The next morning I saw Mr S.K. Kooka, the then Commercial Director of Air-India, and suggested that I take up the task of promoting Himalayan Tourism. Mr Kooka, without any hesitation, accepted my suggestion and asked me to go ahead full-speed. Within a few weeks I wrote *Trekking and Climbing in the Himalayas*, which was later revised as *Trek the Himalayas*.

For the first promotional visit I chose Japan. This was primarily because I had met a very large number of Japanese mountaineers visiting India during the past few years and also knew that there was mass interest in mountaineering and trekking in Japan. In Tokyo alone, I was told, there were over 1,000 mountaineering clubs. The response to my tour was even better than expected; it resulted in over 300 Japanese registering for various Himalayan treks. I was naturally delighted.

I followed Japan up with visits to Germany, Switzerland, France, Belgium, Australia, New Zealand and the USA. On a few occasions Tenzing

Norgay, the first Everest climber, or his nephew, Nawang Gombu – the first man in the world to climb Everest twice – accompanied me. I even visited the Scandinavian countries whose people had never before been to the Himalayas. My visit to Stockholm in 1971 resulted in the Swedish Alpine Club deciding to send a team of climbers to Nun Kun. The next year, I was again invited by this club to attend their press conference in Stockholm called on the eve of the departure of its team to the Himalayas. As I took the plane for Paris the next morning, I noticed my photograph with the team under banner headlines. Could the departure of a small mountaineering expedition for the Himalayas be so important? On my request, a Swedish lady in an adjacent seat translated this for me. It read: THE SWEDES ARE BECOMING CRAZY – THEY ARE GOING TO THE HIMALAYAS.

However, the concept of a journey into the Himalayas received acceptance everywhere. I was invited to address several mountaineering and adventure clubs, as well as to appear in prestigious TV programmes such as the David Frost Show and To Tell the Truth.

In two years over 10,000 trekkers were visiting the Himalayas, and the number kept growing steadily every year. The credit for such a phenomenal growth does not go to me; it is the beautiful Himalayas which have drawn them all. My contribution was perhaps that of a catalyst.

The number of mountaineering expeditions to different parts of the Himalayas has also been going up considerably. For peaks like Everest there is a long queue and one has to wait for six to seven years for a booking. With an influx of trekkers, some popular trekking-trails are showing signs of pollution. As this edition goes to press, the Nanda Devi Sanctuary has been declared a National Park and temporarily closed to all trekkers and climbers. While some fragile areas in the Himalayas may need special attention, it is my belief that the Himalayas are too vast to be polluted like several other tourist-infested destinations in the world.

Besides trekking and mountaineering, there are other adventurous Himalayan pursuits such as river-running. In 1967, Sir Edmund Hillary introduced jet-boating in the Sun Kosi River in Nepal. In 1977, I joined him in another jet-boat expedition up the Ganges, from the Bay of Bengal to its Himalayan source. An exciting film and a book on this, *From Ocean to Sky,* has aroused world-wide interest in rafting and jet-boating in the Himalayan rivers. Several Himalayan expeditions and trekking groups today include rafting in their programmes. In 1981, the Himalayas witnessed a new concept – a traverse along its length from east to west. The first two major traverses were by the Indian Army and joint Indo-New Zealand teams. Today, several teams are engaged in such traverses which take from six to 15 months. In 1983 two Britons introduced yet another concept – a Run Across the Himalayas. With such new trends gaining popularity I have included in this book opportunities for river-running, climbing and other adventures in the Himalayas.

In 1981, I was invited to the first ever International Trekking

Convention in Rawalpindi. This gave me an opportunity of visiting Haripur Hazara, a beautiful mountainous town nestling in the hills of the Kaghan Valley, barely 50 miles from Rawalpindi. It was here that I was born and spent the early years of my life. I was returning to Haripur after 34 long years and was naturally full of emotion and excitement.

It was during this Convention, which was attended by several leading mountaineers from different parts of the world, that I decided to include the beautiful Himalayan region of Pakistan, as well as all other Himalayan countries in this book. The Himalayas straddle eight countries, Russia, China, India, Afghanistan, Pakistan, Nepal, Bhutan and Burma. Of these I have not included Russia and Burma as not much trekking activity is noticeable in these eastern and western extremities of the Himalayas.

I also realised that trekkers and mountaineers are easily the greatest repeat-travellers in tourism — those who visit the Himalayas once keep coming back, be it to India, Pakistan or Nepal. And those who have never visited the Himalayas can never really understand fully the meaning of a journey into them. No words or description of the Himalayas can ever do full justice to the beauty and majesty of this enchanting environment; one has to experience this white and timeless world to fully realise its impact. It is also my firm belief that the promotion of Himalayan tourism could become a shining example of regional cooperation among the countries sharing the Himalayas.

Today the Himalayan scene has undergone a great change. Every year, there are around a score of people engaged in a long and arduous Himalayan traverse: around a hundred or two indulging in river-running and about 3,000 climbers attempting various Himalayan summits. But the number of trekkers has gone even beyond 50,000. And the number of those just visiting the numerous hill stations and simply enjoying the cool climate and magnificent scenic views, is still larger. This guide is meant for all such categories of tourists.

In writing this book, I have received considerable help and assistance from several persons, particularly from Mr M.C. Motwani, the Administrative Officer of the Indian Mountaineering Foundation, and Mr S. S. Khera, a former President of the Indian Mountaineering Foundation. The title of this book has also been chosen on the advice of Mr Khera.

I am most grateful to them all.

M.S. KOHLI

CONTENTS

* All three are under the illegal occupation of Pakistan.

INTRODUCTION

The Discovery

"... I hurried still more not to miss the vision for which we had come so far. Then the miracle happened. Folded in light mist, hill after hill rolled away into the distance from beneath my feet, and over this green ocean sparkled the vast icebergs of the Himalaya. Never in my remotest dreams had I imagined such beauty could exist on earth ... time effaces all memories, but the feelings of that moment are branded in me while I live .... Looking back today I see more, that it was not only the revelation of my dreams of youth, but the beginning of an experience which has influenced me more than almost any other ... the discovery of ... a world outside our time."

Lionel Terray, 'Conquistadores of the Useless'

In the summer of 1955, while holidaying in Kashmir, I happened to meet a middle-aged gentleman who was on his way to the Amarnath Cave, a sacred Hindu shrine situated at about 13,000 ft. His wife had knitted him special woollens for the freezing Himalayan weather, and he had made elaborate arrangements for the trip. He was, however, alone and wanted a companion for this arduous journey.

I did not need much persuasion, and promptly decided to join him. With a gabardine suit and thin-soled dancing shoes, however, I was far from being properly equipped for this, my first Himalayan journey. On the advice of some local experts I bought a pair of jute bootcovers and a bottle each of brandy and honey.

Little did I know then that this maiden and brief Himalayan venture would unfold to me an altogether new world whose beauty and charm I had never known before. It was early May and there was plenty of snow en route. On the second day we started sinking ankle-deep and later, waist-deep, in soft snow. My colleague, thinking of his wife and children, decided to return. For me, this was my first experience of going through snow, and I was too excited to give up. Fortunately, a hermit, bare-footed and scantily clad, appeared on the scene, and in his company I completed my first Himalayan trek.

The impact of this three-day trek was overwhelming. The experience of going through snow and ice, the sight of icebergs floating in the Sheshnag Lake — possibly due to falling chunks of ice from the snow-covered mountain face rising from the far end of the lake — the majesty of Himalayan peaks glistening in the sky, the caress of soft and soothing snow which fell on my sweltering face which I experienced in dangerous situations, the spiritual impact of closeness to Amarnath, and above all the sense of achievement, the self-confidence and physical fitness that I felt on my return to Pahalgam, made me a changed man.

I made a silent decision to return to this beautiful world of the Himalayas, whenever possible.

There has been no looking back since. After that year, almost every year I returned to the mountains. During the next ten years, I was on as many expeditions, which included three attempts on Mount Everest, and expeditions to Saser Kangri, Nanda Kot, Kabru Dome, Ratong, Annapurna-III, Trisuli, Nanda Devi East and Nanda Devi. Though a naval officer I was now more in the mountains than at sea — surprisingly, I felt at home in both scapes. The fury of the elements as well as the realisation of one's insignificance in the midst of the mighty Himalayas or deep seas was common to both. The Sino-Indian border conflict in 1972 resulted in my volunteering to serve with the Indo-Tibetan Border Police. For over seven years I continuously wandered in the Himalayas. This afforded me rare opportunities to see the mountains in various seasons and moods, and thus enjoy in full measure this paradise on earth.

It was during these years of intense activity in the Himalayas that I realised that the climbing of a Himalayan summit is three-fourths torture and one-fourth fun. The real pleasure, in fact, lay in the approach and the return marches, which is plain trekking. While trekking, climbing and any other adventure could be a rewarding experience anywhere in the world, it has a special significance in the Himalayas. Here you see unparalleled views of the high peaks and a great variety of flora and fauna. Equally interested are the colourful and innocent mountain people of the Himalayas in whose company one not only enjoys but learns to appreciate some of the finest human qualities, which today are missing in what we call civilised people.

The majestic Himalayas have always held a strange fascination for men all over the world, and have drawn people from all walks of life — artists, writers, poets and scientists. There are blue and emerald lakes and pine forests, slow-moving rivers and swift mountain streams, rugged rocks and snow-covered peaks, grassy downs and meadows resplendent with multi-coloured flowers, snow bridges spanning angry torrents, deep and narrow gorges, high passes enveloped in mist, or a mountain peak rising above masses of clouds, reaching out to the deep blue sky.

There is no fragrance so delightful and so wholesome as the resinous odour of a pine forest, there is no sound so soothing and comforting as the music of pine needles. It has been said that the

2

air of the Himalayas has the sparkle of champagne, for the higher you go the purer it is, the farther you travel the safer you are from the ills of a crowded city.

It is the grandeur, the beauty and the splendour of the Himalayas that will captivate you. The glitter of the morning sun on a snow peak, the majesty of a rugged monolith, the infinite peace of a meadow strewn with daisies, forget-me-nots, buttercups, and wild primulas, the silence of a starry night, the sensuous joy of bathing in the cold waters of a mountain stream will leave a great impact on you.

There are, in the Kulu Valley, the hottest springs in the world. They are said to be radioactive and have amazing curative properties. The local residents cook their food by letting their pots stand in the waters of the spring for an hour or two. Rice is cooked in twenty minutes by tying it in a piece of muslin and keeping it suspended in nature's boiling pan.

In the Himalayas you will be overcome by a strange sense of peace and a feeling of spiritual joy. Some people believe it is a kind of magic worked by sages and rishis who have gone and lived in the mountain solitude since time immemorial and invoked the blessings of the Gods. The call of the mountains is alluring, but the call of the Himalayas is irresistible.

To me, my very first Himalayan journey in 1955 was the greatest discovery of my life; and the experience of several visits to this magnificent region during the subsequent 28 years, my greatest treasure and possession.

PRINCIPAL PEAKS IN THE HIMALAYAS

No.	Peak	Height (m.)	(ft.)
1	Everest	8,848	29,028
2	K 2	8,611	28,250
3	Kangchenjunga	8,598	28,146
4	Shartse Himal	7,502	24,613
5	Lhotse	8,501	27,891
6	Roc Noir	7,485	24,556
7	Makalu	8,475	27,790
8	Dhaulagiri	8,167	26,826
9	Cho-oyu	8,153	26,750
10	Nanga Parbat	8,126	26,661
11	Manaslu	8,125	26,658
12	Annapurna	8,091	26,502
13	Gasherbrum-1 (hidden Peak)	8,068	26,470
14	Broad	8,047	26,402

3

15	Gasherbrum-II	8,035	26,363
16	Gosainthan (Shisha Pangma)	8,013	26,291
17	Annapura-II	7,937	26,041
18	Omi Kangri	7,922	26,132
19	Gyachung Kang	7,922	25,990
20	Kangbachen	7,902	25,926
21	Himalchuli	7,892	25,894
22	Nuptse	7,879	25,851
23	Dakura	7,837	25,713
24	Masherbrum	7,820	25,657
25	Nanda Devi	7,817	25,647
26	Ngojumba Ri Kang	7,806	25,611
27	Rakaposhi	7,788	25,552
28	Namche Barua	7,756	25,447
29	Kamet	7,756	25,447
30	Ulug Mustagh	7,724	25,340
31	Kungur	7,719	25,326
32	Jannu	7,710	25,296
33	Tirich Mir	7,706	25,230
34	Saser Kangri		25,170
35	Minyag Gongkar	7,587	24,893
36	Annapurna-III		24,857
37	Changtse	7,553	24,781
38	Mustagh Ata	7,546	24,757
39	Peak-29	7,514	25,705
40	Jhomsom	7,473	24,522
41	Kommunizma	7,495	24,590
42	Noshaq	7,492	24,581
43	Pobejda	7,439	24,407
44	Ganesh Himal	7,406	24,299
45	Istor-o-Nal	7,403	24,289
46	Churen Himal	7,375	24,184
47	Saraghrar	7,349	24,112
48	Talung	7,349	24,112
49	Tent Peak	7,365	24,162
50	Kabru	7,338	24,076
51	Chamlang	7,319	24,014
52	Chomolhari	7,314	23,997
53	Langtang Lirung	7,245	23,771
54	Langtang Ri	7,230	23,750
55	Baruntse	7,220	23,690
56	Sharphu	7,200	23,623
57	Glacier Dome	7,193	23,599
58	Gurza Himal	7,193	23,599
59	Melungtse	7,181	23,561
60	Nepal Peak Central	7,168	23,500

4

61	Amne Machin	7,160	23,492
62	Gyari Peri	7,150	23,459
63	Gauri Shankar	7,150	23,459
64	Gangapurna	7,150	23,457
65	Pumori	7,145	23,443
66	Nun	7,135	23,410
67	Lenina	7,134	23,407
68	Tilicho	7,132	23,405
69	Api	7,132	23,399
70	Saipal	7,032	23,070
71	Himlung Himal	7,128	23,380
72	Trishul	7,120	23,360
73	Kangto	7,090	23,262
74	Kun	7,087	23,250
75	Big White Peak	7,083	
76	Santopanth	7,075	23,213
77	Rakhiot	7,070	23,197
78	Nupchu	7,028	23,052
79	Khan Tengri	6,995	22,950
80	Machapuchare	6,993	22,944
81	Lamjung Himal	6,931	22,741
82	Siniolchu	6,887	22,596
83	Nanda Kot		22,510
84	Ama Dablam	6,856	22,494

The Himalayan Range

The Himalayas — or if one prefers it, the Himalaya — are the greatest physical feature of the earth. Extending in a 2,400 km curve across southern Asia from the Pamirs, west of the great bend of the Indus River and eastward to the great bend of the Brahmaputra River, this range is over 300 kms. wide in its north-western extensions — the Karakorams and the Hindu Kush — and its stupendous white rampart is composed of hundreds of peaks higher than the highest summits of Europe, Africa and the Americas.

The Himalayas which are shared by India, Nepal, Pakistan, Bhutan, China, U.S.S.R. and Burma, are much more than great snow ranges. They are the source of many great rivers and determine the weather in this subcontinent. They sustain a rich treasure of flora and fauna, and are inhabited by a variety of interesting and simple mountain people. They constitute a watershed of race and empire.

The Himalayas, at one time, were under sea. Geologically

speaking this was not too far back — even today the fossilized
mains of sea life are found on the higher reaches of Everest and
other mountains. It is said that under the stress of elemental forces
the Himalayas rose to their present eminence

The word "Himalayas" is an ancient Sanskrit compound: *hima*,
snow; and *alaya*, abode. The names and legends of the Himalayan
peaks indicate their association with mythology In the Kumaon
Himalaya there is Swargarohini, "the path to heaven," Mount
Kailash in Tibet is considered "the abode of Shiva," and Annapurna
the "goddess giver of food." Chomolungma (Everest) is the
"goddess mother of the world," and Cho-oyu "the turquoise
goddess," and so on.

The names of the Karakoram peaks are also quite interesting,
Masherbrum is translated as "Day of Judgement" or "Doomsday
Peak." Rakaposhi is known as "Dragon's Trail," while Sia Kangri
means "the Ice Mountain of the Rose."

The southern edge of the Himalayas rests against the Indo-
Gangetic plain while the northern edge extends to the high plateau
of Tibet. In between there are three distinct and roughly parallel
mountain zones — Outer Himalayas, Middle Himalayas and the
Great Himalayas. For the trekker and the mountaineer this
three-fold division is so vast that it can be distinguished only from
a high-flying aircraft.

There are six main mountain divisions:

(*a*)   Punjab Himalaya;
(*b*)   Trans-Himalaya (Karakoram and Hindu Kush);
(*c*)   Kumaon Himalaya;
(*d*)   Nepal Himalaya;
(*e*)   Sikkim Himalaya and
(*f*)   Assam Himalaya.

With the exception of Karakoram and Sikkim Himalaya all
other divisions have three zones: (*a*) Shiwalik; (*b*) Lesser Himalaya
and (*c*) Great Himalaya.

The Punjab Himalaya is roughly 300 miles long and 150 miles
wide lying between the Indus on the north-west and the Sutlej
on the south-east. It contains the mountain basins of four rivers:
Jhelum, Chenab, Ravi and Beas. It contains Nanga Parbat,
Nun Kun, the Zanskar Range, Harmukh and Kolahoi

The Trans-Himalaya range consists of Karakoram and its
associated ranges. The Karakorams consist of the mountain region
between the lower Shyok and Indus Rivers to the south, and the
Shaksgam tributary of the Yarkand River to the north. Beyond
the Karumba River on the west, the mountain chain is known as
the Hindu Kush. This region is most heavily glaciered outside
sub-polar latitude and is famous for several peaks including the
second highest mountain in the world, Gasherbrums, K-2,

Masherbrum, Rakaposhi, Saltoro Kangri and Saser Kangri. The Karakoram also contains some of the longest glaciers outside sub-polar regions.

The Kumaon Himalaya is bounded by the Sutlej on the west and the north, and by the Kali on the east, which here forms the western boundary of the kingdom of Nepal. This region includes the peaks of Nanda Devi, Nanda Kot, Kamet, Panchuli Gangotri, etc.

The Great Himalaya in Nepal is surrounded by three large rivers, Karnali, Gandaki and Kosi which form three distinct sections. It contains some of the highest mountains in the world including Everest, Makalu, Cho-oyu, Annapurna, Dhaulagiri and Manaslu.

The Sikkim Himalaya is the smallest of the five, containing the Kanchenjunga massif, the third highest peak in the world. It is less than 50 miles from Darjeeling. The large massif of Kanchenjunga, from west to east, consists of Janu (25,294 ft.), Kangbachen (25,782 ft.), Kanchenjunga-I (28,146 ft.) and Kanchenjunga-II (27,803 ft.). East of this massif there are two fine mountains, Simreu (22,360 ft.), and Siniolchu (22,600 ft.) — known as the most beautiful mountain in the world.

The Assam Himalaya has not been explored much, and very little is known of this region. The western half of it is around the border between Tibet and Bhutan, and the eastern half extends to the frontier between Tibet and Assam and Burma. It contains Chomolhari (23,997 ft.) and Kulha Kangri (around 24,784 ft.). At the eastern end of the Assam Himalaya is Namche Barua.

A Day on a Trek

You are woken up by your mountain guide or his kitchen assistant with the welcome greetings, "Tea, Sahib, tea." Having walked about ten miles and climbed a couple of thousand feet the previous day, you had slept like a dog.

With some effort you stir out of the sleeping bag, undo the zip of your tent and see the smiling guide outside holding a mug of steaming hot tea. With just a three-day trek your appetite has sharpened and you are feeling hungry at six in the morning — a new experience! With each sip of hot and refreshing tea and the rays of the morning sun hitting your tent, your body springs to life. You had never felt so good getting up in the morning.

There is no morning newspaper or disturbing phone calls which may leave you tense even before you start your day. You are completely cut off from the world. Momentarily, you have even forgotten about your job and your daily routine at home. Though only three days have gone by, on a trek it seems like ages.

On getting out of the tent you are greeted by your companions, some of whom are already dressed up. This is no casual or artificial greeting — the human warmth you had forgotten has now come back to you. You have genuinely made some friends amongst the group and you feel really happy in their company. You soon notice a group with eyes set on a Himalayan summit, glistening in the early rays of the sun. You are left speechless for a moment. A hot debate ensues about the identity of the peak. Could it be Everest, Makalu or Ama Dablam? Could it be Nanda Devi, Trishul or Nanda Kot? A few consult their guide books but finally your guide comes to your rescue. He knows all the peaks, and even the history of their various climbs.

After an enjoyable breakfast you are on the move. The going looks difficult in the beginning but you soon get into the rhythm. You stop off and on to hear a bird or photograph a wild flower. Terraced fields across distant slopes, mountain people with happiness and entertainment written on their faces, an ever-changing landscape and mountain peaks, all fire your curiosity. You find the local people, though poor, happier than people in the city.

After three of four hours of walking it becomes quite warm. The sun is now shining bright and you start sweating. Soon, you come across a glacier stream, its waters crystal clear. No persuasion is needed; you take a dip, and are refreshed. No swims in pools at home have ever been so enjoyable as a bath in a cool Himalayan stream. Your mountain guide has already chosen this site for lunch. You feel awfully hungry; it is a simple rice-dal-mutton curry lunch but you relish it much more than a sumptuous dinner in a five-star hotel.

During the leisurely afternoon walk you suddenly confront a colourful building — it is a Buddhist monastery. Your guide takes you inside. You turn the prayer wheel with Buddhist prayers written on it. Prayer flags on tall poles outside the monastery are fluttering continuously. The whole atmosphere is replete with spiritual joy and tranquillity. You move on.

Despite the fact that you have just completed an ascent of over 1,500 ft. you are delighted at the sight of a small village which nestles in an idyllic setting. It is perched on a ridge commanding a view of great scenic grandeur. You stop for a while and find the local people gay and captivating.

Courtyards of houses are full of various fruit trees. One local patient requests you for some medicine. Fortunately there is a doctor in your group and he dispenses the necessary medicine. To say "thank you" the women of the household turn out in gorgeous dresses, carrying big brass plates laden with a variety of fruit. The expression of their gratitude is touching and you are exalted by the peace, contentment and happiness of their lives.

8

You have an irresistible desire to linger awhile but you still have another four miles to go and so, reluctantly, move on. Leisurely you meander along. It is the month of May. You see a riot of colour all along. Rhododendrons are in full bloom; the green of the forest, the passionate glow of the blossoms and the grey and brown of the trees is overpowering. You see all nature's beauty welcoming you.

As you pass through another small village, a groaning and moaning sound is heard from the courtyard of a large house. It is a pig being slaughtered. Two men are attacking the animal with sharp-edged bamboo sticks. Your guide tells you that this is the best method of slaughter to get a delicious quality of meat. You cannot stand the torture and move further.

Much before dusk you arrive at your destination for the day. A cup of hot tea awaits your arrival. Tents are already pitched and the camp comes to life. As the sun sets in the western sky the high peaks in the distance turn crimson-red in the evening twilight. Are they on fire? Could you have imagined such sights? You feel highly pleased with your decision to undertake this trek.

Your guide had purchased some *chhang* and *rakshi* — local brews. The Sherpas and Sherpanis have already started helping themselves and soon they all start dancing around a camp fire. You also join them.

Appetite for dinner is even sharper than that for lunch. You really feel on top of the world. You eat more than twice your usual quantity. As you get your sleeping bag your thoughts go back to your home. Your love for immediate family members has intensified and you look forward to being back with them soon. You are also looking forward to some of the amenities of life to which you have been accustomed, but have missed on the trek. You begin to realise that for years you were just being driven by hectic city life and had no time for introspection. You now think of several new ideas and plans that you would want to act on, on your return.

Just before you fall into deep slumber the realisation becomes stronger and stronger that if one wishes to offset the strains and stresses of this materialistic society, and keep in touch with the simplicity and beauty of nature, if one wishes to possess a healthy body, alert mind, and master one's weakness, both physical and mental, and also to affirm faith in your fellow beings, the Himalayas are there to offer all this and much more.

Ways and Means

Once you have decided in favour of a trekking holiday you will want to make plans and preparations and tackle the problem of ways and means. The first thing to do is to ask yourself a few

9

simple questions. How much time have you at your disposal? What are your powers of endurance? What is the strength of your purse? What do you want to see and do and experience? These are matters which must be settled first.

Having decided upon the length of your trek or climb and just how strenuous you would like it to be, you will need to buy your international passage. Many a time, if you are going to have your arrangements fully organised by a specialised travel agency, it works out better if you buy a full package including the air-fare. Basically there are two major approaches to trekking — with or without a trekking agency. There are several variations and it is useful to know all.

Through a trekking agency: Comprehensive trekking arrangements are possible through several professional and specialised trekking agencies available today, both in the Himalayan countries as well as in most tourist-generating countries.

There are reputed agencies in U.S.A., U.K., Europe, Australia, New Zealand, Japan, and several other countries. They publish attractive brochures offering a variety of treks in almost all Himalayan countries, and use local professional agencies in India, Nepal and other countries for all trekking arrangements.

Though somewhat costlier, this mode of travel is more suitable for first-comers who have no knowledge of the terrain and local conditions or who have no experienced companions with them. Food and accommodation arrangements by trekking agencies are also much more luxurious, and one does not have to spend any time or effort on organisational matters.

These agencies have the services of experienced guides, and their routes and schedules are predetermined. They are also well-equipped to handle such medical problems or emergencies.

With a guide: In India, Nepal and Pakistan, experienced professional guides are available. If one is prepared to spend some time in organising the logistics it would work out much cheaper just to secure the services of a seasoned guide. In Tibet, Bhutan and Afghanistan, however, a complete package is encouraged. These guides, at times, also serve as cooks. They ensure that the party remains on the right trail, and act as liaison officers for interaction with the locals, and also for making day-to-day purchases.

Such an arrangement allows considerable flexibility in the choice of the route, additional stoppages wherever desired, and any diversions. There is also more opportunity for mixing with the local people.

For trekkers with any special interest, such as flora and fauna, photography, geology or anthropology, this approach works out better. You can stop whenever you like and resume your trek at will.

Trekking without a guide: This naturally can be possible either if one is reasonably knowledgeable about the route or if one is on a well-beaten trail such as the one to Mount Everest. In this case you just live off the land. This is the cheapest mode of trekking and is well-suited to budget-conscious travellers.

On popular treks you may meet a number of fellow-trekkers and strike up acquaintanceship. On popular trails in India and Nepal, hundreds of trekkers every year pick up their rucksacks with a sleeping bag, some food, and a stove and set off on a trek. On such popular trails there are several wayside restaurants which also provide shelter and one need not carry a tent.

On these situations one has maximum scope for mixing with local people, learning their customs and traditions and, perhaps, picking up a few words of the local language. While travelling without a guide, it is desirable to follow more populated routes in order to purchase food from villages. If you plan to travel into the higher regions, you must carry with you one tent, a sto⋅ and food.

Travelling with families: Walking in the Himalayan regions does not require any technical ability. You just need to be physically fit. Age is no bar — you may be 70 or just ten. On most of the treks at medium altitudes it should be possible to take all members of your family along. Of course, persons suffering from heart ailments, asthma and diabetes should avoid altitudes beyond 10,000 ft.

With children, perhaps you will need to avoid a strenuous and high-altitude trek but it could be great fun. A strict schedule may not be possible with small children and it is desirable to keep schedules and routes flexible. Amazingly, children are capable of covering large distances, like adults, though special medical and health care for them is necessary.

Infants and very small children can be carried on back carriers or conical baskets such as those used by the hill people. Disposable diapers, if needed, should be brought along as they are not locally available.

Food for children should not pose any problem. After a while children normally get used to the simple local food of rice and dal, although it may be desirable to bring any special favourites such as chocolates etc., with you. If arranged properly a family trek could be a most exciting, rewarding and memorable experience.

River Running

Man has always been dreaming up new adventures. In 1967, Sir Edmund Hillary brought two New Zealand built jetboats and went up the Arun River in Nepal. One of his boats capsized but

11

the four members of the crew managed to swim to safety. Next year, he returned to go up the Sun Kosi, venturing 250 miles upstream to the outskirts of Kathmandu. It was a remarkable adventure.

In 1976 an eight-member team of the Indo-U.S. expedition, led by Lute Jerstad and Avinash Kohli of Wild Life Adventure Tours, successfully completed a 120-mile run on the upper coast down the River Ganges. The expedition used two inflatable rubber rafts with steel rowing frames and wood and fibre-glass oars.

In 1977, Sir Edmund Hillary decided to take another jetboat expedition up the Ganges. This required a lot of assistance from India and finally took the shape of the joint Indo-New Zealand expedition. The Indian side was represented by H.C. Sarin, President of the Indian Mountaineering Foundation, Cdr. Jogindar Singh and myself. The film and book on this expedition have aroused worldwide interest in river running in the Himalayas.

The same year an Indo-German Indus expedition which included the well-known Indian climber, Col. N. Kumar, came down the River Indus in a tiny rubber boat measuring 3.1 to 3.5 m. and weighing only 12 kgs.

In 1979, an Indo-New Zealand expedition led by Col. Balwant S. Sandu climbed Rataban, the 22,000 ft. Himalayan peak in the Central Himalayas and then rafted down the Mandakini, using two fibre-glass skanners and two rubber rafts, from Rudraprayag to Haridwar. The skanners were launched at 28 kms. above the confluence of the Mandakini with Alakananda.

In 1980 I joined an Indo-French expedition using a hovercraft in the Yamuna — a first experience· in the Himalayan rivers.

During the past 15 years or so, many of the great rivers in India and Nepal have been run by rubber rafts, canoes, kayaks and other craft. Apart from the logistic arrangements regarding the transportation of boats to the starting points, and again at the end of the journey to transport them back, there are no serious problems in river running. River running in the white waters is extremely thrilling, but can be risky.

One of the great advantages of rafting is to travel leisurely through the varied terrain and enjoy interaction with the locals and take photographs. In river running each day could hold promise of new discoveries.

In Nepal river running may be done in Trisuli, Seti, Sun Kosi and Narayani. In India there are great rivers like the Ganges, Indus and Yamuna. In Pakistan, the Indus can be very exciting specially during its course through the North West Frontier Province.

Most travel agencies have included rafting in their trekking itineraries. They use the most modern unsinkable rubber rafts and have a set of reasonably trained river guides who have also developed some expertise in cooking and first aid.

River running is usually organised early in the morning until mid or late afternoon when the camp is set up on some secluded area on the beach. Travel agencies have fairly good logistic support and delicious meals are cooked in the camp.

River trips are generally safe and can be enjoyed by families and holiday-makers of all ages. It would be desirable to ensure that the inflatable rubber rafts are of reasonably good quality and are specially meant for river running. Most rafts are specially outfitted for safety and are virtually unsinkable, with an independently inflatable compartment. Each traveller is provided with a life-jacket as well as water-proof kitbags for clothes and water-tight boxes for cameras, etc.

The rowing of these rafts is done by a trained crew, arranged by travel agencies, and they usually conform to international standards.

Some of the river running programmes currently being handled by various travel agencies are:

1. Ladakh Sarai-Stok: One- to four-day trips are organised in this run. Accommodation is arranged in twin-bedded "Yurts." Apart from river running, a sightseeing tour of Stok Village in Ladakh, Stok Palace and Museum are also included in this programme.

2. Journey to Ladakh: A day on the Indus River presents the visitor with a different perspective of the scenic attractions of this city. The river passes through canyons in the Ladakh and Zanskar Ranges; the landscape is breathtaking. From the river, ancient gompas and monasteries, many containing frescoes and statues 700 or 800 years old, can be seen.

3. The Ganges Trip: Deoprayag to Rishikesh is an exhilarating two-day trip and the most exciting of all the river running trips in India. Tourists normally drive from Delhi to Deoprayag where a camp is set — this is the junction of the Alakananda and the Bhagirathi. It is an exciting river run and a two-day programme is planned, with an overnight camp arranged on the banks of the river.

Some of the rapids are dangerous but this area gives you the thrills of fast water, deep gorges and silver sands.

4. The Bagmati River: All through the winter months the Bagmati River is reduced to the size of a stream. But with the monsoon rains, the Kathmandu Valley and the holy Bagmati come to life.

Rising in the foothills to the north of the valley, the Bagmati meanders through the rice fields of the Thimi area before passing along the sacred Hindu temple of Lord Pashupatinath.

It is just below here that the Himalayan river exploration trip begins, offering unique views of this beautiful valley. A peaceful glide through standing rice crops, incredibly green in the summer months, and a long sweep down leads to the Patan Shankamul temple with its magnificent 800 m. river frontage. You slowly drift through the heart of the great cities of Patan and Kathmandu before emerging into the rolling countryside at the southern end of the valley.

Both in India and Nepal travel agencies are marketing several treks which include river rafting as a part of their programme; for example, a 21-day Sun Kosi expedition includes a trek and a nine-day rafting trip.

White water rafting conditions are based on the Himalayan weather pattern. Because of incessant monsoons, no rafting tours are marketed during the summer monsoon season. Post-monsoon conditions are most favourable for rafting in the Himalayan rivers. Even in winter rafting is good fun though at times it can be fairly cold.

The most popular rivers for rafting in Nepal are Trisuli and Sun Kosi. The Trisuli is well suited to adventurers who have limited time at their disposal. Here the road runs along the side of the rivers ensuring speedy availability of provisions and medical aid.

Running the Himalayas

Running the Himalayas is the latest in adventure. With the advent of mountaineering in the Himalayas the institution of mail runners had started; these porters virtually run between the base camp and the mail point. On Everest expeditions, mail runners covered the distance between Kathmandu and base camp from the usual eighteen days to eight days only. No trekkers or mountaineers ran, except that many covered return journeys doing double marches.

In 1952, when I was President of the International Youth Organisation, I came across several adventurers who used to embark on round-the-world journeys on bicycles or motorcycles. There were also a couple of instances of persons embarking on walking trips from one end of the country to the other, taking a couple of years on the trip. In one solitary case, a young man sent in a proposal for running around the world, and just to prove his point, ran from Delhi to Ludhiana, a distance of about 190 miles. But I never imagined this concept would one day spread to the Himalayas.

Running, which has been fairly popular in the West during the past few years, has come to the Himalayas only recently. Some three years ago an American runner completed the journey from Kathmandu to Kala Pathar near Everest Base Camp, in a little

14

over four days — about twice the speed of a mail runner.

In early 1983 two young brothers from Britain embarked on an ambitious project of running across the length of the Himalayas from Darjeeling to Rawalpindi via Kathmandu, keeping as close as possible to the ridge line of the Himalayas.

It is a fascinating journey covering mountain passes and endless valleys, raging rivers and dense forests, Sherpa families and Buddhist monks. But personally I would prefer a leisurely walk, when you can enjoy your surroundings much more than those who run.

Runners have to be careful on steep and precarious slopes. Running downhill could be fun but one has to master the technique. To avoid falling a runner must take short strides and strike heel first with knees slightly bent. Logistic support in these runs is not quite easy and it is desirable that runners get used to live off the land.

In running, the problems of high altitude illness are very vital. In running or hurried walking one may not get properly acclimatised; in such cases there could be serious risks of pulmonary oedema and in such cases it is desirable to descend to lower altitudes as rapidly as possible.

For running in the Himalayan terrain, proper shoes are an absolute must. Ripple-soled running shoes are preferable to waffle-soled shoes which wear quickly and cause blisters. Running without socks may not be comfortable but it helps in preventing blisters and in wading through Himalayan streams.

Runners are bound to sweat a lot. To avoid dehydration one should consume as much liquid as possible. On completing the run, and during stopovers, one should immediately put on a pullover or down jacket to conserve body heat. Exposure in the mountains can be serious.

Seasons for Trekking and Climbing

Mountaineers often blame the weather for failure, and more often than not they are right. The major enemies in the Himalayas are violent blizzards, high winds, and intense cold. The first are rarely predictable and may cause disaster to the careless, but high winds and low temperatures follow more general rules, and trekkers and climbers should know that there are seasons which are more favourable than others, and these may vary according to the altitude of the climb.

Knowledge of Himalayan weather has been gained by analysis of experience in the Himalayas during the last few years.

During most of the year, the prevailing wind at high altitudes throughout the Himalayas and Tibet is westerly and strong, often blowing at gale force. On Everest, especially at South Col, we

.have experienced winds well over a hundred miles an hour. Towards the second half of May, the monsoon sets into action winds from the east. And just before the monsoon hits the Himalayas there is a period of comparative calm known as the pre-monsoon lull, which is ideal for attempts on high peaks. Most of the climbs in the Himalayas have been made during this period.

In general, the season from mid-September to the end of May is ideal for trekking and climbing in Himalayas. Broadly speaking the four seasons are:

Winter   : December to February
Spring   : March to May
Monsoon: June to September
Autumn : October to November

Monsoon: The rainy season in the Himalayas is associated with the summer south-west monsoon. The eastern Himalayas come under its influnce in the first week of June and the western Himalayas, by July. There are spells of intense rainfall separated by periods of comparatively clear weather. This situation depends on the position of the monsoon trough over the Gangetic plains. Whenever the axis of the monsoon trough runs close to the Himalayas, heavy to very heavy rains occur, leading to flooding of some of the tributaries originating in the Himalayas. The reverse is true when the trough moves southward away from the Himalayas, and heavy rains occur over the plains. The duration of each rainy spell is generally three to four days. The monsoon withdraws from the western Himalayas by the first week of September and from the eastern Himalayas by the first week of October. During these three and a half months of rain, the weather is characterised by low and dense clouds, high temperatures and humidity, muddy and slippery trails and an abundance of leeches, especially in Nepal and the eastern Himalayas. The rainfall is higher over the eastern Himalayas and Nepal to the order of 100-250 cms. with the higher ranges in the north receiving about 50 cms. The western Himalayas receive 100-150 cms. along the lower ranges with rapidly decreasing rainfall over the higher ranges in the north which record 10-20 cms. of rain. Ladakh receives just 5 cms. of rain during this season and in Tibet the monsoons are non-existent. Travel is by no means impossible or hazardous during this season, but the general absence of clear views of the Himalayan peaks makes trekking unsatisfactory. In the Kulu-Manali sector and Kashmir rainfall is milder compared to the Himalayas and Nepal.

Autumn: Post-monsoon or autumn (October to November) is a fair weather period, ideal for trekking. The sky is a clear blue and the views of distant peaks in the Himalayas are absolutely unclouded. There may, however, be a few days in October when the eastern Himalayas and eastern Nepal have cloudy weather with thunderstorms, due to the retreating monsoon. The temperature begins to come down, with the minimum dropping to 0°C. At highe elevations of about 10,000 ft. the temperatures drop below zero. Rainfall over the eastern Himalayas and Nepal varies from 10-30 cms. and over the western Himalayas from 5-15 cms., with the higher ranges in the north receiving less than 5 cms. Ladakh receives about 1 cm. of rain or snow during this season.

Winter: The winter season which extends from December to February is characterised by fair weather on most days. However, low pressure systems from the west called "western disturbances" move across the Himalayas four to six times a month. The weather is characterised by extensive cloudiness, rain or snow and occasional hailstorms or snow blizzards. This is also the period when the wind is very strong and avalanches occur in avalanche-prone areas. The temperature during this season generally remains very much below 0°C. Rainfall in the form of snow varies from 15-30 cms. over the western Himalayas. During these coldest months of the year, the clearest views are available and the trekking is probably the most comfortable during this season, except for days when the western disturbance is active.

Spring: During spring, March to May, the Western Himalayas and western Nepal are still prone to two or three western disturbances. Eastern Nepal and the eastern Himalayas may experience thunderstorms late in the afternoon on a few days in a month. During this season the temperatures begin to rise although temperatures over higher ranges continue to remain below 0°C till mid-April. The eastern Himalayas receive from 40-100 cms. of rain whereas it is 15-50 cms. over the western Himalayas and Tibet. Ladakh receives only 5 cms. of rain. Early spring is characterised by excellent views and beautiful flora in the Himalayas. The rhododendron begins to bloom at altitudes of over 1,829 m. (6,000 ft.). These two months are suitable for trekking in Nepal, a start in early February being as good a compromise as any for an Everest trek. Distant views in March may become rather hazy, and the days towards the end of the month are warm in Pokhara Valley and at altitudes below 1,524 m. (5,000 ft.).

For trekking in the Manali area and even in Nepal, April and May are excellent months, after October and November. But at altitudes lower than 2,134 m. (7,000 ft.) these two pre-monsoon months can, at times, be oppressively hot. The aspect, however, may be hazy, a mixture apparently of dust and smoke blown up from the plains, and may conceal views of high mountains, and even the closer wooded hills, for days on end. These months are, however, very good for several species of plant and animal life.

One year in every two or three, on an average, is marked by heavy snowfall above 3,963 m. (13,000 ft.) in late October and

November, and in such a year snow melting may not take place until spring. For climbing expeditions there are normally two suitable seasons — pre-monsoon and post-monsoon. For climbing in the Nanda Devi Sanctuary and further north, where the monsoon has no effect, the entire period from May to October is suitable.

During the winter months there are frequent snowfalls in the outer Himalayas down to below 5,000 ft., in most years, and roads to hill stations may be temporarily blocked. Passes are closed and inhabitants move down from the summer grazing grounds to the valleys.

In some parts, deep in the Himalayas and the Karakoram, there are advantages in winter travel. In Hunza[1] and surrounding areas, for instance, where in the late summer and autumn travellers are driven high up the valley walls, the river-beds and flood-plains become passable, and it is possible to explore regions that earlier in the year are inaccessible; but the cold can be too great for high climbers.

The monsoon is stronger in the east, and its effect is greater on Kanchenjunga and Everest than on Nun Kun or Nanga Parbat; some places where there is a broad valley, as the Vale of Kashmir, there is a marked drop in the rainfall.

There is hardly any rain beyond the Great Himalayas, except in Kashmir, but the main axis is a climatic divide between India and Central Asia, particularly in the east. Tibet is not seriously affected by monsoon conditions, so that an approach to the Great Himalayas from the north can be most deceptive.

Dras, beyond the Zoji-La in Kashmir, and Leh have negligible rainfall. Incursions of the monsoon are infrequent into the Karakoram and Gilgit[1] Nanga Parbat; the extreme western end of the Great Himalayas, however, is somewhat affected by the monsoon.

With regard to avalanches in the Himalayas it may be added that during almost any season in the high Hiamalayas they are an ever present danger. Snow slopes at inclines of over 40° are usually prone to avalanches within about 48 hours of fresh snowfall.

A Word of Advice

Trekking in the Himalayas does not require any special technical ability. The trails used are generally safe and anyone with a little trekking experience and in a physically fit condition can undertake a trek without fear. Age is, in itself, no bar although persons over 60 should normally avoid strenuous and long treks.

An average day may entail eight to 12 miles of trekking, lasting six to eight hours including halts for rest and meals. Medical

[1] Under the illegal occupation of Pakistan.

facilities in most trekking areas, except in towns such as Kathmandu, Pokhara, Kulu, Manali, and Darjeeling, are unavailable. It is, therefore, desirable that a small first-aid kit be carried by intending trekkers. It will also be wise to consult your physician before you finalize your trekking plans.

While in the mountains, always make an early start. This has many advantages. Early morning is the best time for trekking, the air being fresher and more invigorating than later in the day. It has a clear, crystalline quality which adds to the beauty and colouring of the mountain-scape. Photographs taken in the forenoon are usually better than those taken in the afternoon. Streams are easier to ford in the morning, before the melting snows have added to the volume of water. Further, afternoons in the Himalayas are usually cloudy and gusty with drizzle or snowfall. Perhaps the greatest advantage of an early start is an early arrival, for this enables you to rest at the end of the day's march, look around and make a good start the next morning. To begin the day's march when you are fresh, it is desirable that you march steadily for the first two hours and rest for about 15 minutes. Thereafter take a ten-minute rest every 50 minutes or so and don't forget to carry some hot tea or coffee in your thermos flask!

Whether you ride or walk, the man who carries your lunch must have strict instructions to stay with you. He can also carry your spare jersey or windbreaker, which you may need when you stop for a breather.

A good mule will normally carry a load of about 120 kgs. (2,461 lbs.), but on high altitudes and some difficult routes, they may not carry more than 75 kgs. (164 lbs.), as the paths are narrow, the passes steep, and the streams (which have to be forded), treacherous. The only thing to do is to assign a reasonable load to each muleman. The Himalayan muleteer is essentially a cheerful man; he likes his job and is not one for belly-aching.

Riding ponies is a different business. You cannot do anything about their load. If you are a lightweight the pony will smile; if you are not, he will just have to grin and bear you. Of one thing you may be sure — the hill pony will not run away with you. If he does not like you, he will sit down and refuse to go further. When this happens, you must finish the journey on foot or go back for another mount.

The Himalayas are very photogenic. At every step you come upon the breathtaking beauty of a colourful valley, a lake, a mountain, a snow bridge or a roaring cataract. Take a camera and plenty of films. Do not skimp on films. You may never be able to pay a second visit to the place and very often an unpromising scene gives a prize photograph owing to its peculiar composition or some unusual feature. Colour photography is an expensive hobby, but if carefully and judiciously practised, it yields correspondingly greater profit.

If you are a collector of wild flowers you will find here a hundred varieties. Buttercups and daisies, kingcups and wild roses, forget-me-nots of a dozen different colours, violets, anemones, irises, columbines, harebells, blue poppies, primulas, verbenas, lilies of the valley, and cactus roses are all there. Tall, white lilies, ferns of many varieties, wild jasmine, bright blue larkspur, campanula, monkshood, honey-suckle and white clematis delight the eye. You may see a whole bank of white peonies, a cluster of tiny brilliant blue gentians. The alpine flower, edelweiss, grows in such abundance that you will see entire fields covered with it. Goats and sheep feed on it and shepherds use its fluffy wool to catch the sparks from their little fire-making contrivance of flint and steel.

June and July are the months for lovers of wild flowers. At lower heights there are rhododendrons which bloom in March and light up the forest with their scarlet flashes till the middle of April. There is yet a third and rarer variety of rhododendron found on windswept meadows at 3,658 m. (12,000 ft.) also. This is no more than a low scrub clinging to the ground, bearing diminutive flowers of a pale cream colour. On the meadow, you will find anemones of indescribable beauty in shades of light yellow and sky blue. A whole mass of march marigolds growing near a streamlet lights up the grassy bank. An occasional spring crocus winks at you and potentillas in red, salmon, pale pink and orange astonish you by the diversity of their colours. Primroses and rock-roses grow in abundance and the tiny flowers of the wild garlic intrigue you till you crush the stalk and smell it. Take a book on wild flowers with you and add to the fun of the trek by picking and identifying the flowers you see.

The bird-watcher can spend many fascinating hours in the Himalayan forests. The golden oriole with its colours of golden yellow and black, the blue magpie with its long tail performing low-flying acrobatics, the white-cheeked bulbul, the paradise flybutcher and the scarlet minivet, perhaps the most beautiful bird of all, will make you crazy with delight. The effortless soaring of the golden eagle rising higher and higher with the help of air currents it seeks instinctively, the static pause of the kestrel in mid-air before it swoops on its prey like a flash of lightning, the haunting call of the cuckoo and the cries of the whistling thrush rising above the dull roar of a mountain torrent are joys you can experience only in the Himalayas. Whether you are an experienced bird-watcher or a complete novice, you will make your holiday richer and more rewarding if you take with you a pair of binoculars and a book on

Himalayan birds.

Both in India and Nepal stepping over the feet or body of a person is not done; always walk around the person. Also do not offer any food which has already been tasted or bitten into.

In the eastern countries, specially in India and Nepal, it is customary to cleanse oneself with the left hand after a bowel movement. It is, therefore, desirable that you do not offer anything with the left hand only. Either do it with the right hand or perhaps with both.

It is also customary with the local people to take off their shoes before they enter their homes. It is, therefore, desirable to follow this or at least keep this in mind and act according to the situation; particularly in regard to the kitchen or cooking/eating places, one must follow this rule strictly. Most of the villagers often eat squatting on the ground. It is proper not to stand in front of them while they are eating.

On various trekkings you will come across *chortens* and *manewalls*. It is always customary to pass these from the left side in a clockwise direction. Similarly, in case of prayer-wheels around the *chortens* and *manewalls* and also outside the monastery, turn them in a clockwise direction.

Some trekkers inadvertently pick up stones from the *manewalls* with the inscription "Om Mani Padme Hum" and take them home as souvenirs. This is considered a sacrilege and should not be done.

At some crossroads you may come across bits and pieces of a coloured cloth box, a bamboo framework with coloured threads woven in an intricate design lying on the ground. You should be careful not to touch them or step on them. These are the offerings made to various deities. These should also be passed from the left.

In Nepal avoid touching a local person dressed completely in white clothes, white shoes and white cap — this signifies a death in his family.

Equipment, Clothing and Food

Provision of proper clothing and equipment on a trek or an expedition is of vital importance and cannot be over-emphasised. Requirements of clothing for the Himalayan journey are quite different from a weekend backpacking trip. Some items of personal clothing such as down clothing, boots and sunglasses are not very easy to get in the Himalayas, and it is desirable that you bring these along.

Many items of clothing are available with a few mountaineering firms in Delhi, and some good second-hand equipment may be available in Nepal. For Afghanistan, Pakistan and Tibet one should make full arrangements before departure. In the case of mountaineering expeditions it is wise to make complete arrangements for your entire requirement of clothing and equipment before departure.

For both climbers and trekkers, the most important single item is footgear. Blisters and sore feet can ruin a trip. Boots or shoes must be well worn and comfortable.

Shorts are more comfortable in warm weather. In winter and at heights of above 10,000 ft., in all seasons, climbing trousers or warm ski-pants should be worn.

Whatever the time of the year or the altitude at which you are hiking, a considerable range of temperature is experienced during the course of a day. Even in the winter you may, in warm sunshine, be comfortably clad in shirts or a T-shirt at one moment, and be hunting for a warm sweater and windproof coat moments later, should the sun get obscured. It follows that spare clothing must either be carried or be readily on hand. It is as well, too, to be prepared for rain or even snow.

On no account overburden yourself, but on the other hand bear in mind that the porters carrying the beddings and tents may reach camp an hour or more after you in the evenings and it would be annoying to be without, for instance, a small towel if bathing facilities are nearby; and extremely trying to be without warm clothing if the sun sets or a cold wind springs up.

You should be careful to choose your personal clothing keeping in mind that while trekking through the valley it can be warm during the summer and very cold in heights, particularly in bad weather. The following list of personal clothing should serve you as a guideline:

Light rucksack	1
Sleeping bag	1
Shirts	2
Hard-wearing trouser/slacks	1
Woollen trouser for the evening	1
Cotton shirts	2
Pullover (light)	1
Pullover (heavy)	1
Windproof jacket	1
Feather jacket	1
Light raincoat	optional
Sun hat or French beret	1
Woollen mittens	1 pair
Scarf	1
Under-garments	as required
Nylon/woollen socks	2 pairs
Thick socks (woollen)	as required

Handkerchiefs	as required
Toilet requisites	as required
Bathing suit	as required
Sunglasses	as required
Trekking boots (properly fitted)	1 pair
Camp shoes/*chappals*/flat sandals	1 pair
Light nylon duffel bag lined with polythene	1
Polythene bags for cigarettes, books, camera and films	as required
Pocket-knife-cum-tin-opener	1
Torchlight with batteries	1 set
Plastic water bottles	1
Binoculars (optional)	1

Food: Except on popular trails you will not be able to obtain food along the trekking routes. It is, therefore, desirable that you carry adequate supplies with you from the starting point. Tinned or packed food including dehydrated pre-cooked items are available in most places in India and Nepal. Through the Defence Laboratory in India even freeze-dried items can be obtained with adequate notice. In Ladakh, Zanskar and Tibet it is essential that a stove, etc., be carried on the trek.

Food available on the trekking trails depends on the area and season. Generally, rice, lentils, eggs and tea are available in all parts of the Himalayas. In most villages in Nepal and India chicken is also freely available. Mutton may be available only in bigger villages or towns. It would be handy to carry some powdered drinks, soup packets, biscuits, jams, nuts and sugar with you. Vegetables are also available in most places in the Himalayas. For larger groups it would be desirable to take along a skilled cook. Many Sherpas are great experts in cooking.

Specialised travel agencies, who look after trekking arrangements, usually arrange freshly cooked, piping-hot food.

Health and Medical Care

Although trekking in the Himalayas does not require any special technical ability it is important that one should be in good physical shape. Apart from major towns like Srinagar, Pahalgam, Darjeeling, Manali, Leh, Rawalpindi, Peshawar, Abbottabad, Karnal, Paro and Lhasa, most of the villages and small towns with trekking trails do not have medical facilities. It is, therefore, desirable to carry a first-aid kit and also have simple protective innoculations against cholera, typhoid and tetanus.

While on the trek it is important to avoid faster ascents of over 2,5000 m. and spend four to five days acclimatizing oneself before attempting to ascend places of over 3,000 m.

Before embarking on a trek, a few days of jogging and deep-

	of the eyes
Chloromycetin Applicaps	10 for eye infection
Cholomycetin Topical	1 bottle for ear trouble
Crepe bandage — 6" wide	1 for sprains
Relaxyl ointment	1 tube — for sprains, muscle pulls, etc.
Sticking palster — 4" wide	1 roll — various uses, medical and non-medical

Small scissors

Anything you fancy. (But remember you are going to have to carry it!)

N.B.: Blisters — do not open or puncture them.

Apply tight-sticking plaster.

Acute mountain sickness: Mountain sickness depends entirely on individual susceptibility: physical fitness is not a factor. The two main forms of the disease affect (a) the lungs, causing breathing difficulty and blue lips, and (b) the brain, causing drowsiness and unconsciousness.

Rescue Facilities in the Himalayas

In the event of any accident in the Indian Himalayas requiring ground or air evacuation, the Indian Mountaineering Foundation takes suitable action. Air evacuation is arranged with the assistance of the Indian Air Force.

All foreign expeditions to the Indian Himalayas have to take along a liaison officer appointed by the Indian Mountaineering Foundation. The officer is fully briefed regarding the action to be taken in such an eventuality. The nearest police or army post is used for sending telegraphic messages to the Indian Mountaineering Foundation, who promptly get in touch with the Indian Air Force.

Helicopter lifts in the past have been organised within 24 to 48 hours after receipt of the message. At times the local Army posts while sending the message to the Indian Mountaineering Foundation simultaneously inform the Indian Air Force. This expedites evacuation arrangements.

The expedition has to pay the actual cost of the airlift which it can meet from insurance funds. Expeditions are therefore advised that prior insurance must be taken to cover such cases. The usual cost of an evacuation comes to US $2,500.

In Pakistan also similar arrangements for evacuation are organised by the authorities.

In Nepal the Himalayan Rescue Association looks after the rescue work. The HRA is a voluntary non-profit organisation which strives to reduce casualties in the Nepal Himalayas. The Association runs a Trekkers' Aid Post at a height of 14,000 ft. (4,300 m.) in Pheriche, with the cooperation of the Tokyo Medical

breathing exercises help a lot. Cycling, swimming and cross-country runs are also useful in this respect. About a month or two of such training is of considerable help in toning up the body and muscles.

A thorough medical examination by your physician, prior to your departure from home for the trek, is very desirable. Persons suffering from diabetes, asthma and pulmonary hypertension should not travel to high altitudes.

People till the age of 60 and 70, who are physically fit and with some experience of trekking and mountaineering, will have no problems. Those who are not used to it have to be careful and should at no cost rush about.

For precaution against infectious hepatitis, it is generally useful to take a Gamma Globulin injection before departure. This certainly lessens the risk.

To prevent stomach and intestinal problems it is helpful to keep your hands clean and eat in clean places. The following items are useful for inclusion in a first-aid kit:

Chloroquin, Paludrine or Fansidar tablets for malaria.
Sleeping pills for use at high altitudes.
Pain-relieving tablets with codeine for high-altitude headache.
Lomotil or other tablets for diarrhoea.
Moleskin or Telfa pads for blisters.
Tape and band-aids.
Decongestants/antihistamines for high-altitude congestion.
Throat lozenges and cough drops.
Aspirin for mild pain and discomfort.
If you are allergic to any medicine (penicillin for example), bring your own substitutes.
Any special medicines you require. Have your doctor prescribe them on the medical certificate.

In the case of organised treks, these medicines will usually be available with the group leader. For expeditions and very high altitude treks the following medicines may be carried:

Aspirin tablets (5 gms.)	100 for headaches, bodyaches
Mexaform tablets	50 for diarrhoea
Strepto-Paraxin	30 for severe diarrhoea
Stemetil (5 mgms.)	20 for vomiting
Largactil (10 mgms.)	10 for severe vomiting
Penitraid (if you are not allergic to penicillin	30 for mild infections
Terramycin SF (250 gms.)	20 for severe infections
Baralgan	30 for colicky pains
Nebasulf powder	2 tubes for dressing all wounds
Bandages (preferably sterile)	½" & 4" — 3 each
Cotton (sterile)	1 kg.
Locula solution	1 tube for redness, irritation

25

College. It is manned and equipped to treat Mountain Sickness (MS). A new post high up in Manang is also planned.

The following procedure may be adopted in case of emergencies in Nepal:

If a trekker becomes sick or is injured, and is incapable of walking out from the trek, the following options for evacuation are available:

(a) Carriage of patient by porter or pony (if available) to the nearest town, roadhead, or STOL airfield. Airfields are listed below:

(b) In the case of more serious injury or illness needing early hospitalisation, a helicopter may be called.

Whist the medical requirement and location of the patient will naturally determine the course of action chosen, very serious consideration must be given to calling for helicopter evacuation. For example:

(a) Whilst RNAC and the army helicopter service normally react with urgency to a request for helicopters, there are times when they are not immediately available, and it can be a number of days before a rescue flight can be initiated.

(b) The patient's location may not be suitable for a helicopter evacuation because of altitude, terrain or adverse weather conditions.

(c) The cost of helicopter evacuation is extremely high and payment is solely the responsiblity of the patient. Under no circumstances will your travel agency accept liability.

(d) Calling for a helicopter for a case that is shown subsequently to have been unnecessary, jeopardises the chances of future rescue for real emergencies.

The decision to call for helicopter evacuation will start with the despatch of a Sherpa runner with a message to the nearest radio station. A list of these stations is given below. A list of STOL landing grounds is also given.

Radio Stations in Trekking Areas

Jumla Treks
Jumla, Simikot, Gum, Pokhara, Kusma, Rara, Baglung, Beni, Dunahi (checkpost west of Tarakot).

Kali Gandaki/Manang
Pokhara, Kusma, Baglung, Beni, Jhomsom, Hongde, Chame.

Between Pokhara and Kathmandu
Gorkh, Kuncha, Trisuli Bazaar (roadhead and telephone to Kathmandu), Jagat, Namlung.

Langtang
Rasua Garhi, Dhunche.

Helmu
None (Kathmandu).

Everest Treks and Rolwaling Valley
Jiri, Mache Bazaar, Salleri (south of main route: close, if on trek near Junbesi).
Charikot (south of Rolwaling), Lamobagar (Dudh Kosi Valley).

Everest-Biratnagar/Dharan Treks
Chainpur, Taplejung, Phidim, Bhojpur (one fast "Sherpa day" south of Dingla).
Tehrathum, Dhankuta, Dharan (British Army Depot linked to British Embassy).
Kathmandu (civil radio station), Ilam, Chandragarhi (in Terai, south of Ilam).

Arun Valley and Kanchenjunga Treks
Khandbari (three hours north of Tumlingtar), Chepua (Arun Valley, northern checkpost).
Chainpur, Taplejung, Phidim, Bhojpur, Tehrathum, Dhankuta, Dharan, Ilam, Chandragarhi.

Airport/Stol Landing Grounds
Jumla Treks

Jumla	Regular STOL schedule service, radio in town and airport.
Dhorpatan	Pilatus Porter aircraft only, no radio.
Rara Lake	Pilatus Porter aircraft only, airstrip often snowbound in winter.
Simikot	Pilatus Porter aircraft only, no radio.
Dunai	Twin Otter.

Kaligandaki Treks

Balewa (near Baglung)	Regular STOL schedule service once or twice a week. Radio.
Jhomsom	Regular STOL scheduled but often cancelled due to high wind. Radio at police post and at town airport.

Between Pokhara and Kathmandu

Pokhara	Regular AVRO scheduled service. Radio.
Gorkh	Regular STOL service.
Manangbhot	Pilatus Porter aircraft only. Radio.

Helmu-Langtang Treks

Thangjet	West of Trisuli River, roughly opposite Syabru Bensi. No radio.
Langtang	High altitude strip, marginal, for serious cases only. No radio.

Everest Treks (all STOL strips)

Jiri	Scheduled flights once or twice a week. Radio.
Lukla	Regular RNAC scheduled flights. RNAC SSB communiciations at strip.
Tyangboche	Regular flights October to May. Radio at Namche checkpost and Tyangboche.
Phaplu	Fairly frequent scheduled flights.
Lamidanda	(South of Aisyalukharka and Rawa Khola.) Regular scheduled flights once or twice a week.

Phaplu is one day and Lamidanda three days south of the regular route from Kathmandu to Everest.

Everest-Biratnagar/Dharan Treks

Tumlingtar	Between Dingla and Chainpur on the east bank of Arun River, scheduled flights once or twice a week, radio at strip.
Bhojpur	Scheduled flights once or twice a week.
Dharan	Helipad inside British Army Camp. Radio.
Biratnagar	Daily AVRO scheduled flights.
Lamidanda	(South of Aisyalukharka and Rawa Khola.) Regular scheduled flights once or twice a week.

Arun Valley and Kanchenjunga Treks

Tumlingtar	Between Dingla and Chainpur on east bank of Arun River. Scheduled flights once or twice a week. Radio at strip.
Bhojpur	Twin Otter scheduled service once or twice a week.
Taplejung	STOL Pilatus Porter/scheduled service once or twice a week. Radio
Chandragarhi	Twin Otter scheduled service once or twice a week. Radio.

28

You can roughly calculate that a runner will cover three normal day stages in 24 hours provided the total distance does not exceed five or six normal day stages.

If on a Pokhara-based trek or when Kathmandu is reasonably close (such as during the early stages of a walk in an Everest trek or on treks to Helambu or Langtang), and Pokhara to Kathmandu is only slightly more distant than some minor radio station, then send the runner directly to Pokhara or Kathmandu.

Address radio messages for helicopter to HELICOPTER SERVICE, ROYAL NEPAL AIRLINES, TELEPHONE 14511, or to your travel agent.

India

The Country and the People

India, it is often said, is not a country but a continent. It is the seventh largest country in the world, and one out of every seven persons in the world lives in India. From north to south and east to west the people of India are different, the customs are different, the country is different — there are few countries on earth in fact with the enormous variety that India has to offer.

The people of India belong to many different races and religions. They speak about 180 languages, including 14 major ones, and more than 700 dialects.

Many aspects of life in India have stayed the same for hundreds of years; ancient customs may be seen side by side with the latest advances in civilisation and science. For centuries, India meant mystery, wealth and excitement to people of the western world. Early European explorers, traders and adventurers travelled in India for jewels, rugs, silks, spices and other valuables.

India is a sort of inverted triangle with its top formed by the mighty Himalayas. Here, from west to east, you will find the beguilingly beautiful areas of Jammu and Kashmir that include the Zanskar and Ladakh districts; Himachal Pradesh containing Kinnaur, Kulu, Manali, Lahaul, Spiti and Chamba; Uttar Pradesh containing the Garhwal-Kumaon Himalaya with peaks such as Nanda Devi; Darjeeling and its surrounding trekking areas of Sandakphu and Phalut which afford unparalleled views of Everest, Makalu and Kanchenjunga; and Sikkim.

Besides the Himalayas, India is made up of deserts, thick jungles, the world's rainiest areas, a long coastline and tropical lowlands.

On account of its regional and religious variations, India has a great number of interesting and colourful festivals. Most of them follow the lunar calendar and thus fall on different dates each year.

Once you are in India it is desirable to spend a few days seeing a few of its fabled attractions. Apart from the Himalayas it is worth visiting Agra to see the Taj Mahal — a marble monument to an Emperor's love; Varanasi, for the holy Ganges, temples and Buddhist shrines; Amritsar for the Golden Temple of the Sikhs; Kerala for its Kovalam Beach and Periyar Wildlife Sanctuary; Rajasthan for its medieval fort palaces; Tamil Nadu and Mysore for their temple towns; Maharashtra for its fantastic cave temples; and Madhya Pradesh for its forts and wildlife sanctuaries.

Delhi and Bombay are the main gateways to India. For visiting the Himalayas, Delhi, the capital of India, is the ideal starting point. In its monuments, Delhi still carries the impress of Hindu, Muslim, Mughal and British rulers who built their own cities, each a few miles apart. New Delhi is the twentieth century city whose original plan was laid by a British architect, Sir Edwin Lutyens. Parliment House and Rashtrapati Bhawan (the President's Residence) are the architectural summit of a city that is laid out along wide avenues, fountains and gardens. The most breathtaking is Rajpath, a ribbon of asphalt with emerald green lawns on either side, running straight down from Rashtrapati Bhawan to India Gate, where people pay homage at the Memorial of the Unknown Soldiers. Nearby is the National Museum, with a rich collection of Indian art spanning the country's history, as well as the National Gallery of Modern Art.

The splendour of Mughal India is evident all through Delhi; the towering thirteenth century Qutab Minar (238 ft. high), Humayun's Tomb — prototype of the better-known Taj Mahal — the Red Fort containing the Diwan-i-Am (Hall of Public Audience) which once held Shah Jahan's jewel-encrusted Peacock Throne and the Diwan-i-Khas (Hall of Private Audience) representing the chiselled perfection of Mughal architecture in white marble, Jama Masjid, the largest mosque in India which is a poem in redstone and white marble, and Chandni Chowk (Silver Square), congested today, but where descendants of the old silversmiths and ivory workers still carry on their trade. Amidst this bustle stands the legendary Sikh shrine, Gurudwara Sis Ganj. Nearby is Rajghat, the spot where Mohandas Karamchand Gandhi, father of the Indian nation and prophet of non-violence, was cremated after his assassination. Adjoining Rajghat is Shantivana (Grove of Peace) where Jawaharlal Nehru, India's first Prime Minister, was cremated in 1964.

Old and New Delhi can be seen ir a day, though it is better to set a day apart for each.

Passports, Visas and Permits

Passports: Nationals of all countries (other than those specified below) including citizens of Sri Lanka (Ceylon) and Pakistan, holders of U.K. and Colonies passports ordinarily resident in Kenya, and British passport holders who are shown as "British Subjects" or "British Protected Persons," require a valid passport with entry, transit or tourist visas for visiting India.

Other citizens of Commonwealth countries and the Republic of Ireland (barring missionaries) and nationals of Nepal (except when coming overland from Tibet when a visa is also necessary) require only a valid passport without a visa. Special endorsements in the passport are required for missionary work.

Nationals of West Germany, Yugoslavia and the Scandinavian countries (Norway, Sweden, Denmark and Finland) do not need visas for a stay upto 90 days in India.

Nepalese and Bhutanese, when proceeding from their respective countries, need no passport or visa.

South Africans of Indian origin do not require visas but should be in possession of valid passports or certificates of identity endorsed for India.

Individuals without nationality or of undetermined nationality (stateless persons, I.R.O. refugees, persons receiving legal and political protection, holders of Nansen Passports, etc.) should have valid passports, identity documents or sworn affidavits with visas for which they should apply at least two months in advance.

Family passports issued by other governments are recognised without discrimination.

Visas: The Government of India issues three kinds of visas, viz. tourist, entry and transit, according to the purpose of visit.

Visas are issued by Indian representatives abroad. In countries where there are no Indian representatives or consular officers, the nearest British representative will advise on the obtaining of Indian visas.

Tourist visas: Effective for a three-month stay in India. Tourists must arrive within six months of the date the visa was issued. The tourist can extend his stay for a further period of three months if he applies to the Foreigners' Regional Registration Offices at Delhi, Bombay, Calcutta or Madras, or any of the offices of the Superintendent of Police in the district headquarters.

An application for a tourist visa should be made on the prescribed application form with three passport-size photographs along with a return or through ticket. Tourists travelling in organised groups by chartered aircraft/ship can obtain a collective visa. Four copies of the list of the passengers with passport particulars should be furnished.

Note: Diplomats when travelling as tourists are granted the same facilities as those given to other tourists.

Entry visas: Entry visas are issued to persons who wish to visit India for purposes of business, employment, permanent residence, profession, etc. Applications for such visas should be accompanied by the following documents: (*a*) three passport-size photographs; (*b*) full particulars of the purpose of visit; (*c*) either a sponsorship letter from the applicant's firm or evidence of the financial status of the applicant or a return/onward ticket.

Entry visas initially issued for a period of three months are like tourist visas, extendable for a further period of three months. For visits exceeding six months, applications should be made two months in advance.

A foreigner resident in India who wishes to make short trips abroad of not more than three months, can obtain a "return visa" from the Foreigners' Regional Registration Offices of the state governments. If the visit abroad is of longer duration, "no objection to return" endorsements can be obtained. Such endorsements are valid for one year in the case of missionaries and six months in the case of others, and within these periods Indian missions can issue re-entry visas on the strength of such endorsements.

Transit visas: Visitors passing through India en route to some other destination are granted transit visas on presentation of through tickets for the onward journey. Holders of transit visas must enter India within three months from the date of its issue. The maximum stay in India permitted is 15 days provided the visa for the country of destination is valid for this period. Two-way transit visas can also be obtained for two journeys through India permitting a maximum stay of 15 days on each visit.

Applications for a transit visa should be made on the prescribed form along with three passport-size photographs.

Passengers in direct transit who do not leave the precincts of the airport or the ship do not need transit visas.

Landing permits: Tourists who arrive without a visa may be allowed by the immigration authorities at the port of arrival to land and stay in India for a period of upto 30 days. Known as landing permits, such permission, which will be available for air and sea passengers, may also be made valid for departure from India from a port other than the port of entry. Collective landing permits may also be issued to tourists travelling in organised groups. Temporary landing permits are not granted to tourists entering by land.

Foreigners require special permits to visit areas declared "Restricted" or "Protected."

Restricted and protected areas: There are special regulations regarding restricted and protected areas. For Darjeeling and Jaldapara (West Bengal), Kaziranga and Manas (Assam) and Shillong (Meghalaya) permission for one week can be given by Indian missions abroad by making endorsements in the passport as well as by the foreigners' regional registration offices at New Delhi, Bombay, Calcutta and Madras.

Permits for Darjeeling can also be obtained from the Immigration Officer, at the international airports at New Delhi, Bombay, Madras and Calcutta and from the special officer at Bagdogra airport.

Permits to visit Kaziranga and Manas can also be obtained from the Trade Adviser and Director of Movements, Assam House,

8, Russel Street, Calcutta and for Shillong from the Trade Adviser and Director of Movements, Meghalaya House, 9-10 Russel Street, Calcutta.

Foreign tourists can visit Darjeeling town and nearby places of tourist interest without permits for periods of upto 15 days, provided they travel upto Bagdogra and back by air. Such tourists will be permitted to trek in Sandakphu and Phalut areas provided they inform the Foreigners' Régistration Officer, Darjeeling, 24 hours before departure, and report at police checkpoints at Sandakphu and Phalut on arrival.

Foreign tourists can visit Shillong and the Kaziranga Wildlife Sanctuary for periods of upto 15 days and seven days, respectively, provided they travel upto Gauhati and back by air and travel to Shillong/Kaziranga from Gauhati by the following routes:

For Shillong: Gauhati-Jorhat-Shillong Road,
                 NH 37-Kaziranga.

For Kaziranga: Gauhati-Jhalukbari-NH Division-Jorhat.

Individual foreign tourists can visit Gangtok, Rumtek and Phodang (Sikkim) for upto four days on permits. Foreign tourists travelling in groups of upto 20 can, in addition, visit the Dzongri area for trekking upto 15 days provided they travel from Calcutta to Bagdogra by air and follow one of the following: Bagdogra-Naya Bazar-Pemayangtse-Yaksum-Dzongri, or Bagdogra-Rangpo-Gangtok-Yaksum-Dzongri. The groups will be accompanied by a liaison officer or guide provided by the Sikkim government, who will join them at Rangpo or Naya Bazar or be with the group during their stay in Sikkim. The date and expected time of arrival of the group at Naya Bazar or Rangpo, as the case may be, should be intimated to the Sikkim government in advance.

Applications for permits to visit Sikkim should be made to the Deputy Secretary, Ministry of Home Affairs, New Delhi, at least five weeks in advance from the date of the expected visit. For permits to visit other restricted and protected areas, applications are to be made at least six weeks in advance of the date of the visit to the Ministry of Home Affairs, North Block, New Delhi. For visiting Bhutan, visitors require a visa from the Royal Bhutan government through their missions in New Delhi and New York. They also require transit permits to pass through the restricted areas of India. Applications for transit permits should be made to the Ministry of External Affairs, New Delhi, sufficiently in advance of the date of the visit.

Note: The above-mentioned immigration formalities for foreign tourists travelling in India are not exhaustive and should not be quoted as an authority while discharging legal obligations by foreign or other agents. The factual information included in this and subsequent sections is liable to change from time to time.

Tourists are therefore advised to consult their travel agents or the nearest Government of India tourist office for up-to-date information.

Domestic Flights

Indian Airlines one of the largest regional airlines in the world, transports tourists to various points in the Himalayan ranges, from Jammu and Kashmir in the north-west to Arunachal Pradesh in the north-east.

Indian Airlines has 70 stations on its network, including eight in the six neighbouring countries. Its fleet of 10 Airbuses, 25 Boeing 737s and 20 turbo-prop aircraft criss-crosses over 71,100 unduplicated route kilometres on its network every day, transporting 23,000 passengers daily.

Vayudoot, the feeder airline, which has been launched by the Goverment of India to link inaccessible areas, tourist centres and industrial towns hitherto unconnected by air, covers another 19 points. This vast network includes almost a dozen destinations in the Himalayan ranges which serve as the launching points for all activities connected with trekking, climbing and adventure in the ranges.

Leh, the capital of Ladakh, is the highest point to which Indian Airlines operates its services, both from Srinagar and Delhi (via Chandigarh). This northern-most district of India is 10,400 ft. above sea level, and is the highest altitude in the world where a commercial airline operation is undertaken. This region was thrown open to foreign tourists in June, 1974; since then Leh has become an important and busy centre.

Srinagar, another famous tourist centre, is an important station on the Indian Airlines network and is well connected with the rest of the country by air. Srinagar has a daily airlink with Amritsar, Jammu and Chandigarh and a direct airlink with Delhi, and same-day connecting flights round the year to some of the major metropolises.

Another important and popular spot in the Himalayan ranges is Bagdogra, which provides access to the land-locked mountain state of Sikkim and the kingdom of Bhutan. The famous hill resorts of Darjeeling and Kalimpong are also approached from here. Indian Airlines operates regular daily flights to Bagdogra from Delhi, Patna, Gauhati, Imphal and Calcutta. Indian Airlines flights connect Kathmandu with Delhi, Varanasi, Patna and Calcutta.

The eastern parts of the Himalayan ranges are connected by regular flights to various points like Gauhati, Shillong, Tezpur, Lilabari and Dibrugarh. Vayudoot operates flights beyond Dibrugarh to Tezu in Arunachal Pradesh, with connections to Indian Airlines flights.

In the north-west, Vayudoot operates regular services to Kulu in Himachal Pradesh and Dehradun at the foot of the Kumaon hills. Unscheduled helicopter services by private operator are also available for a hop from Chandigarh to Simla.

Treks in Jammu and Kashmir

Kashmir conjures up before one's mind's eye a land of matchless beauty. It has been variously called "paradise on earth," "an emerald set in pearls," "the Garden of Eden," and so on. Travellers and tourists have spoken in one voice extolling its charms which are varied and, as we shall see, appeal to every want and taste with its alpine pastures, shimmering sapphire lakes, snow-capped mountains and sheer Himalayan pageantry.

The state has three main consituents — Jammu, the Valley, and Ladakh. Geographically, the trekking area can be divided into three parts, as is the case with all Sivaliks. First the Vale, next the gentle mountain resorts such as Gulmarg, Sonamarg and Pahalgam, and finally, rugged vertical country as in Ladakh-Zanskar.

The Vale: The Vale is an oval amphitheatre of irregular contour, broken by ridges and broad receding valleys, 129 kms. long and 40 kms. wide, just 883 kms. north-west of Delhi, the capital of India. The Vale marks the site of an old lake bed. South-west, the Pir Panjal Range, snow-capped and rising in many places to about 5,000 m., stands like a wall between the Vale and the plains, with an entrance across a 2,975 m. gap, the Banihal Pass. The Pangi Range of great beauty flanks the Valley on the north-east. Its chief summits can be seen from many parts of the Valley. Harmukh (5,184 m.) dominates the Wulla Lake, Mahadeo (13,013 ft.) rises above the Dal Lake towards the east. The Kolahoi massif is situated at the head of Lidder Valley. The chain of mountains, though beautiful, cannot rival the grandeur of the range to the north where the Great Indus curves east to west traversing large areas.

Cradled thus in the foothills of the Himalaya, the Vale holds a wealth of attractions: meadows (*margs*), wooded and grassy slopes alive with a wide variety of wildly exquisite flowers, shady fir forests, rivers and lakes, glinting snow peaks, all under the canopy of a crystalline blue sky.

Bountiful nature has willingly allowed herself to be tended by the hand of man. The Mughal gardens with pavilions, terraces, water cascades, reflecting pools, fountains, flower-beds, and rows and clusters of trees, are a sheer delight. Nishat Garden (Garden of Light), Shalimar (Abode of Love), and Nasim Bagh are worth a visit. Blue Lakes with a magnificent backdrop of mountains make the loveliness of the surroundings almost magical, restful

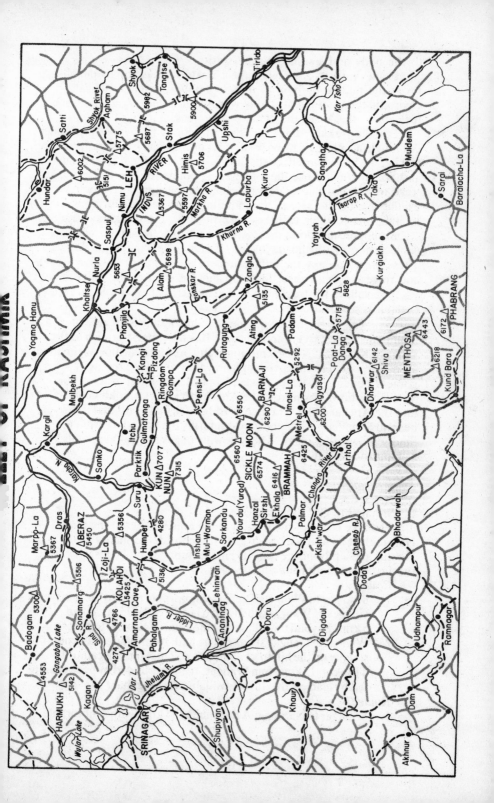

to the body and soothing to the spirit.

From April to November the climate of Kashmir is delightful. From the middle of June to mid-September, Srinagar and its environment are uncomfortably warm and humid. Four thousand feet above the Vale, the climate is perfect.

For the trekker, however, the attractions lie beyond the Vale. Although all places can be visited from Srinagar, it is easier for a trekker to base himself at the hill resorts of Gulmarg, Pahalgam and Sonamarg and use them as staging points for one-day or longer treks to various places, depending upon the time and money available. For the active, the mountains are more alluring, inviting one to their vastnesses. In them lie the trekkers' paradise.

Mountain meadows are scattered all over Kashmir. There is a succession of upland meadows all along the Pir Panjal Range. These *margs* occupy the depressions between the fir-covered slopes and ridges of the highest foothills and the crest of the main range.

The valleys for trekking are the Lidder Valley and Sind Valley. Ladakh is a world apart.

Sind Valley: North of Srinagar the Sind Valley is an area of mountains, lakes, rivers and glaciers. It is the longest branch of the valley of Kashmir, over 96 kms. long, and presents the most diversified aspects, ranging from narrow upland valley and deep rock-girt gorges to open grassy meadowland and village-dotted slopes. The Sind River flows down from the Amarnath and Harmukh Glaciers into the Anchar Lake. The Leh road from Srinagar follows this river beyond Sonamarg while the Zoji-La forms the boundary from the Sind Valley with Ladakh. The following pages list trekking trails in Jammu and Kashmir.

From Srinagar

I. Srinagar to Gangabal Lake
    The lake is one of the longest in the area and lies at the foot of Harmukh at an altitude of 3,572 m. It is considered sacred by the Hindus and a pilgrimage too. It is made annually in August. It can be reached by the following routes:
    Route (a)
    1. Srinagar to Wangat: There is a motorable road to the pretty villages of Wangat situated at a height of 2,075 m. About 5 kms. beyond the village are the ruins of two old temples.
    2. Wangat to Gangabal Lake: The path from Wangat ascends steeply up the hill to a height of 3,657 m. One can camp at Trunkol, 15 kms. fom Wangat. It is surrounded by peaks and fed by glaciers. No fuel is available at Gangabal.
    Route (b)
    1. Srinagar to Naranag: A distance of 54 kms. with a motorable

road.

2. Naranag to Gangabal: A distance of 19 kms. to be covered on foot. Above the ruins of Naranag a path runs steeply uphill to a height of 3,292 m. When the path is wet, it becomes too slippery for ponies or dandies to negotiate. Another 8 kms. bring one to Gangabal Lake.

Route (c)

1. Srinagar to Chattargul: Through Ganderbal and Wayul to Prong where a path branches off to Chattargul.
2. Chattargul to Mahalesh: A steep climb of about six hours. The camping site is exposed and windy. Wood and water can be found in a ravine ten minutes away.
3. Mahalesh to Gangabal: A three-hour hike along the grassy ridges and over the pass at about 3,962 m., a turn to the left and down to the stream, takes one to the Lake.

Route (d)

1. Srinagar-Erin: Situated at a height of 1,983 m., it is about 80 kms. from Erin to Srinagar via Bandipur. There is a rest house and river-bank camping sites at Erin.
2. Erin to Chuntimula to Poshpathis: The 11 km. trek starts by crossing the Erin River near the rest house. The first three or four kilometres of the route, which ascends in stages, is in good condition. It passes the village of Kudara, where there is a rest house, and reaches Poshpa (at 2,440 m.).
3. Poshpathis to Sarbal: A difficult 8.5 m. ascent takes you to Minimarg after which the rest of the 11 km. route to Sarbal is not so difficult. There is a good campsite on the banks of the Sarbal Lake at the foot of Harmukh.
4. Sarbal to Kundsar Lake: The day's 9 km. trek starts off from the left of the Gujar huts. It follows a steep ascent for about 2.5 kms. and then climbs gradually the rest of the way to the Lake at 3,800 m.
5. Kundsar Lake to Gangabal Lake: The 11 km. trek first follows the bank of the Kundsar, then, after about 1.5 kms. climbs over a glacier and dips into a depression for nearly 3 kms. After a further 3 kms. the route veers left and descends 150 m., climbs about 500 m. to the top of the ridge, then drops to the Lake. You need rope, ice-axes and U-bolts for this day's trek because of the crevasses in the glacier. You can camp at the lake (3,572 m.) or at Nund Kol about 1.5 kms. away.

II. Srinagar to Harmukh

Harmukh is reputed to be the abode of the gods.

1. Srinagar to Bandipur: Accessible by bus or car. Ponies

and porters for further travel can be hired here.

2. Bandipur to Erin: About 5 kms. The road is jeepable.
3. Erin to Kudara: 2.5 kms. from Erin is Sumlar, up to which a jeep can be used. From here Kudara is 7.5 kms. away.
4. Kudara to Sarbal: 9.5 kms. on foot. In an hour, a bridge is reached at the junction of two valleys. To the right begins a gradual ascent to Ganaspatra. Sarbal Lake is set in a beautiful valley. There is another lovely lake about one and a quarter hours away.
5. Sarbal to Harmukh: The route for climbing is up the ridge to the north. From Sarbal to the summit and back is a stiff climb of about 12 hours.

III. Srinagar to Narmarg

Narmarg is a favourite resort of tourists situated on the flat grassy summit of a range overlooking the Wular Lake above Alsu Village. It is surrounded by pine forests and in many respects is similar to Gulmarg. There is a forest hut, reached by a fairly easy ascent of about 3,500 ft. from Alsu. It is advisable to make the trek in the early morning.

IV. Srinagar to Yusmarg

Yusmarg is a small meadow, set in the heart of the mountains south-west of Srinagar at a distance of 20 miles. It can be reached via Nagam and Tsar. The road is motorable. Yusmarg is an ideal picnic spot, with huts and a rest house. From Yusmarg short treks can be made to Sange-Safed (Chitta Pathar), Dodha Patri and Sunset Peak (15,576 ft.). Sange-Safed is a rivulet and a tributary of Dudhganga Nallah which flows through Srinagar. Sunset is the highest peak in the Pir Panjal Range.

V. Srinagar to Mahadeo

Mount Mahadeo rises behind the Haewn water reservoir. From Srinagar to Dara Village, the site of an annual Hindu pilgrimage, then towards the east on foot up a narrow ravine following the path on the right bank of the stream. The path then crosses the stream and ascends through sparse forests. Lidwas, a *marg*, is reached; it is surrounded by a pine forest. The western summit of Mt. Mahadeo is easily accessible from here. A higher peak, Handil (4,046 m.), has a fine central position overlooking the Sind Valley.

VI. Srinagar to Kounsernag (72 kms.)

1. Srinagar to Aharabal (72 kms.): Aharabal is situated at an elevation of 246 kms. and is accessible via a good motorable road. The journey takes one through a number of

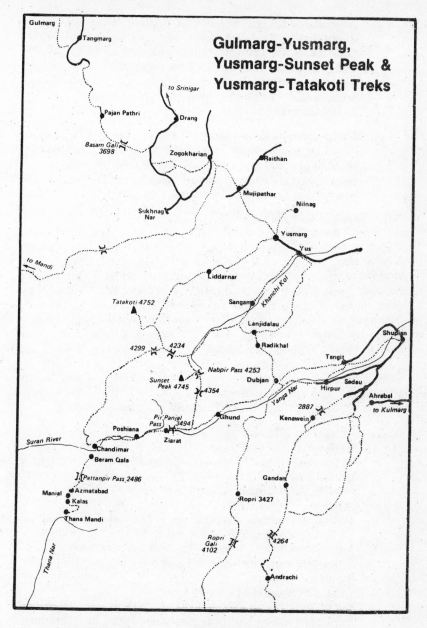

**Gulmarg-Yusmarg,
Yusmarg-Sunset Peak &
Yusmarg-Tatakoti Treks**

Gulmarg

Tangmarg

to Srinigar

Pajan Pathri

Drang

Basam Gali
3698

Zogokharian

Raithan

Mujipathar

Nilnag

Sukhnag
Nar

Yusmarg

Yus

to Mandi

Liddarnar

Khanchi Kol

Tatakoti 4752

Sangam

Lanjidalau

Shupian

4299   4234

Radikhal

Tangit

Nabpir Pass 4253

Sedau

Sunset
Peak 4745

4354

Dubjan

Hirpur

Yanga Nar

Ahrabal

2887

to Kulmarg

Pir Panjal
Pass   3494

Ghund

Kenawein

Suran River

Poshiana

Ziarat

Chandimar

Beram Qala

Pattanpir Pass 2486

Gandan

Manial   Azmatabad

Kalas

Ropri 3427

Thana Mandi

Ropri
Gali
4102

4264

Thana Nar

Andrachi

picturesque villages and rice fields. There is a rest house
and a campsite with water and wood supplies. There is a
waterfall 10 kms. from Aharabal on the conifer forest near
the rest house.

41

2. Aharabal to Kungwattan (9 kms.): This 1½ km. meadow is situated at a height of 2,559 m. The walk starts through thick forest, then climbs gradually along the Vishav River. The plateau of Mahinag (2,989 m.) is reached, surrounded by lovely mountains and a group of ice-cold springs. There are a number of climbing opportunities here for mountaineers.

3. Kungwattan to Kounsernag (13 kms): A straight climb of 914 m. to Kounsernag. The lake is 3½ kms. long and is situated at 3,700 m. in a beautiful high dale. Provisions have to be carried from Srinagar and ponies can be arranged at Shopian or Aharabal.

VII. Srinagar to Lolab Valley

Travel from Srinagar via Bandipur and Alsu. The Lolab Valley is very picturesque but should be visited preferably before July or after August, as it gets very hot in summer. There is a motorable road via Sopore upto Cheridigam, about 97 kms. from Srinagar, with linking roads to different parts of the Valley. The road in Alsu ascends for about three and a half hours. Leaving Nagmarg on the right, descend an equal distance through a fine forest landscape. The Lolab is about 5 kms. wide and four times that in length, with several nullahs. Its beauty lies in its wide park-like expanse of meadow and fields dotted with groves of walnut trees and orchards, among which villages are almost hidden from sight. The valley is fringed with low cedar-clad hillocks and shut in by dense forests where formerly bears abounded.

VIII. Srinagar to Kishtwar (Ladakh)

1. Kashmir Valley to Daksum (100 kms.): The distance can be covered by bus or taxi in three hours. There are camping facilities with wood and water in Daksum and ponies can be hired here. Accommodation has to be booked from Srinagar.
2. Daksum to Sinthan Pass (16 kms.): The trek takes about six hours; wooden huts and wood and water are available.
3. Sinthan to Chatru (8 kms.): The trek takes two hours. Wood and water are available and there is a camping ground.
4. Chatru to Mughal Maidan (9 kms.)
5. Mughal Maidan to Dadpath (8 kms.): There are daily buses from Dadpath to Kishtwar. Accommodation and camping facilities are available to Dadpath.
6. Dadpath to Kishtwar: There are notable waterfalls at Kishtwar. It's a popular take-off point for other treks and mountain climbing.

From Gulmarg

I. Gulmarg to Alpathar Lake

Situated in the Pir Panjal Range, Gulmarg used to be the summer resort of the English officials in Kashmir. Gulmarg, the "Meadow of Flowers," is the queen of hill stations. It is situated at 2,730 m. and occupies an area of about '3 sq. kms. In the spring it is a rolling meadow dotted with countless flowers. It is a base for trekkers. In winter it is a skiing centre, with ski lifts on the slopes. In summer it turns into one of the highest golf courses in the world. There are many huts and hotels around. Situated 45 kms. from Srinagar, it may be reached by way of a village called Tangmarg. Vehicles can be driven all the way to the outskirts of the meadow. Ponies can be hired at Tangmarg for a three-mile trip up a winding trail shaded by giant conifers. From here Nanga Parbat (8,137 m.) is clearly visible.

1. Gulmarg to Khilanmarg (3,045 m. and 5 kms.): Directly above Gulmarg is another meadow called Khilanmarg, from where magnificent views can be had. Khilanmarg has ski fields and is a botanist's paradise. It affords glorious views of the Vale and its surrounding mountain ranges, including Nanga Parbat. It has a fine pony track.
2. Kilanmarg to Alpathar Lake (8 kms.): A picturesque blue lake, a good pony track leads up to it.

II. Gulmarg to Tosa Maidan

One of the most beautiful *margs* of Kashmir, three marches from Gulmarg via Ferozepur Nallah. The path is steep but fit for ponies, and winds through forest ·and meadows. Tosa Maidan can be reached in stages:
1st camp at Danwas
2nd Camp at Tejjan
3rd camp at Tosa Maidan; or
1st camp at Khag,
2nd camp at Riyar,
3rd camp at Tosa Maidan.

III. Gulmarg to Lienmarg (16 kms.)

A day's trek through lovely forests.

IV. Gulmarg to Ningle Nallah (10 kms.)

Issuing from the melting snows and ice, Apharwat and the Alpathar Lake, this stream continues down into the valley below and joins the Jhelum River near Sopore. The path crosses the Ningle Nallah by a bridge and continues on the Lienmarg, another grassy meadow and a good spot for camping.

V. Gulmarg to Ferozepur Nallah (5 kms.)

Accessible from the Tangmarg road or from the outer circular walk, this mountain stream meets the Bahan River at a popular picnic spot known as Waters Meet. The stream is reputed for trout fishing. From here one can continue on to Tosa Maidan, a 5 km. walk.

From Sonamarg: Sonamarg is set high in the Sind Valley. The Nichnai and Thajiwas valleys from the north and south run alongside the harder strata to join the Sind just below Sonamarg. At a height of 2,740 m., Sonamarg is the last major point in the Kashmir Valley before the Zoji-La into Ladakh. Sonamarg is thus a good base for treks and a take-off point for trips to Ladakh. Sonamarg means "meadow of gold" and although this could be due to the profusion of flowers that carpet the meadow in spring, it is also possible that the name derives from Sonamarg's strategic trading position in the days when this was a major route into Central Asia. One of the most popular short walks from Sonamarg is the 4 km. route to Thajiwas, a small valley at the foot of the Sonamarg Glacier. Sonamarg is 80 kms. from Srinagar and is connected by a good, motorable road. Vast camping grounds and a rest house are situated here.

I. Sonamarg to Vishansar and Krishansar Lakes
1. Sonamarg to Nichnai (13 kms.): The march involves a steady ascent of 5,250 ft. to the Nichnai grazing ground. The path is rough, passable for ponies in dry weather. Fuel and water are available in abundance. Nichnai is situated at 3,620 m.
2. Nichnai to Vishansar (13 kms.): The ascent starts by crossing the 4,080 m. Nichnai chain followed by a descent of 2,000 ft. to the lake which is at an altitude of 3,519 m. Water and fuel supply is abundant. Krishansar is good for trout fishing.

II. Sonamarg to Thajiwas (Valley of Glaciers)

The Valley of Glaciers runs south-east to north-west to join the Sind River below Sonamarg. There are interesting walks and scrambles available. Sonamarg to Thajiwas Nar is an easy walk of one and a half hours. Gujar camping ground is available for camping. A three-hour walk takes one to the Nar and the campsite below Glacier 3. The scenery is superb with a great variety of Himalayan flora. It is possible to ski the whole of Thajiwas Nar, particularly in May, June and early July.

III. Sonamarg to Zabnar

A splendid day's walk affords one of the finest viewing points for peaks such as Nanga Parbat, Nun Kun, Amarnath, etc. and also of high rock peaks, steep glaciers and buttresses on the opposite side of the valley. Taking a trek about a mile and a half from the village among the woods near the new tourist bungalow, one can ascend to Zabnar. An ascent can also be made from the Thajiwas Valley at a point where two rivers meet. Of the six glaciers, Number 3 is the longest. There are a number of small peaks. The glaciers are good for skiing in late May, June and July.

IV. Sonamarg to Wangat

Following the same route up to Krishansar as mentioned under Trek I above, the following route may be followed:

1. Krishansar to Dubta Pani: Crossing the Razbal Galli at 4,191 m., following the right bank of the Lake, the route descends to the Gadsar Lake at 3,680 m. and crosses the river at Gadsar Maidan. There is no wood available at Dubta Pani. The camp is at 3,280 m.
2. Dubta Pani to Gangabal Lake (17 kms.): The trek starts with an ascent to the Satsaran Gali at 3,680 m. It is open from June to October. A fine view of Satsar Lake at 3,600 m. can be had. The climb follows the 4,081 m. Zojibal Gali from where can be seen Nund Kol Lake at 3,501 m. The campsite at Gangabal Lake (3,570 m.) has wood, water and trout fishing. The lake at the foot of Harmukh is the site for a major pilgrimage in the month of August.
3. Gangabal Lake to Wangat (19 kms.): The trek descends 1,500 m. to Wangat, situated at 2,050 m.

Lidder Valley: This is one of the most picturesque valleys in the area and is easily accessible. The point where the trekker must station for walks around, is Pahalgam, the village of shepherds. It is a famous tourist resort, 96 kms. from Srinagar, connected by an excellent motorable road. One can reach Pahalgam from Srinagar by car in two hours. The route follows the Jammu road out of Srinagar, then turns up the Lidder Valley through a number of villages with fine views of rice fields and snow-capped peaks all along. Situated at an altitude of 2,134 m., it is lower than Gulmarg, hence night-time temperatures do not drop too low. It has the added advantage of the beautiful Lidder River running right through the town.

Pahalgam is located at the junction of the Lidder and Sheshnag Rivers and is surrounded by fir-covered mountains with bare snow-capped peaks rising behind them. Pahalgam is noted for mountain springs, streams and rivers. The Lidder boasts of some of

Kashmir's best trout fishing. Set at 3,124 m. it is surrounded by forested mountains. From here long and short treks can be planned into the interior; the most famous among these are to Kolahoi and Lidderwat Glaciers and to the Amarnath Cave. Camping equipment is available for hire at Pahalgam from private agencies. Hotels, cottages and camping grounds are available.

I. Pahalgam to Amarnath Cave (3,962 m., 45 kms., five days' return trek)

Amarnath Cave is one of India's most famous pilgrimages, visited by pilgrims in August at the time of the full moon. Inside the Cave is a natural ice *lingam*, the symbol of Lord Shiva, the presiding deity of the Himalaya. The *lingam* forms to its full height during this period. The following is the route.

1. Pahalgam to Chandanwari (13 kms.): Chandanwari is situated at an altitude of 2,900 m. The road is jeepable. There is a PWD rest house where the Sheshnag and Chandanwari Rivers meet. Chandanwari is known for its snow bridge.
2. Chandanwari to Sheshnag (11 kms.): Sheshnag is at an altitude of 12,200 ft. A pony trek is good. One route passes the Pisu Hill and the other lies via Pisu *ghati* (the pilgrim route). Sheshnag Lake, a beautiful freshwater lake, is at 3,700 m. One can camp at Zojibal or at Wanjan, 1½ kms. ahead, off the lake, where a PWD hut and a couple of pilgrim sheds are available.
3. Sheshnag to Panchtarni (11 kms.): Panchtarni means "Five Streams"; a good pony trek from Sheshnag leads to it. There are pilgrim sheds and PWD huts available. Sheshnag Peak with three heads from 5,000 m. to 5,100 m. can be reached from the pilgrim road between Pahalgam and Amarnath Cave.
   Nichhang (5,445 m./17,862 ft.) lies south-east of Panchtarni. It is in view all the way from Sangam to Amarnath on the pilgrim route from Baltal.
4. Panchtarni to Amarnath Cave (8 kms.): The Cave is at an altitude of 12,729 ft. There are several peaks of around 15,500 ft. across the *nullah* south-east of Amarnath. About 6 kms. from the Cave is a high pass leading over into Ladakh. The pass is the lowest point on the north-west ridge of the peak (17,061 ft./5,202 m.) on the Ladakh border. From Amarnath Cave there is a straight trek to the Baltal area close to the Srinagar-Leh road. The distance of 13 kms. can be covered in two hours on pony or in three to four hours on foot. Sonamarg is another 21 kms. from this

point. Hence, the return to Srinagar from the Cave can be made in one day via Sonamarg.

II. Pahalgam to Kolahoi Glacier

1. Pahalgam to Aru (11 kms.): Aru is a little picturesque village at an altitude of 9,270 ft., situated at the confluence of two small rivers. There is a jeepable road which runs right along the right bank of the Lidder River through pine forests. It has grassy mountain slopes which make the walk along the river, upstream, very pleasant. The scenic grandeur — thick, fir-clad mountain slopes and pinnacled ridges — is simply breathtaking. There is a PWD rest house and a forest hut.

2. Aru to Lidderwat (11 kms.): A good pony trek leads to Lidderwat at an altitude of 10,000 ft. One can stay in the PWD rest house but beautiful camping grounds located at the meeting point of the Kolahoi Glacier stream and the stream from the Tarsar Lake, offer better sites.

3. Lidderwat to Kolahoi Glacier (13 kms.): The altitude of the glacier is 11,000 ft. The stretch to the glacier leads east through a pine forest upto Sataljan where the landscape opens out. To the north-west, beneath the glacier, is the Dudh Nag Lake at 4,267 m. The Kolahoi Peak, from which the glacier descends, is 5,485 m..high. One can camp at the base of the glacier. The route follows the river to its main source at the glacier. There are good campsites about 1½ kms. from the snout. Trekkers will have to arrange for ponies and provisions at Pahalgam itself.

III. Pahalgam to Yem Har

Follow the same route up to Lidderwat as described above. From there the route goes from:

1. Lidderwat to Sekiwas (11 kms.): Turning west at Lidderwat, one enters the *nullah* leading to Sekiwas, a pleasant meadow set at 3,420 m. A good camping ground with water and fuel is situated at Sekiwas. To the south are many points over 4,250 m. and pretty little lakes such as Tarsar. To the west is an easy peak, Deo Masjid (4,440 m.).

2. Sekiwas to Yem Har (6 kms.): North of Sekiwas you have to ascend to the pass of Goddess Yem. The hills around form a gigantic rock bowl. The east wall of the bowl sweeps round to a peak, Sekiwas (4,700 m.), the west side curves to the peak, Sentinel (4,609 m.). On the south side is a small lake suitable for camping. From this lake across the Yem Har is Zaiwan, 11 kms. away.

IV. Pahalgam to Tarsar and Marsar Lakes

After reaching Lidderwat as mentioned in Trek II above, a pony trek takes you to the two lakes. The altitude at Tarsar is 12,450 ft. and that of Marsar, 12,530 ft.

From Lidder Valley to Sind Valley

I. Pahalgam to Sonamarg
   1. Pahalgam to Sekiwas: Reaching from Pahalgam via Aru and Lidderwat you have to ascend the Sekiwas Nallah and then take the route.
   2.ˑ Sekiwas to Khemsar (11 kms.): Altitude, 4,115 m. You have to cross the Yem Har Pass (13,500 ft.), an easy descent. No fuel is available. July and August are the best months for a visit.
   3. Khemsar to Kulan (Sind Valley, 14 kms.): Altitude, 7,300 ft. Descent is through a forest to the Sind River. One has to cross the Kulan Bridge at 2,226 m. Fuel is available here.
   4. Kulan to Sonamarg: Good path up the Sind Valley.

II. Pahalgam to Zaiwan area

After reaching Yem Har as in Trek III above, Zaiwan is reached by crossing the river at Kuler, 6 kms. beyond Gund and ascending through pleasant conifer forests for 900 m. The place is ideal, for within range of a day are many fine peaks and glaciers. Ponies, porters, and food are available; camping grounds are fine.

III. Pahalgam to Durin Nar

From the camping ground at the foot of Kolahoi Glacier (see Trek II under Lidder Valley), a route to the north goes over the glacier at the head of Durin Nar which descends to Sarbal in the Sind Valley, 8 kms. east of Sonamarg. The glacier is at a height of 4,400 m.

From Lidder Valley to Ladakh

   1. Pahalgam to Pannikar (Suru Valley): Take the same route as for the Amarnath Cave trek upto Sheshnag, and then follow the route from:
   2. Sheshnag to Rangmarg: The route ascends to the 4,406 m. Gulal Gully (pass) then descends along the left bank of the Gulal Nar down to the mouth of the Sain Nar. Along the right river bank a 7.5 kms. walk takes one to Rangmarg.
   3. Rangmarg to Hampet: The trail follows the Sain Nar until it joins the Kanital Nallah on the left. Then it goes along

the left bank to Hampet, a total distance of 5.5 kms.
4. Hampet to the foot of Lonvilad Gully (22 kms.): The trek
continues along the left bank of the Kanital Nallah to
Baziram. Here the route divides with a long route leading
straight ahead of Pannikar. Following the right bank, the
Lonvilad Gully is reached.
5. Lonvilad Gully (4,460 m.) to Pannikar: Ascending the
Gully, the descent takes one to a glacier which comes from
the Chalong Nallah From here Pannikar is 15 kms. From
Pannikar a road leads north to Karjal or east to the
Zanskar Valley.

Ladakh: Tucked away in the folds of the Himalayas is this lofty
land of mountains, monasteries, monks and myths. Ladakh, the
Moonland, is the highest region in India, comprising two districts:
Leh and Kargil. The average height ranges between 10,000 ft. to
12,000 ft. ASL. Situated approximately between 32-35' north
latitude and 75-80' longitude, Ladakh is a frontier province, and for
centuries the trade routes of Central Asia passed through this
area. Two of the world's mightiest mountain systems surround
Ladakh: the Karakoram in the north and the Great Himalaya in
the south. The Himalayan range, running along its southern
fringes, does not allow any precipitation to filter from the humid
areas of Kashmir and Himachal Pradesh. Consequently, rainfall is
scant and the general terrestrial feature of the area is dry and
desert-like. The draught and the incredible elevation combine to
produce a highly rarefied atmosphere wherein both the seasonal
and diurnal temperatures fluctuate from one extreme to another.
Thus while the mercury levels may shoot up to the 30°C mark at
certain places during the summer, it can dip down to as low as
40°C during the dead of winter.

Culturally, Leh is the seat of Buddhism, while Kargil is made
up of Shia Muslims. The greatest attraction of Leh and Zanskar is
its Buddhist culture, akin to Tibet, with monasteries all over full
of statues, scrolls, wall and canvas paintings, masks, costumes, etc.
In Kargil one can see some of the finest examples of Turkish
architecture in the form of mosques and *imambaras.* Apart from
this, the costumes of the people, their language, food habits, etc.
give them a distinct and unique identity. There are numerous high
peaks with massive glaciers. Some of the famous treks are:
Leh-Kargil via Suru Valley.
Kargil-Zanskar-Manali.
Kargil-Suru-Wardhwan Valley-Pahalgam.
Leh-Markha Valley-Zanskar.
There are many other short treks around Leh.
Trekking in the mountains does not require any special

permission, but all mountain climbing requires written permission from the Government of India, through the Indian Mountaineering Foundation, New Delhi. All unauthorised mountain climbing in India is a violation under the Foreigners' Act and can result in arrest and prosecution.

Porters and ponies can be arranged in various trekking/climbing areas with the assistance of local tourist officers.

Approach: Indian Airlines operates a Boeing service to Leh thrice a week, on Wednesday and Friday from Srinagar, and on Monday from Chandigarh. The road link to Ladakh from the Valley passes over the 11,200 ft. high Zoji-La Pass which remains open from mid-May to mid-November. Depending upon snow the pass may sometimes open in early June also. Daily buses operate from Srinagar to Leh with a night's stopover at Kargil.

Both Leh and Kargil have regular bus services to various points in the district. Jeeps and taxis are also available for full-day or half-day engagements. Further information can be obtained from the tourist transport officers in Leh and Kargil.

Special advice for first visitors: As the region of Ladakh is not only very high but also extremely dry, it is advisable to carry some anti-sun-tan creams, lotions, etc. People going on treks should carry sufficient warm clothing, provisions, juices, medicine, etc. Those travelling in their own vehicles should carry enough fuel and spares. Petrol and diesel are available only at Leh and Kargil and there are no service stations en route.

Restricted area regulations: Tourists are allowed to visit Kargil, Leh and Zanskar only. The limit of the free area is an imaginary line drawn one mile north of the Zoji-La-Kargil-Leh road, one mile east of Leh-Upshi, and one mile west of the Upshi-Manali road. As such a Leh-Manali trek via the Shingo-La Pass is allowed for tourists. Foreigners are not permitted to enter any restricted area without written permission from the Ministry of Home Affairs (Government of India) at New Delhi.

I. Sonamarg to Leh (350 kms. from Leh, 80 kms. from Srinagar)

One can go direct from Srinagar to Leh but Sonamarg, the last village in Kashmir, serves as a take-off point for treks in Ladakh. The important places on the Sonamarg to Leh trek are:
1. Sonamarg to Zoji-La: The 3,505 m. Zoji-La Pass is the ethnographic frontier between Ladakh and Kashmir. Once past the Zoji-La, the terrain also changes: the green valleys suddenly become barren. The wind becomes brisker, the sun warmer. During spring the snow melts and after the rainfall, landslides take place and the road is blocked. From the heights of the Zoji-La, the road passes through the region where the River Dras has its source.

The first settlement after the pass is the town of Matayan on the Gumbar River. The road then passes through the villages of Prandrass and Murad Bagh before reaching Dras.

2. Zoji-La to Dras: 288 kms. from Leh, and 146 kms. from Srinagar, Dras is a 15 sq. kms. valley. Dras Village is situated on the River Dras. There is a PWD rest house here. It experiences heavy snowfall in winter and freezing temperatures. Dras is the second coldest inhabited place in the world.

3. Dras to Kargil: 190 kms. from Leh, and 204 kms. from Srinagar, the road follows the river. Outside Dras stands Maitreya, an equestrian figure. Beyond Tashgam the valley narrows; the road goes to Kharbu, Channingund and then Kargil. Beyond Tashgam the landscape becomes more rocky, with the mountains on both sides of the river soaring to 5,000 m. Kargil is the second largest town in Ladakh, and is the approach base for the Zanskar region.

4. Kargil to Mulbekh: 190 kms. from Leh, and 244 kms. from Srinagar, Kargil was once an important trading centre due to its strategic location at the intersection of old trade routes at the junction of the Dras and Suru rivers, 20 kms. from the Indus. It is a good halting point with hotels, camping facilities and a service station on the road to Leh. The buses from and to Leh stop for the night here. A kilometre beyond Mulbekh is a huge figure of the Maitreya cut into the rock.

5. Mulbekh to Lamayuru: 125 kms. from Leh, and 309 kms. from Srinagar, from Mulbekh the road climbs to the 3,713 m. high Namik-La. The first village beyond the pass is Kargil where it is possible to obtain fuel. The road then winds its way to the 4,091 m. high Fatu-La (139 kms. from Leh, 295 kms. from Srinagar), cool and windy. This is the highest point on the Srinagar-Leh road. The Drogpo Valley and Lamayuru Gompa first come into sight 14 kms. beyond the Fatu-La. The road leads to the village of Lamayuru and on into the valley a short distance beyond. There is a rock relief sculpture of Maitreya, Kushan period.

6. Lamayuru to Leh: 434 kms. from Srinagar, beyond Lamayuru the road winds round many sharp curves. The route lies through Khalatsi (98 kms. from Leh, 336 kms. from Srinagar) and Saspule (62 kms. from Leh and 372 kms. from Srinagar), which is the approach base for Alchi, Likir and Rizong monasteries.

Leh, the capital town of Ladakh, lies about 10 kms. north-east of the Indus at a height of 3,505 m. In and around Leh there are a number of interesting places to visit. Leh was the major halting point on the Asian Silk Route. It is the largest town in the region.

II. There are several places of interest in and around Leh. These are:

1. Hemis Gompa: 49 kms. from Leh, Ladakh's biggest monastery is situated on the Leh-Manali road. It contains quite a few statues in gold and stupas decorated with precious stones. It has a superb collection of *tankhas*, including one which is supposed to be the largest in existence and is exhibited only once every 11 years. On the tenth day of the fifth month of the year of the Fire Dragon, Ladakh gives itself up to the Hemis festival — a ritual to ward off evil and to bring peace and prosperity; and once every 12 years the Hemis festival is celebrated. On this occasion the most precious *tankhas* and other antiques, gold statues and gem-studded stupas are exhibited and dances are held.

2. Thiksey Monastery: 17 kms. from Leh, en route to Hemis Gompa, the Thiksey Monastery provides a panoramic view of the green Indus Valley from its vantage point atop a hill. It has chambers full of statues, stupas and *tankhas*. There are 60 resident lamas and, allegedly, a nunnery.

3. Shey Palace and Monastery: 15 kms. from Leh, also on the way to Hemis Gompa, is the summer palace of the erstwhile Raja of Leh. Set upon a hill, and housing the largest golden-topped victory stupa, the monastery has a 2-storeyed statue of the sitting Buddha, wrought in copper and gold, that stuns the senses. Since the monastery is exclusive, it is preferable to make arrangements for a visit beforehand with the lama.

4. Sankar Gompa: Just 3 kms. from Leh is this monastery that has a formidable collection of statuettes in pure gold and a number of exciting paintings. It is well-lit and may be visited in the evening as well.

5. Spituk Monastery: Just before Leh on the Srinagar-Leh road, on a hilltop overlooking the Indus, the Spituk Monastery boasts of not only some prized *tankhas*, but also a chamber with enormous images of Kali, whose faces are unveiled only once every year. The chamber contains an ancient collection of masks, too. It is recommended that the monastery be visited on Puja day.

6. Fiang Gompa: The monastery of the red sect of the Buddhists, Fiang Gompa lies 20 kms. short of Leh on the Srinagar-Leh road, and possesses some exquisite statues

and *tankhas*.

7. Alchi and Likir Gompas: These two monasteries are to be found near Saspol on the Srinagar-Leh road. They house a great deal of gigantic clay statues of the Buddha in various forms. The primary attraction of these monasteries is, however, their 1,000-year-old wall paintings, which make a visit more than worthwhile.

8. Lamayuru Monastery: On crossing Fatu-La, the highest point on the Srinagar-Leh road, if you take a winding road that descends into the Indus Valley, a sudden bend in the road will reveal a strange villa with a monastery atop it. This is Lamayuru, Ladakh's oldest monastery, with fascinating caves carved out of the mountains.

9. Mulbekh Monastery: The village of Mulbekh, on the way to Namik-La, is a unique sight: a huge rock image to the right of the road. Its monastery is perched on a high rock over the village and the valley, and contains some prized relics.

10. Stok Palace: After crossing the Indus at Choglamser the 200-year-old Stok Palace is reached. It is the only royal palace still in use in Ladakh. The last king, Kunsang Namgyal, died in 1974.

Longer Treks

I. Kargil to Padam: Zanskar area — 240 kms.

Padam, the headquarters of Zanskar, is the central trekking point in Ladakh. It is equidistant from all important stations such as Leh, Kargil, Kishtwar, Lamayuru and Manali (Himachal Pradesh). Each of these places can be reached from Padam in an eight days' trek.

There is a fair weather road that links Zanskar area with the Srinagar-Leh highway at Kargil. It can take vehicular traffic and remains open from early July till late October.

1. Kargil to Sanko (40 kms.): Motorable road. Trucks ply regularly. There is a dak bungalow at Sanko.

2. Sanko-Panikhar (27 kms.): Motorable road. Trucks ply regularly. Panikhar is the approach base for trek routes to Kishtwar and Pahalgam.

3. Panikhar to Tangole (10 kms.): Approach base for Nun Peak. A short cut, steep trek over the saddle. Affords an excellent view of Nun Kun massif.

4. Tangole to Parkachik (12 kms.): Approach base for Nun G.1.

5. Parkachik to Shafat (20 kms.): Approach base for Nun

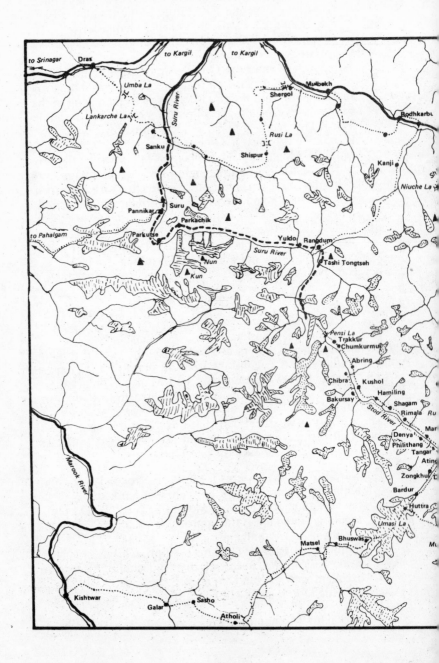

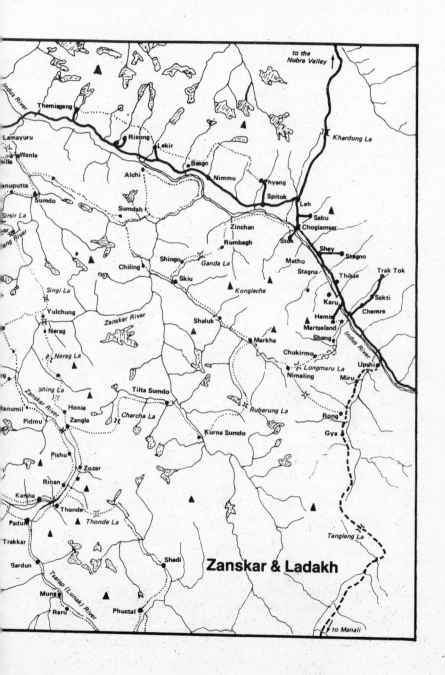

Zanskar & Ladakh

Peak.

6. Shafat to Ringdum (21 kms.): Trek camp at the gompa, seat of an imposing eighteenth century monastery.
7. Ringdum Gompa to Pensi-La (20 kms.): Trek, cross Pensi-La (4,401 m.) and camp on the other side of the pass.
8. Pensi-La to Trakkur (16 kms.): Trek along Doda River downstream, camp at Trakkur. Vehicles can come upto this point beyond which progress is prevented due to unbridged river.
9. Trakkur to Abring (20 kms.): Trek along Doda River downstream, camp at Abring, the first village of Zanskar.
10. Abring to Tungri (32 kms.): The trek passes along the Doda River downstream through Hamilung and Phe (14 kms. from Abring). From Phe one can see the valley leading to Umasi-La on the way to Kishtwar. But one has to cross the Doda River and reach Ating on the opposite bank camp at Tungri. From Tungri a 17 km. long fair weather road leads into the Karsha Valley.
11. Tungri to Sani (6 kms.): Sani is the seat of a famous castle and the Kamika *chorten*.
12. Sani to Padam (6 kms.): Trek along Doda River downstream. One can camp at Padam, the capital town of the Zanskar region.

II. Kargil to Dras

1. Reach Sanko (40 kms.) as mentioned in Trek I above.
2. Sanko to Astakap (14 kms.): The trek from Sanko is upstream along a glacial stream, through the villages of Gona and Thangbo.
3. Astakpa to Umba (13 kms.): The trek continues along the glacial stream through the villages of Masar, Yuljik and Mat.
4. Umba to Umba-La (8 kms.): The trek to Umba-La consists of steep and loose rock. Camp after crossing the Umba-La, about 3 kms. downhill.
5. Photaksar to Chumpado Gongma: The trek follows a stream from Umba-La and is a gradual descent to Dras. One may walk this in two days, camping at Watakular.

III. Lamayuru to Padam; Zanskar

1. Lamayuru to Chila: Cross Wanla (3,245 m.) en route. Chila is a small village with a small gompa and an old castle.
2. Chila to Hanupata: A very steep pass of 4,265 m. with loose rock on trail to Hanupata. Water is a problem as the river is

56

saline. A freshwater well is located half-way to Hanupata, a settlement of 20 houses and a gompa.

3. Hanupata to Photaksar: The route is good with a gradual ascent of 10 to 12 kms. to Sirsir-La (4,900 m.) and a descent to Photaksar. The village is located on a river and is surrounded by steep mountains, and has a gompa. The area is full of yaks.

4. Photaksar to Chumpado Gongma: Another crossing over Singila (5,200 m.), ascent to which is gradual, the trail becomes steep descent for an hour and ascends again for two hours. One may camp here, or take shelter in one of the three houses situated an hour's walk from here.

5. Chumpado Gongma to Linshat Gompa (4 kms.): The trail traversed along mountainside gradually ascends to Linshat Gompa, which is a religious and cultural centre of the area with 60 lamas. A festival is held in July (18-20th). Eggs, meat and *tsampa* are available.

6. Linshat Gompa to Snertse (41 kms.): The trail passes Hulumala (5,000 m.). After the pass the descent is through a wild valley with glacier, snow and water; shepherds spend summer here and wood is available.

7. Snertse to Pidmu (24 kms.): This trail fords a 4 m. wide stream (Omachu) and descends into Zanskar Valley via Hanumil. An easy walk.

8. Pidmu to Pishu (12 kms.): The trail runs upstream along Zanskar River via Zangla Gompa. The river has a rope bridge with a span of 130 to 150 m.

9. Pishu to Padam (30 kms.): The easy trail keeps following River Zanskar upstream and passes the village of Thonde (16 kms.), having a large gompa. Padam can be approached the same way.

IV. Padam to Kishtwar

1. Padam to Tungri (12 kms.): Trek to Tungri along upstream of Doda River.

2. Tungri to Ating (12 kms.): A few kilometres before Ating an extremely dirty glacial stream has to be forded; this must be done as early in the morning as possible.

3. Ating to Huttra (24 kms.): From Ating up a side valley along the left bank of the stream, one can see Zunkool Gompa on rocks after about a 4 km. walk. The path is vague and loses itself among boulders, disappearing into the river at the foot of a cliff. But the river is slow and the bed firm. Two to three hours after passing the gompa there is a huge glacier. At about 1 km. from the snout of

the glacier turn into a hanging valley by crossing a river through a remarkable rock construction, and steep ascent. A good camping site for a night halt.

4. Huttra to Buswas (17 kms.): The locals and monks walk with their sheep from Huttra to Buswas in a single day, taking about 13 hours. The trek involves walk on hard ice, snow and boulder stream moraine across Umasi-La. But keep to the trek in the snow. There is a long descent into the Bhut Nadi Valley. Buswas is an excellent campsite.
5. Buswas to Machail (27 kms.)
6. Machail to Athole (30 kms.)
7. Athole to Galar (32 kms.) From Buswas to Galar the path is well-defined and well used. But one must be careful to cross the river at the right place. One can do this in three days, camping en route or staying at Machail and Atholi.
8. Galar to Kishtwar: From Galar one can take any of the two buses leaving Galar — at 10 A.M. and 5 P.M.

V. Kishtwar to Lehinwan (Kashmir Valley)

1. Kishtwar to Palmar (16 kms.): Palmar (1,650 m.) is a famous old village ahead of Dadpath. The night will have to be spent in tents.
2. Palmar to Akhala (10 kms.): Trek on to Akhala (1,800m.); overnight at the forest rest house.
3. Akhala to Sondar (17 kms.): This trail is through forest, traverse is along the ridge and opens to the beautiful Sondar Village (2,575 m.). A diversion of 16 kms. takes one to the base of Brammah peaks. Overnight in tents.
4. Sondar to Hanzal (16 kms.): Trek to Hanzal (3,000 m.) takes one through breathtaking flora; this is of tremendous interest for flower enthusiasts. Overnight in tents.
5. Hanzal to Yurdu (11 kms.): The trek takes about six hours. From here the route deviates to the Nun Kun peaks, in the east. Overnight in tents.
6. Yurdu to Inshan (18 kms.): The trek consists of a level walk along the River Marwah. Inshan is a meadow bifurcated by the river. From Inshan one can continue along the river to the upper reaches of Wadwan Valley. One can turn to Humpet for going to the Suru Valley or Rangmarg/ Galol Gali for Pahalgam via Sheshnag. Overnight in the forest rest house.
7. Inshan to Lehinwan (16 kms.): A gradual climb leads to the Margan Pass (4,210 m.) and descends to the beautiful and enchanting Valley of Kashmir through Lehinwan. The

distance is covered in about eight hours. Overnight in the forest rest house or straight by bus to Kokernag/Srinagar.

VI. Zanskar-Manali

Drive from Srinagar-Kargil-Tungri. Then trek from Tungri to Shingo-La (5,100 m.), to Darcha. Drive from Darcha via Keylong to Manali.

Nubra Valley

One of the most exciting areas in Ladakh is the Nubra Valley. This valley takes you to the base camp of Saser Kangri and to the famous Karakoram Pass.

I had the pleasure of visiting the Valley in 1956, while on an Indian expedition to Saser Kangri. I can do no better than to produce an extract from my diary which I wrote at that time:

The party left Leh on June 25 and reached Pulu, our first stage. Forty yaks with our baggage had arrived there earlier. Next day we had a long and tiring march over the "Kharding La" (18,380 ft.) on to the village of Kharding Serai, a formidable stage of 17 rigorous miles. Stages in this area are not dictated by the number of miles or terrain difficulties but by availability of small grazing patches in a singularly barren countryside. We left at 3.30 A.M. so that we might cross the Kharding La while the snow was still firm. This was made necessary because of the fact that ours was the first party to cross the pass that season. Incidentally this is the main obstacle on way to Tibet and Yarkand (China) from Leh. Unfortunately, it was cloudy and we could not get the view of Saser Kangri.

The performance of the yaks descending the deep 2,000 ft. snow on the north side of the pass was delightful to watch. At some places I saw them with their bellies on the snow making swimming motions to propel themselves on. What an animal! This shaggy sure-footed animal serves a multitude of purposes. Easily domesticated, the yak is an ideal beast of burden on the high altitudes. Although he moves slowly and rarely covers more than 15 miles a day, he carries heavy burdens and is unfalteringly steady-footed on the steepest and most dangerous trails. This accommodating beast also ploughs the fields. He yields an almost indestructible wool. Boots are made of yak skin and leather, and a suit of yak cloth lasts a lifetime. Finally and most important, the yak provides milk, butter and meat.

One of the most attractive aspects of Himalayan travel is the march between 9,000 and 13,000 ft. There one finds bush green alps, imposing forest, beautiful flowers in colourful carpets, bubbling streams, and butterflies and birds fitting around. In the Karakorams the terrain is quite different, but exciting.

On the third day we entered the famous Shyok Valley, where we stopped under a tree for lunch on the bank of River Shyok, a tributary of the Indus. Khalsar, our halt for that t evening, is situated in the deep ravine, green and distinct with its long line of *maneys*. A *chorten* is a monument erected over the remains of any important local personage, while a *maney* is a long wall fenced with flat stones inscribed with "Om Mane Padme Hum," the mantra of Buddhism.

In Leh and also everywhere else we were greeted by the local people with the words *jooleh*, a general term for greetings. The dress of the Ladakhis is salwar and kamiz covered by an ample woollen gown, fastened at the waist by a bright red sash. The boots of embroidered wool in bright designs, with leather soles and carved toes, are called *papphus*. The headgear of the women is enchanting. Viewed from the back it is like a cobra-head, poised to strike, studded with bright green turquoise, with elephant-like ears of curled black wool on either side. Looking from the front it provides a fascinating frame to fair, frail faces. Theirs are, without doubt, the cleanest of Himalayan villages, which in general are cleaner than those in the plains. The men have very attractive faces, a keen sense of humour and a smile always playing on the edges of their lips, ready to break out into unrestricted laughter at the slightest provocation.

The journey down the Shyok Valley and up the Nubra was very hot, the most exacting of all our marches. A broad sandy valley, it has little vegetation and hot wind blows about. It was more like desert travel for us than an approach to high hills. At Triggur we camped in the school compound by the side of a freshwater channel. We were refreshed en route by bowls of *tarah* (buttermilk) and *shod* (curd) insistently pressed on to us by the hospitable villagers.

Our next halt was to be Panamik, the last village before we got off the old Central Asian trade route. This morning, when we left Triggur the only addition to our caravan was a camel on which was seated a young Ladakhi girl in colourful costumes. Behind her were yaks, horses, coolies and the members of our party. As we left the village, we found villagers singing and dancing in their fields; and the lady on camelback looked as though a queen was travelling in state. A tall, tough Ladakhi, who had lost one arm during the invasion of Ladakh by tribesman in 1947, led the way with the only animal he owned: a little donkey which lugged as much as the rest of the animals!

At Panamik we paid off our caravan and looked forward to a day of rest. The population at Panamik was not sufficient to provide us with the 90 odd porters required to move us up to base camp. By 11 A.M. on June 1 we had 30 porters collected, so that the advance party could leave. It was hoped that the rear party would move up in a couple of days when more porters arrived from the Nubra and Shyok Valleys.

I happened to be in the rear party and fortunately or unfortunately the party could not move up till June 7, when we were able to get the required number of porters. The porters who came back from the base camp refused to make the second trip. They had found the trek very risky. The week I spent in Panamik will remain unforgettable in my life. Our camp was situated in a garden studded with poplars on the bank of a brook and hardly a few yards from the great Nubra River. We received the greatest hospitality from the local village folk, maybe because of the presence of the doctor in our party who proved very useful to the local population. They supplied us with chicken, buttermilk, curd, cheese and vegetables every day. In return we used to distribute *khara* (sweetmeats) to the local *thos* (children).

We learned a lot about the culture and the way of living of Ladakhis in Panamik. There is a hot water spring there which became very popular with us. Of all my travels in the Himalayas, the visit to the Nubra Valley will remain one of the most beautiful trips.

Treks in Himachal
Himachal Pradesh extends from the plains of the Punjab and Haryana to the snowy mountains separating it from Tibet. It lies between north latitudes of 30°-22'-44" and 33°-12'-40" and east longitudes of 75°-45'-55" and 79°-04'-20". Most of the tract lies in the Himalayan region with only some of the lower areas in Siwalik ranges. The elevation varies from 350 m. in the foothills to 6,975 m. in the high hills. Between these elevations, there are a number of mountain ranges of different heights, traversing the tract and enclosing between them valleys of varying width. The topography varies from undulating hills in lower valleys to lofty and precipitous mountains in the interior. Himachal Pradesh is a picturesque country with lofty mountains, perpetual snows, beautiful valleys, extensive forests, alpine pastures and a number of perennial streams and rivers.

Wide range in altitude results in marked variation in the climatic conditions met within different parts of the state. The climate is tropical and sub-tropical in the lower areas, temperate in the middle portions and arctic in the high mountains, snow-clad throughout the year. During winter it snows down to an elevation of about 1,500 m. but does not lie for a long period below about

2,000 m. At elevations of about 3,000 m., the average snowfall is about 3 m. and lasts for about four months, from December to March. The hills above an elevation of about 4,500 m. remain almost perpetually under snow.

The people of Himachal Pradesh are bound together by ties of common religion, tradition and culture. The large majority is Hindu by faith, devoted to traditional gods for whose worship more than 2,000 temples exist in the state. Each village has its own *devta*. Buddhism is largely confined to the Lahaul and Spiti district.

Like all hill people the inhabitants of Himachal Pradesh have to struggle very hard for a living, and like all hill people they forget their hard life in laughter and songs. In the finest of natural settings, the people have developed a high aesthetic sense which expresses itself in their handicrafts and items of daily use.

Himachal Pradesh, with its snowbound recesses, its vistas of unsurpassable beauty, green meadows and pastures, forests rich with fauna, mountain peaks of stark grandeur, and natural ski slopes, is a trekker's delight.

With Manali as the base, treks can be made to various places. The best seasons are early April to end of June and again mid-September to mid-December.

Indian Airlines operate two services a week between Delhi and Kulu. A regular bus service also operates between Delhi and Kulu via Chandigarh, a distance of 539 kms. from Chandigarh and Pathankot to Kulu is 283 kms. and from Simla to Kulu 229 kms. In addition deluxe coaches can be hired from the India Tourism Development Corporation or through any regional travel agent.

Kulu and Manali area: The district of Kulu lies between North latitude 32°-20' and 32°-26' and East longitude 76°59' and 77°-50'. On its west lies the Bara Bhangal range of mountains, separating it from Kangra proper, on the south-west by Dhauladhar (the Outer Himalaya). It is the source of the River Beas and its two major tributaries, the Parvati and Sainj. On the north-east and east, Kulu is separated by Central Himalayan ranges dividing it from Lahaul and Spiti. It contains a total area of 1924 sq. ft. miles — 80 miles long and of varying width, running north to south along with the western side of the great snow range known as mid-Himalaya. There are several trekking-trails.

Chandrakhani to Malana
I. Manali to Bhuntar

1. Manali (1,928 m.) to Rumsu (2,060 m.): A 24 km. trek. Buses ply upto Naggar, 20 kms. from Manali.
2. Rumsu to Chandrakhani (3,650 m.): An 8 km. trek. The

valley is known as the "valley of Gods," and offers a
striking view of Deo Tibba, overlooking the Malana glen
and other snow-crowned giants on the Spiti border.

3. Chandrakhani to Malana (2,100 m.): A 7 km. trek. Malana
comprises two villages, about a hundred yards apart.

4. Malana to Rashol (2,390 m.): A 13 km. trek. Rashol affords
a fine view of the Pin Parbati Range of mountains.

5. Rashol to Kasol (1,580 m.): An 8 km. trek. Kasol has a
charmingly situated rest house. A broad expanse of clean
white sand, it offers a striking view.

6. Kasol to Jari (1,560 m.): Jari nestles on a hillside shelf well
above the Parbati River; there is a clean comfortable and
welcome resting place after a 15 km. march.

7. Jari to Bhuntar (900 m.): A 12 km. trek. Confluence of the
Beas and Parvati. Above, on a projecting bluff, is the site
of the most striking temple — Bijli Mahadev. This trek is
operational from 15 May to 15 October.

II. Manali to Chandrakhani to Malana to Mankaran to Bijli
Mahadev

The trek offers much variety in the landscape and is of great
historical, geological and sociological interest. The Chandrakhani
Pass (3,657 m.) is crossed to get to Malana Village.

III. Manali to Banjar to Jalori Pass to Seraj Valley

This is a 15-day trek. The highest point reached is Jalori Pass
(3,133 m.). This is an easy, low altitude trek to Seraj Valley towards
Simla through villages and fine cedar forests. Alpine flowers bloom
during April-May.

IV. Manali to Keylong to Udaipur to Miryarnala to Mt. Menthosa
Base Camp

A 14-day trek, the maximum height you can reach is 5,030 m.
This is a most rewarding trek through the famous Lahaul Valley.
After crossing Rohtang Pass, a number of monasteries can be
visited. The best season for this trek is from the middle of June
to the middle of October. Lahaul Valley is not affected by monsoon
rains and the entire valley is bright with alpine flowers during June-
July.

V. Kulu Valley to Lahaul

A 16-day trek, the highest point reached is Hamta Pass
(4,268 m.). This unique route presents a magnificent contrast in
landscapes, a view of the emerald blue glaciated lake of
Chandratai and very close views of Mount Deo Tibba (6,001 m.)
and Mount Indrasan (6,221 m.). The trek is followed by a tour/of

the Buddhist monasteries of Lahaul.

VI. Palampur to Laka Pass (5,100 m.) to Manimahul Lake
(4,200 m.) to Chambo

An 18-day trek, the maximum height reached is Laka Pass
(5,100 m.). This trek is fairly strenuous and presents yet another
interesting and beautiful area of Himachal Pradesh.

VII. Across Baralacha through Chandratal

1. Manali (1,928 m.) to Chhika (2,960 m.): Situated on a long,
    grassy bank sloping down from the cliffs, it is an ideal
    location for the end of the day's march (13 kms.). The
    impressive grandeur of immediate surroundings, the
    nearness of the Tokru-Shakru peaks, the wonderful
    colouring of rock and mountainside, the deep purple early
    morning hues and the golden glories of the setting sun
    constitute this halting place.
2. Chhika to Chhatru (3,360 m.): Over Hamta Pass at a height
    of 4,268 m. in the Lahaul Valley, distant and massive
    mountains dominate the landscape, their serrated peaks
    silhouetted against the deep blue horizon. Offers close
    views of Deo Tibba and the fabled Indrasan Peaks (16
    kms. altogether).
3. Chhatru to Chhota Drara (3,740 m.): A walk through the
    rugged valley (16 kms.).
4. Chhota Drara to Batal (3,960 m.): A 16 km. trek. Batal is
    situated at the foot of Kunzam Pass, which provides the
    main approach to Spiti from Lahaul. The panorama as
    viewed from the top of the pass is enthralling and inspiring.
    On the way is Bara Shigri (*bara* meaning big and *shigri*
    meaning glacier, in Lahauli dialect). The view of the Shigri
    stream emerging from beneath a huge iridescent archway
    of solid ice is a never-to-be forgotten sight. Behind the
    archway lies the Shigri Glacier climbing upto a dizzy height.
    The glacier is a mountainous mass of solid ice, more than a
    kilometre wide and extending over a distance of 10 kms.
5. Batal to Chandratal (4,270 m.): Chandratal means "the lake
    of moon." This lake of exquisite beauty is set on a large
    meadow of edelweiss between a lower ridge and the main
    Kunzam Range, with an outlet into the Chandra River. A
    beautiful view of the Samudra Tapoo Glacier and of the
    Mulkila Range is obtainable. An 18 km. trek.
6. Chandratal to Tokpo Yongma (4,320 m., 12 kms. *Tokpo*
    means river and *Yongma* means lower. *Gongma* means
    upper. The river is to be forded and the water is waist deep.

64

7. Tokpo Yongma to Tokpo Gongma (4,640 m.): An 11 km. trek.

8. Tokpo Yongma to Baralacha (4,883 m.): A 10 km. trek. This pass is 8 kms. long. *Baralacha* means "pass with crossroads on summit" (roads from Zanskar, Ladakh, Spiti and Lahaul meet on the top of the pass). On the north-west is the Bhaga River, on the north the Yunan and on the south-east the Chandra.

    Return, through the same route, upto Chhatru, involves six days of trekking. From Chhatru one can cross over to Kulu Valley via the Rohtang Pass in three days.

9. Chhatru to Gramphoo: A 16 km. trek. This is at the foot of the Rohtang Pass. From Gramphoo one can visit, by bus, Keylong — the headquarters of Lahaul and Spiti district. Sha Shur monastery standing nearly 600 m. above the village provides a wonderful view of snowy ranges and glacier fields. On a mountain above the confluence of the Chandra-Bhaga rivers is the most noted monastery in Lahaul — the Guru Chantal or Gondola Gompa.

10. Gramphoo to Marrhi (Grassland) (3,320 m.): A 10 km. trek. The crest of the Rohtang Pass (3,980 m.), affords a widespread panorama of mountain scenery. Looking into Lahaul the eye meets a range of snow-clad peaks, pinnacles, ridges and precipitous cliffs of stark rock, huge glaciers piled with moraine, and deep ravines, the slopes of which are bare and treeless. Almost directly opposite is the well-defined Sonepani Glacier; slightly left are the twin peaks of the Gyephang — jagged pyramid of rock, snow-streaked and snow-crowned.

11. Marrhi to Mandi: A 23 km. trek. The return journey passes through Rahla, where the Beas, after hurtling over a sheer drop of more than 30 m., assumes a respectable size and gets a powerful start on its long journey of about 560 kms. Kothi is a quiet but picturesque spot. Below Kothi for more than 1 km. the Beas flows through a deep gorge, almost a subterranean passage 30 m. or more in depth. The trek is operational during July and August.

    You often listen to the soft muttering of the pious invocation "Om Mani Padme Hum" by the Lamas and religious Buddhists while trekking in these areas of Lahaul.

VIII. Manali to Solang Valley

1. Manali to Solang (2,480 m.): For a lavish spread of natural beauty Manali is the principal showplace of Kulu Valley. Famous for the Hadimba Devi temple and Vashisht hot

springs, Solang offers a view of glaciers and snow-capped peaks.

2. Solang to Dhundi (2,840 m.): A level trek of 8 kms. An alpine plateau. Glimpses of Indrasan and Deo Tibba can be had. The track is along the bank of the Beas River and one turbulent steam has to be forded.
3. Dhundi to Beaskund (3,540 m.): A 6 km. trek. An interesting alpine meadow. Source of the River Beas, the place is associated with the sage Vyasa, author of the *Mahabharata*. The walk lies over loosely held boulders on dying glaciers.
4. Beaskund to Shigara Dug (3,600 m.): An 8 km. walk through dense and enchanting forests. There are chances of seeing red bears from close quarters.
5. Shigara Dug to Marrhi (3,380 m.): A 10 km. trek. Remnants of dying glaciers are visible while getting into Sheila Goru Nallah. Holds views of Rohtang Pass, Bhrigu Lake and Shelasa; the trek upto Marrhi is precipitous, over patches of loose soil over perennial snows.
6. Marrhi to Rohtang (4,200 m.).
7. Back to Manali: A 17 km. route.

IX. Manali to Deo Tibba

A comfortable trek, the route is full of panoramic views along thick forests and alpine plateaux to the base of Deo Tibba.

1. Manali (1,928 m.) to Khanul (2,020 m.): A 10 km. trek. Motorable upto Jagatsukh and then a 3 to 4 kms. walk among luxurious walnut trees on the bank of Bhuhangan Nullah.
2. Khanul to Chhika (3,000 m.): A 6 km. walk through alpine plateaux and a beautiful rock-climbing area.
3. Chhika to Seri (3,900 m.): A breathtaking view of Deo Tibba appearing with magical suddenness. One of the loveliest alpine walks with an untiring gradient, Seri is a beautiful remnant of a once glaciated lake. The campsite lies among abundant alpine flora. With an extra day here, one can visit the heights of Taina alpine plateau (4,077 m.), and visit Chandra Lake (4,480 m.), famous for its emerald waters.
4. Seri to Sarach (3,000 m.): An 11 km. walk. There is a comfortable camping round and a big rock cave wherein 1,000 sheep are accommodated during the grazing season. At Bhanara, 3 kms. away, there is a beautiful camping site outside the temple.
5. Bhanara to Manali: After getting down to Jagatsukh or to Prini, Manali can be reached the same day in a vehicle.

X. Manali to Kalath

1. Beaskund to Tentu Pass (4,996 m.): The 3.5 km. trek is arduous as it goes over moraine. From the Tentu Pass one can look into both the valleys of Bara Bhangal and Kulu and get a close view of Hanuman Tibba. The pass is windy and temperatures drop substantially at night. It is advisable to camp a little lower on the other side, say between 4,000 m. and 4,800 m.

2. Tentu Pass to Camping Ground (3,856 m.): A 10 km. trek through the valley.

3. Camping Ground to Phulangot (4,000 m.): A trek upstream along Tantagiri Nullah. The area is largely uninhabited except for the shepherds, who are in the valley from mid-June to early September.

4. Phulangot to below Manali Pass (4,998 m.): A 6 km. walk. One should camp at the head of the Tantagiri Glacier at a height of 4,840 m. just above the subsidiary pass. Views of a number of peaks including Indrasan, Deo Tibba and Hanuman Tibba are available.

6. Rani Sui to Bhogi Thatch (2,820 m.): A 6 km. trek through beautiful grazing ground at 1,800 m.

7. Bhogi Thatch to Kalath (1,800 m.): Situated on the right bank of River Beas, 8 km. from Manali. One can drive from here to Manali.

XI. Chamba to Manali via Sach Pass

Pathankot to Chamba, a distance of 120 kms. can be covered in almost five hours by coach.

1. Chamba to Trella (1,829 m.): An early morning five-hour drive takes one to Trella at a distance of 90 kms.

2. Trella to Bhanodi (2,744 m.): A 13 km. trek. This, the first stage of the trek, can be covered in about six hours.

3. Bhanodi to Satrundi (3,658 m.): Situated at the base of Sach Pass, at a distance of 13 kms. Trekking here involves the usual ascents and descents. The last kilometres involve a steep climb. A PWD rest house is situated at Satrundi.

4. Satrundi to Sach Pass (4,867 m.): One must start early morning for Sach Pass to avoid high winds at the top. The 5 km. trek takes three hours.

5. Sach Pass to Brindabani (4,367 m.): The descent to Brindabani covers a distance of 16 kms.

6. Brindabani to Kilar: A 13 km trek. At Kilar the route bifurcates, one goes to Jammu-Kishtwar and the other to Manali via the Rohtang Pass.

7. Kilar to Cheri (2,184 m.): A 12 km. trek which takes five hours, the route is quite tough and involves frequent

ascents and descents. Accommodation is available at the forest rest house.

8. Cheri to Purthi (2,256 m.): A 15 km. trek. It can be covered in about five hours. A forest rest house is available.
9. Purthi to Camping Ground: An 8 km. trek.
10. Camping Ground to Rohli (2,591 m.): A 16 km. walk.
11. Rohli to Tindi (2,822 m.): A 17 km. walk which takes seven hours.
12. Tindi to Salaram (2,553 m.): An 11 km. trek, taking five hours. A rest house is situated here.
13. Salaram to Udaipur: The last lap, covering 22 kms., takes about six hours. The walk is almost a stroll. A PWD rest house has a staging hut.
14. Udaipur to Triloknath (2,802 m.): A pleasant trek to the famous temple. The distance is about 6 kms. and can be covered in three to four hours.
15. Udaipur to Manali: A 150 km. route, it runs through the Rohtang Pass (3,970 m.) and can be covered in five hours in a vehicle.

XII. Chamba to Manali via Kalicho Pass
1. Chamba to Bharmour (2,100 m.): A 70 km. drive by vehicle. Takes about five hours. Bharmour is the land of a legendary goddess on the bank of Brammah s Nallah. Famous for its ancient temples.
2. Bharmour to Sirar (2,045 m.): A 16 km. walk. The first stage of the trek begins with Sirar. The trek is through beautiful meadows and glades. Overnight in tents.
3. Sirar to Bhadra (2,281 m.): A 14 km. trek. Takes seven hours.
4. Bhadra to Bhansargot: A 19 km. trek. Takes seven hours.
5. Bhansargot to Alyas: A 9 km. trek to the base of Kalicho Pass.
6. Alyas to Kalicho Pass (4,800 m.) to Triloknath: A 16 km. trek, which takes seven hours. An early ascent of Kalicho Pass provides breathtaking views. Descent to Triloknath. One can visit Dzohrang Springs, 8 kms. away. Another 10 kms. takes one to Kerring.

XIII. Palanpur to Chamba via Laka Pass and Manimahesh Lake
From Amritsar, a seven-hour journey by road, takes one to Palanpur and from there to Dharamsala by coach, another 55 kms.
1. Dharamsala to Triundi (2,700 m.): A 12 kms. trek. Triundi is situated at the meeting point of three ridges, commanding a magnificent view of the Dhauladhar Range. It is the last village en route.

2. Triundi Camping Ground: An arduous trek of 11 kms. Takes about five hours. Overnight in tents. The camping ground lies at the foot of a pass.
3. Camping Ground to Kaka Pass to Chatta: An early morning start for the pass (5,100 m.), then descent to Chatta. Total 10 kms. Takes six hours to cover.
4. Chatta to Kuarsi: A 12 km. trek.
5. Kuarsi to Jhanata: A 16 km. trek.
6. Jhanata to Bharmour: A 16 km. trek.
7. Bharmour to Hadsar: A 12 km. trek. Takes five hours. Route lies through dense *deodar* forest.
8. Hadsar to Dhanchha: A 11 km. trek.
9. Dhanchha to Manimahesh Lake (4,200 m.): An 11 km. trek, it takes five hours to climb Bhairon Ghat and Bander Ghatti. Manimahesh is an important pilgrimage centre. Return to Bharmour and then proceed to Chamba. The distance is 53 kms.; in a vehicle it takes four hours.

XIV. Trip Around Manali via Hamta and Rohtang Pass
1. Manali to Chika (3,000 m.): Trek 13 kms., to find excellent panoramic views of the mountains.
2. Chika to Hamta Pass (4,330 m.): An 11 km. trek.
3. Hamta Pass to Camping Ground: An 8 km. trek. Initial 5 kms. involve a steep climb and take one to the top of Hamta Pass.
4. Camping Ground to Gramphoo: Descent to Gramphoo, 16 kms. away.
5. Gramphoo to Rohtang Pass (3,960 m.) to Rahla: A climb to the pass and descent to Rahla: 15 kms. covered in six hours.
6. Rahla to Manali: A trek of 13 kms.
7. Triloknath to Manali: A 30 km. drive to Keylong (2,440 m.) along River Chandra and then a 110 km. drive along beautiful mountainscape, over Rohtang Pass, to Manali.

XV. Chamba to Manali via Kugti Pass
1. Chamba to Bharmour (2,353 m.): As already mentioned.
2. Bharmour to Hadsar (2,320 m.): A 12 km. long trek through dense *deodar* forest.
3. Hadsar to Kugti (2,600 m.): A 12 km. trek. Kugti is the last village en route. Overnight in tents.
4. Kugti to Duggi (3,200 m.): An 11 km. trek. The first 3 kms. are quite steep. A beautiful place.
5. Duggi to Alyas (4,000 m.): A 12 km. trek to the base of Kugti Pass (5,215 m.). Camp overnight at Alyas camping ground.

6. Alyas to Kugti Pass (5,215 m.): The first 6 kms. of ascent to the snowbound pass (5,125 m.). Takes six to seven hours.
7. Kugti Pass to Shansha: A 10 km. trek, full of greenery, a heaven for botanists.
8. Shansha to Tandi (2,625 m.): A 15 km. trek. Camp in tents.
9. Tandi to Sissue (3,000 m.): A 2 km. trek into Lahaul Valley.
10. Sissue to Khoksar (3,325 m.): A 16 km. trek en route to Rohtang Pass.
11. Koksar to Rohtang Pass to Murry: A 15 km. trek.
12. Murry to Manali: A trek of 30 kms. can be covered in a vehicle.

XVI. The Dhauladhar

1. Dharamsala (1,350 m.) to Triundi (7,000 m.): A trek of 12 kms. Dharamsala stands on a spur of the Dhauladhar Range amidst magnificent *deodar* and pine forests, tea gardens and beautiful hills. Now the seat of the Dalai Lama, this hill station evokes the days of imperial rule when one visits places like McLeod Ganj and Forsyth Ganj, or the century-old church of Saint John in the wilderness. Triundi affords a breathtaking view of the snows above, and the valley below.
2. Triundi to Lakagot (3,000 m.): A 7 km. trek. Lakagot is at the foot of Indrahar Pass (5,660 m.) and is on the majestic Dhauladhar Range.
3. Lakagot to Chatta (3,300 m.): A trek of 10 kms. While at the base a wonderful view of the Kangra Valley in all its rural loveliness and repose, and a massive view of awe-inspiring Himalayan ranges, can be had.
4. Chatta to Kuarsi (2,192 m.): A 12 km. trek.
5. Kuarsi to Chhanota (2,245 m.): A 16 km. trek.
6. Chhanota to Bharmour (2,100 m.): A 40 km. trek. Once called Brahmpura, as the original capital of the State, Bharmour still retains in its ancient temples the monuments of its one-time glory. Manimahesh, Lakshna Devi, Ganesh and Narsingh are important temples. It is also known as the homeland of the Gaddis, a semi-pastoral tribe.
7. Bharmour to Gehra (1,350 m.): A trek of 23 kms.
8. Gehra to Chamba (1,050 m.): A 56 km. trek. The journey can be covered either on foot or by bus. Perched like some medieval Italian village fortress, on a flat mountain shelf, overhanging the rushing torrent of the River Ravi, the town of Chamba is famous for its temples, for Chaugan, a public promenade, and the Bhuri Singh museum.
9. Chamba to Khajjiar (2,690 m.): A 17 km. trek. Here lies

70

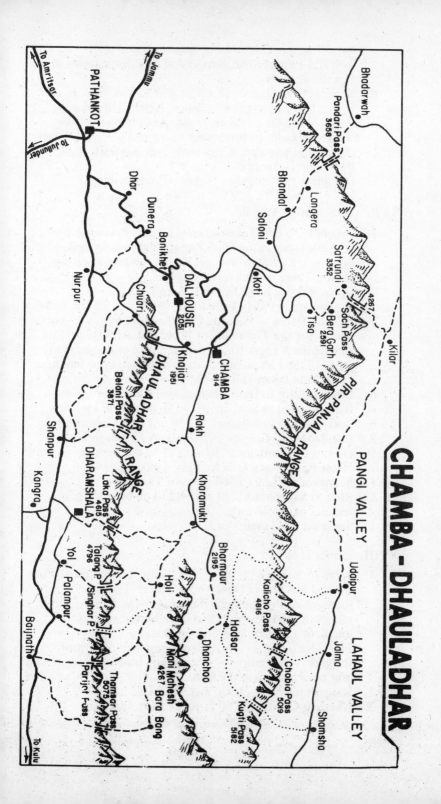

one of the most picturesque saucer-shaped plains, 1.5 kms. long and 1 km. broad, surrounded by a dense forest of gigantic *deodars*.

10. Khajjiar to Dalhousie (2,100 m.): A 17 km. trek. In many ways a hill station par excellence. Nestling in the outer slopes of the Dhauladhar, Dalhousie is known for its bracing climate, picturesque scenery and lovely picnic spots. Dalhousie: You can, if you wish, visit Subhash Baoli, Panjpulla, Bakrota etc.

11. Dalhousie to Pathankot: Takes 80 kms. by bus.

XVII. Palampur to Manali

1. Palampur to Bir: Takes 40 kms. by bus. Palampur is a delightful spot in the main Kangra Valley surrounded on all sides by tea gardens. Neugal Khad is an awe-inspiring chasm. There is a tea factory at Bir.
2. Bir to Rajgundha (2,610 m.): A 16 km. trek.
3. Rajgundha to Palchak Deota (2,700 m.): A 12 km. trek.
4. Palchak Deota to Panardu (3,450 m.): A trek of 10 kms. Cross over the Thanesar Jot (4,665 m.). An exhilarating view of the Kangra Valley and glimpses of magnificent peaks of the Lahaul and Ladakh areas are to be had here.
5. Panardu to Dhan-kall Jot (3,936 m.)
6. Dhan-kall Jot to Bara Bhangal: An 8 km. trek.
7. Bara Bhangal to Sukhaparh (3,000 m.): A 17 km. trek.
8. Sukhaparh to Lambaparh (3,150 m.): A 13 km. trek.
9. Lambaparh to Gowari (3,750 m.): A 13 km. trek.
10. Gowari to Shanghor (3,360 m.): A 13 km. trek across Kali Haini Pass (Black Glacier Pass, 4,680 m.)
11. Shanghor to Raili (3,360 m.): An 8 km. trek.
12. Raili to Sangchur (2,850 m.): A 13 km. trek. There are remains of an old fort.
13. Sangchur to Manali: An 11 km. trek.

XVIII. Simla Hills

1. Solan to Rajgarh (1,385 m.): A 40 km. trek. Named after the goddess Soloni Devi whose temple is situated at the southern end of the town. Solan is situated in the outer ranges of the Himalayas and is well-known for its undulating scenery and bracing climate.
Fast developing as a fruit-developing belt of Sirmur, Rajgarh, it still enjoys a solitude and tranquility which few other places have in the state.
2. Rajgarh to Naura (1,920 m.): A 19 km. trek.
3. Naura to Chaura (3,750 m.): A 13 km. trek. The

Chuhardhar Peak (3,647 m.) dominates the entire landscape of fields, forest ravines all round. It affords a view southwards of the Gangetic plain and the Sutlej River; northward lies Badrinath, and beyond, Tibet. Chuhardhar is also the home of God Shrigul.

4. Chaura to Pulbahl (1,800 m.): A 10 km. trek.
5. Pulbahl to Sainj (1,350 m.): A 19 km. trek.
6. Sainj to Chhailla (1,500 m.): An 8 km. trek.
7. Chhailla to Shalaru (2,400 m.): A 16 km. trek.
8. Shalaru to Narkanda (2,700 m.): It commands a unique view of the eternal snow-capped mountain ranges.
9. Narkanda to Simla: A 64 km. route.

Kinnaur

Between the Garhwal Himalaya and the Punjab Himalaya lies Kinnaur. Kinnaur, a terraced wilderness of the forest-clad, steep-sided ridges of the Great Himalayan and Dhauladhar Ranges and the barren, powdery spaces of the Zanskar is approached from Simla along the valley of the Sutlej River. The river has carved itself a spectacular gorge: lorries ply along the old Hindustan-Tibet road and reach most road terminals in two to three days.

The climbing and trekking area lies north of the Inner Line, entered at Wangtu and except the oft-attempted twin peaks of Leo Pargial (6,816 m. and 6,791 m.), has largely remained unvisited. The valley of the Sutlej is the longest in Kinnaur. It is about 140 kms. long, lying generally north-east to south-west. The Hindustan-Tibet road offers a great walk through vineyards interspersed with fields and apple and apricot orchards, and across the moon-like spaces through the Zanskar Range to Shipki Pass. The road runs a few hundred metres above the turbulent river. Today it is mostly replaced by a metalled lorry road — good for trekking if you happen to be a wheel-barrow! Yet the few intact stretches of the old road are worth a walk. Streams and deep rivers exhausting themselves into the Sutlej still lead to walks high up along the spurs. Here are found huge morina and rye pines, and great forests of the mountain monarch, the *deodar*.

If the trekker persists, far above these are the great *deodars* which for centuries have held the hillsides up. However, the needs of man are now upsetting this delicate balance; the valley has recently witnessed great damage due to landslides. Still, the highlands on the north-western aspect of the valley provide a few high walks.

Spiti Valley: Spiti River joins the Sutlej at Namgia. The lowest villages in the valley are at about 2,800 m. and the highest are below 3,700 m. With the exception of narrow cultivated strips the valley has a sterile aspect. Leo Pargial, 6,816 m., lies at the head

73

KINNAUR

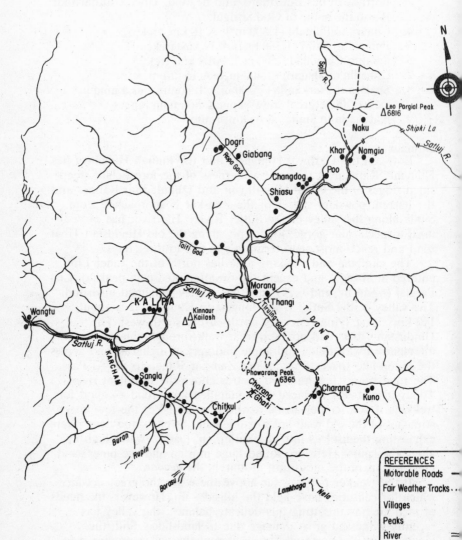

REFERENCES
Motorable Roads ——
Fair Weather Tracks ···
Villages
Peaks
River
Bridge
Note: Distances in km
Heights in metre

of this valley. Above the delightful village Nako is to be found an uneven walk, of two or three days, gradually inclining upwards across moraine wastes leading to the base of Leo Pargial.

Ropa Valley: The stream of this name courses for about 15 kms. through an inhabited valley and then through high alps for about 20 kms. and the occasional vineyards are to be found below the rocky crests of the valley, culminating in the divide with Lahaul. The valley offers access to Lahaul via the Manirang Pass.

Tidong Valley: Tidong Valley offers a rugged landscape along both banks of the deep-sided Tiruing Gad for about 50 kms. At its narrow entrance squats the village of Thangi, above the junction of Shankvi and Tiruing Gad. A large hill village, huddled at the foot of a bare mountain, it looks across cultivated fields to the north face of the Kinnaur massif. A doubtful track leads across tumbling hillside to the village of Charang at 3,600 m.; from here an unused track goes south over the Charang Ghati to Chitkul in the Baspa Valley. At the head of the valley lies Kuno, a perfectly set oasis amidst the wind-beaten brown-draped hills above and the silver sands of the river below. It is a rewarding walk of seven to ten days. The Phawararang mass, 6,365 m., dominates the upper reaches of the valley.

Baspa Valley: Baspa River, a large tributary of the Sutlej, begins at the Indo-Tibetan watershed and empties into the Sutlej above Karchham. From its source (or sources, for these are the many high alpine and glacial petals and basins) the river meanders down an open valley as far as Sangla. The valley floor of grass and boulder lies at 3,000 to 4,200 m.; the hillsides rise to 6,000 m., occasionally even higher.

The valley offers one of the prettiest walks anywhere in the Himalaya. From Sangla (approached by road) to its head the valley is about 70 kms. long. The river generally rolls gently down the open level-valley. The valley is inhabited from Sangla to Chitkul (3,500 m.) on both sides of the river. It is richly cultivated, but pastureland on both sides of the river is diminishing. While hops and spices like cumin seeds and saffron are cultivated at Sangla, the meadows are full of flowers and fruit trees. Among these are also willows, hazel and sweet briar.

From the valley floor of about 4,500 m. rise mountains of an unusual steepness of 6,500 m., offering exciting two- to three-day climbs off grassy base camps. The flatness of the valley recalls local legend, that it was once a lake. It offers easy going for ponies.

The valley can be reached across the Nela (and Lamkhaga) Pass from Harsil, Borasu Pass from Harkidum, and the Rupin and Buran Passes from the Rupin and Pabar Rivers.

In July and August monsoon affects the valley upto Kalpa and is there blocked off by the great Himalayan range. The flora of

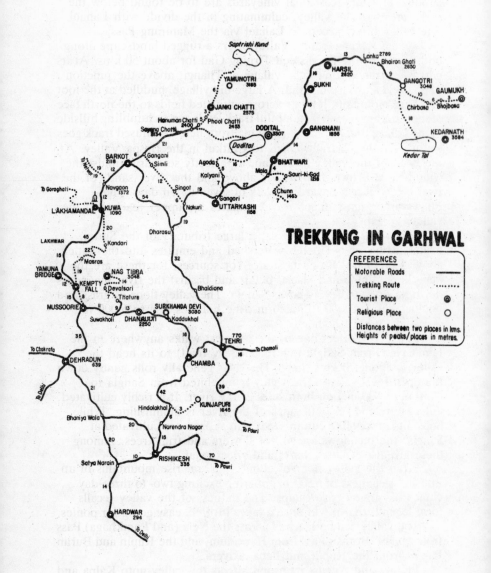

TREKKING IN GARHWAL

REFERENCES

Motorable Roads	———
Trekking Route	·········
Tourist Place	◉
Religious Place	○

Distances between two places in kms.
Heights of peaks/places in metres.

Kinnaur consists of the flora common to moist zones: Pinus roxburgi, Rhododendron arborium, Pinus excelsa, spruce and broad-leaved trees (horse chestnut, hazelnut, walnut) and so on. *Deodar*, ilex and silverfir grow in the dry zone and the neoza pine, *deodar* and blue pine in the arid zone.

The above forests support the sadly diminishing wild life of these areas. The high alps have a wealth of high alpine flowers.

Trekking in Kinnaur is limited to April-June and September-October. Currently the innerline restrictions begin at Wangtu about 120 kms. from Simla.

Treks in Garhwal and Kumaon

Panch-Kedar: Panch-Kedar are five temples respresenting five different forms of Lord Shiva. Each temple is located in a different valley; they are known as the Kedarnath Valley (5,384 m.), Madmaheshwar Valley (3,289 m.), Tungnath Valley (3,810 m.), Rudranath Valley (2,286 m.) and Kalpnath Valley (2,134 m.). All these valleys are rich in flora and fauna. Each valley affords spellbinding views of the Garhwal Himalaya. The following is a 14-day trek in this area.

1st Day: Rishikesh to Muni-Ki-Reti to Pipalkoti
Motorable road; the distance is 220 kms.
Deluxe coaches are available.

2nd Day: Pipalkoti to Urgam .
Motorable road upto Helang (22 kms.) Trek
to Kalpnath Mahadev with packed lunch
(distance: 9 kms.). Return to Urgam Valley.

3rd Day: Urgam to Gopeshwari
Trek to Helang. Then hire a vehicle to
Gopeshwar (53 kms.).

4th Day: Gopeshwar to Naila
By vehicle to Mandal (15 kms.). Trek to
Anusuya Devi with packed lunch, then trek
to Naila (16 kms.).

5th Day: Naila
Trek to Rudranath.

6th Day: Rudranath to Chopta
Trek to Mandal with packed
lunch. Take a vehicle to Chopta.

7th Day: Chopta to Tungnath to Chopta
A 3 km. trek to Tungnath, then on to
Chandrashilla. Return to Tungnath. Halt
for the night at Chopta.

8th Day: Chopta to Gaundhar
By vehicle to Makku (12 kms.), with packed

PANCH-KEDAR TREK

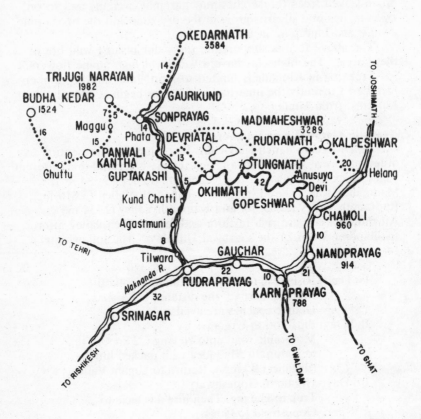

REFERENCES

Motorable Roads	——	Religious Place	○
Trekking Route	••••••	Tourist Place	◎
River	～～	Religious & Tourist Place	●

Note : Distances between two places in kms.
Heights of peaks/places in metres.

lunch. Trek to Gaundhar (19 kms.).
9th Day: Gaundhar to Madmaheshwar
Trek to Madmaheshwar with packed lunch.

78

10th Day: Madmaheshwar to Gaundhar
Trek to Gaundhar.

11th Day: Gaundhar to Kalimath to Guptakashi
Trek to Guptakashi via Kalimath with
packed lunch.

12th Day: Guptakashi to Kedarnath
By vehicle to Gaurikund (31 kms.). Trek to
Kedarnath (14 kms.).

13th Day: Kedarnath to Guptakashi to Rudraprayag
Trek to Gaurikund. Drive to Rudraprayag.

14th Day: Rudraprayag to Muni-Ki-Reti to Rishikesh
You can hire a vehicle to Muni-Ki-Reti and
Rishikesh.

Roop Kund Trek: Situated at a height of 5,029 m. on the Trisul massif, this lake is surrounded by rock-strewn glaciers and snow-clad peaks. The starting point for the trek is Tharali (333 m.), which is easily approachable by road from Rishikesh and Nainital. There is another route from Ghat, connected by a motorable road, with Nandprayag en route to Badrinath on the main highway.

Route	Altitude of Reaching Point (m.)	Distance (kms.)
1. Tharali to Debal	1,218	12 (motor)
Debal to Bagrigarh	1,645	8 (trek)
Bagrigarh to Mandoli	2,134	3 (trek)
Mandoli to Lohaganj	2,133	1 (trek)
Lohaganj to Bedri Bugyal	3,354	10 (trek)
Badri Bugyal to Bistola	4,667	8 (trek)
Bistola to Roopkund	5,029	5 (trek)
Jyurighatindhar to Homkund	4,061	8 (trek)
Homkund to Sutola	2,192	18 (trek)
Sutola to Ghat	1,331	26 (trek)
2. Tharali to Debal	1,218	12 (vehicle)
Debal to Faldiagaon	1,354	8 (trek)
Faldiagaon to Mandoli	2,134	9 (trek)
Mandoli to Wan	2,439	14 (trek)
Wan to Gairoli Patali	3,049	9 (trek)
Gairoli Patali to Patar Nachanni	3,658	11 (trek)
Patar Nachanni to Roop Kund	5,029	10 (trek)

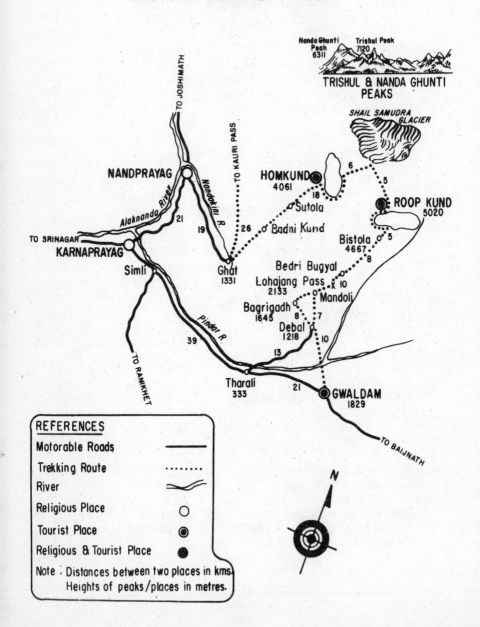

ROOP KUND TREK

TRISHUL & NANDA GHUNTI PEAKS

Nanda Ghunti Peak 6311 Trishul Peak 7120

SHAIL SAMUDRA GLACIER

TO JOSHIMATH

TO KAURI PASS

NANDPRAYAG

Alaknanda River
Nandakini R.

HOMKUND 4061

6

5

ROOP KUND 5020

18

Sutola

TO SRINAGAR

21

19

26

Badni Kund

Bistola 4667

5

KARNAPRAYAG

Simli

Ghat 1331

Bedri Bugyal

8

Lohajang Pass 2133

× 10

Mandoli

Bagrigadh 1645

8   7

Pindar R.

Debal 1218

39

10

13

TO RANIKHET

Tharali 333

21

GWALDAM 1829

TO BAIJNATH

N

REFERENCES

Motorable Roads

Trekking Route

River

Religious Place   ○

Tourist Place   ◎

Religious & Tourist Place   ●

Note : Distances between two places in kms.
Heights of peaks/places in metres.

Valley of Flowers

In Hindu mythology the Valley is associated spiritually with the name of Lord Lakshmana, the younger brother of Lord Rama. The former was believed to have meditated on the banks of Lokpal Lake (Hemkund). The *sanjeewani buti* by virtue of which Lord

THE VALLEY OF FLOWERS
AND
HEMKUND TREK

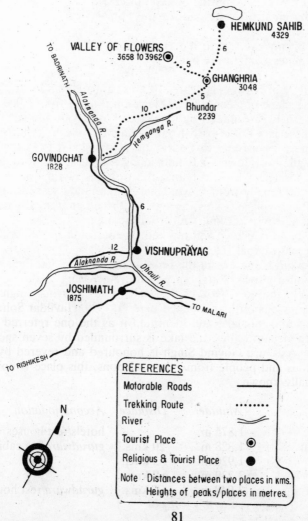

HEMKUND SAHIB
4329

VALLEY OF FLOWERS
3658 to 3962

GHANGHRIA
3048

Bhundar
2239

GOVINDGHAT
1828

VISHNUPRAYAG

JOSHIMATH
1875

TO MALARI

TO BADRINATH

Alaknanda R.

Hemganga R.

Alaknanda R.

Dhauli R.

TO RISHIKESH

N

REFERENCES

Motorable Roads

Trekking Route

River

Tourist Place

Religious & Tourist Place

Note : Distances between two places in kms.
Heights of peaks/places in metres.

81

Lakshmana was brought to life after he was badly wounded by
Meghnath (the son of Ravana), was found here. It is futher believed
to be the place where God showered the flowers that took root.
Officially this Valley, where nature has endowed its bounties
aplenty, was discovered by famous mountaineer and naturalist
Frank Symthe, in the year 1931. Though the Valley was known to
the locals, they dared not enter it because of the superstition that
the fairies who haunted the place would take them away. Joan
Margaret Leggs, inspired by the work of Frank Smythe, camped
here for some time, but as fate would have it, she slipped from
a rock while collecting flowers and lost her life. She was buried in
the heart of the Valley and the epitaph inscribed on her tombstone
expresses the great love she had for the Himalayas:

I shall lift my eyes up to the Himalayas,
from whence cometh my help.

The Valley of Flowers is nearly 10 kms. in length and 2 kms. in
width, in the shape of a cone. In an elevation ranging from 3,000 m.
to 4,000 m., it is surrounded by the River Pushpavati and small
streams. There is a bridle path from Ghanghria; the trek starts
from Govindghat en route to Badrinath. (Govindghat is 19 kms.
from the Valley of Flowers.) It falls along a mule track, through
beautiful landscape flora and fauna; the trek has two major
gradients, one intially from Govindghat-Alakananda suspension
bridge to Pulna village 3 kms. away, and the other from Bhundar
to Ghanghria. After a 3 km. trek from Ghanghria lies the
bifurcation point which is well marked on the route to the Valley
of Flowers and Lokpal (Hemkund).

At Hemkund, apart from the Lakshmana Temple and the lake,
there is a Guru Govind Singh gurudwara. According to the Guru
Granth Sahib, the holy book of the Sikhs, Guru Govind Singh in
one of his previous births meditated here. In 1930, Havildar Sohan
Singh discovered this lake and identified it as the one referred to
in the Guru Granth Sahib; the lake is surrounded by seven snow-
clad peaks. As Guru Govind Singh is honoured and revered by
Sikhs, Hindus and people from other religions, this place is now
internationally known.

Place	Altitude	Distance	Accommodation
Joshimath	1,875 m.		hotels/rest houses
Govindghat	1,828 m.	20 kms.	gurudwara/log cabins
Pulna	1,920 m.	3 kms.	
Bhundar	2,239 m.	7 kms.	
Ghanghria	3,048 m.	5 kms.	gurudwara/rest house

HAR-KI-DOON TREK

Osla 2559 ···· ⊙ HAR-KI-DOON
                8   3566
Taluka ○···11
        ·
12 ···○ Saur
      ·
    ○ NETWAR
       1401
12
    ○ Mori
Jarmola○ 16
        22
Purola○
      19   ⊙ BARKOT

LAKHAMANDAL   ○ Navagaon
        ●   1372
              ○ KUWA

N

TO JAMNOTRI
TO CHAKRATA
Yamuna R.

            ○ YAMUNA BRIDGE
              ● KEMPTY FALL
KALSI ○
      6   ⊙ MUSSOORIE
DAKPATHAR
○
  9   Yamuna R.
TO SIMLA
    Harbartpur

TO CHAKRATA
TO SAHARANPUR

        ● DEHRADUN
              TO HARDWAR
              /RISHIKESH
TO DELHI

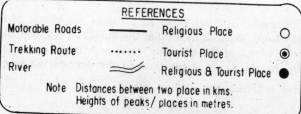

REFERENCES

Motorable Roads ——————   Religious Place   ○
Trekking Route ······· Tourist Place   ⊙
River   ～～～   Religious & Tourist Place ●

Note Distances between two place in kms.
      Heights of peaks/ places in metres.

| Valley of Flowers | | 5 kms. | |
| Hemkund | 4,329 m. | 6 kms. | *gurudwara* |

NOTE: Hemkund Sahib is 5 kms. away from Ghanghria.

Har-ki-Doon Trek: Har-ki-Doon is situated in the western ranges of the Garhwal Himalaya, in the Uttarkashi district, on the base of Fateh Parvat, at an elevation of 3,566 m. ASL. This cradle-shaped valley south-east of the Janundhar Glacier is surrounded by glittering peaks on the north-western side, and in the south-east by dense forests of pine, *deodar* and other coniferous trees. This is a forest rich in wild life and a paradise for bird-watchers and nature lovers. The people of this region worship Duryodhana, the famous character from the *Mahabharata.*

The trek commences from the village of Netwar, which is easily accessible by motor from Dehradun and Mussoorie via Navagaon and Purola. The trek from Netwar to Taluka trails along motorable road on the upper bank of River Supin. This trek presents a panoramic view of the Supin Valley with the Fateh Parbat shadowing it. Netwar to Osla the trek is through very dense forest of chestnut, walnut, willow and *china.* The trek from Oslo to Har-ki-Doon is through terraced mountain fields, lush green grassland and coniferous forests. The best season to visit Har-ki-Doon Valley is during the monsoon, when multicoloured flowers bloom, presenting a heavenly sight. During this season the starting point for Har-ki-Doon is from Purola, since the Purola-Netwar motor road is a foul weather road.

Place	Altitude (m.)	Distance (kms.)
Dehradun	701	
Mussoorie	1,921	36 (motor)
Purola	1,524	97 (motor)
Jarmola	1,800	22 (trek)
Mori		16 (trek)
Netwar	1,380	12 (trek)
Saur		12 (trek)
Taluka	1,900	11 (trek)
Osla	2,559	11 (trek)
Har-ki-Doon	3,566	8 (trek)

Kedarnath-Vasukital Trek: Kedarnath, the abode of the almighty Lord Shiva, is located at the height of 3,584 m. ASL in the Chamoli district of the Garhwal region. A magnificent temple was built by the Pandavas at the base of the peerless Kedarnath Peak

Preceding pages: Machu Puchare in Nepal (Frank Hoppe) and Kanchenjunga in Darjeeling (Indian Mountaineering Foundation). Above:Everest from the north (Chris Bonington). Below: The regular and colourful Saturday bazaar at Namche (Harish Kapadia).

Thyangboche Monastery, Nepal.   H. Swift

Everest, north face, Tibet.   Leo Lebon

Above left: A Himachali belle.

Below: A Shepani porter.

Above: Dard girl, Ladakh.

Nanda Devi in the Garhwal Himalayas.

Bapsa Valley, Himachal Pradesh. Balwant Sandhu

Jet-boating (above) and rafting (below) up the Ganges.

Avinash Kohli

Romesh Bhattacharji

Above: Nubra Valley, Ladakh.

Right: Shivling from Tapoban in the Garhwal Himalayas

Harish Kapadia

The picturesque Lidder valley in Kashmir.

ITDC

Above left and right: The Nun and Kun peaks in the Zanskar range, Kashmir.

Below left: Trekkers in the idyllic Chitral Valley, Pakistan

PTDC

Col. Narendra Kumar

Right: Skiing in Gulmarg.

R. Bali

The Takstang Monastery, Bhutan.   G.N. Mehra

A view of the magnificent Potala Palace, Tibet.   Chris Bonington

Campers in the shadow of Nanga Parbat PTDC

A Himalayan rhapsody.

The Gurla Mandhata Range, Tibet.   Rommel Varma

Chomal Hari, Bhutan.   Col. Narendra Kumar

Kanchenjunga from Darjeeling. (Sunil Janah).
A moraine camp (Frank Hoppe).

Overleaf: The sacred peak of Kailash in Tibet (Romesh Bhattacharji).

KEDARNATH - VASUKITAL TREK

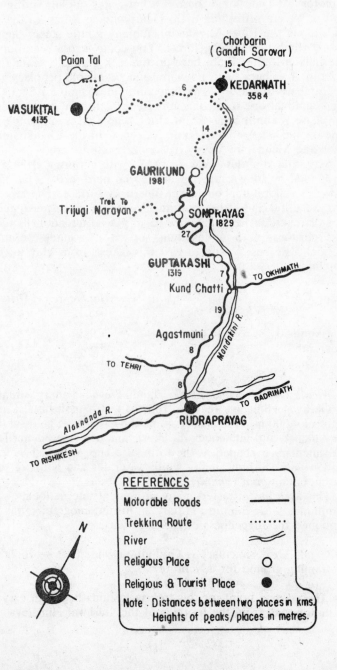

Chorbarin
(Gandhi Sarovar)

Paian Tal

15

KEDARNATH
3584

VASUKITAL
4135

1

6

14

GAURIKUND
1981

5

Trek To
Trijugi Narayan

SONPRAYAG
1829

27

GUPTAKASHI
1315

7

TO OKHIMATH

Kund Chatti

19

Mandakini R.

Agastmuni

8

TO TEHRI

8

TO BADRINATH

Alaknanda R.

RUDRAPRAYAG

TO RISHIKESH

N

REFERENCES

Motorable Roads

Trekking Route

River

Religious Place ○

Religious & Tourist Place ●

Note : Distances between two places in kms.
Heights of peaks/places in metres.

(south-eastern phase) where millions of pilgrims come to offer their prayers to Lord Shiva.

The trek starts from Gaurikund, which is easily approachable by motor. At Gaurikund there is a hot-water sulphur spring where you can have a refreshing bath. Gaurikund to Rambara the trek winds along the River Mandakini, initially a little steep, then a gradual climb through the forest. You come across beautiful waterfalls en route. From here on the trek gradually leads to the village of Rambara, with its warm and hospitable people.

Rambara to Garur Chatti is a continuous climb for 5 kms., and then a gradual one to Kedarnath. Kedarnath to Vasukital for the first phase is continuous ascent along a goat track on to a grassy slope on the west of Kedarnath. The view of the Chaukhamba Peaks and Mandakini Valley is wonderful from here.

Vasukital is about 1 km. in radius with glittering clear waters surrounded by snow-capped peaks. From here to Paiantal, north-west of Vasukital is about 1 km. on rocky surface. The lake is more beautiful and at the bottom of it one can see rectangular slabs of rocks, so neat that they seem placed intentionally.

From Kedarnath to Vasukital, services of a guide are most essential. The best season to visit this lake is from May to September.

Place	Altitude (m.)	Distance (kms.)
Gaurikund	1,981	
Kedarnath	3,584	15 (trek)
Vasukital	4,135	6 (trek)

Nanda Devi Sanctuary Trek: Nanda Devi sanctuary, situated in the Garhwal Himalaya (eastern region) in Chamoli district at a height of 4,500 m. ASL, is surrounded by 70 white, colossal peaks, many named and unnamed, the most famous being Nanda Devi. The sanctuary is shaped in the form of a cup, with lush green meadows and gushing, milky white waterfalls and herds of the blue mountain goat (*bharal*).

This area has attracted many prominent international mountaineers. Sir Edmund Hillary, in his autobiography, has mentioned the ruggedness of this sanctuary:

Nanda Devi Sanctuary is God-gifted wilderness — India's training ground for adventure ....

The starting point for this trek is Joshimath, within easy reach by motor road from the foothills of the Garhwal Himalaya. At

86

NANDA DEVI SANCTUARY TREK

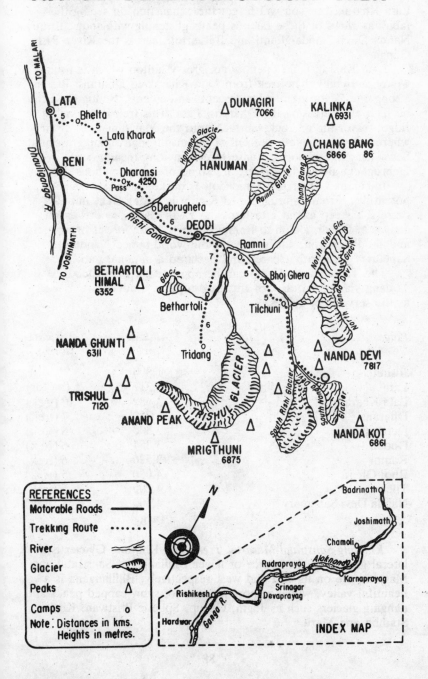

Joshimath arrangements for guides and porters as well as last-minute purchases can be made. Joshimath to the village of Lata, by road, is 25 kms. From here the trek starts, an arduous trek to Lata Kharak, but you will forget the exhaustion on seeing the fabulous views of those famous peaks glistening with snow: Runti, Nanda Devi, Nanda-ghunti and Bethartoli, across the River Rishi Ganga.

Lata Kharak is an open, wide, grassy hilltop which is usually windy and chilly. The trek from Lata Kharak to Dharansi Pass is a long one, featuring regular descents and ascents. Nanda Devi can be seen after crossing the Dharansi Pass. This trek is through a ridge, traversing on rocky surface upto the Malatuni Pass, from where it is a continuous descent of 750 m. through alpine grassland. Snow clinging on slopes, dense forest, inviting meadows of Debrugheta alongside a river, are some of the marvellous sights.

In summer Debrugheta meadow is decked with flowers such as potentillas. From Debrugheta to Ramni is a long trek; initially there is a steep ascent after crossing Rishi Ganga, and then one arrives at Deodi. Deodi to Ramni through dense forests of junipers and rhododendron, and you enter the world-famed Nanda Devi Sanctuary (presently cleared and declared a national park).

The Trishul Base Camp can be approached from Deodi to Tridang via Bethartoli. For this trek ropes are advisable, as well as the services of guides.

Place	Altitude (m.)	Distance (kms.)
Joshimath	1,890	
Lata	2,317	25 (motor)
Lata Kharak	3,689	10 (trek)
Dharansi	4,250	7 (trek)
Debrugheta	3,500	8 (trek)
Deodi	3,354	6 (trek)
Ramni	3,520	6 (trek)
Bhoj Ghera	4,050	5 (trek)
Tilchuni	4,200	5 (trek)
Nanda Devi Sanctuary	4,500 (avg.)	8 (trek)

Khatling-Sahstratal-Masartal Trek: The Khatling Glacier is a lateral glacier, at the source of River Bhillangana. Sahstratal and Masartal are on its east and west respectively. Bhillangana is a beautiful valley, with a panoramic view of snow-capped peaks and hanging glaciers such as Jogin, Group, Sphetic Pristwan, Kirti Stambh and Meru.

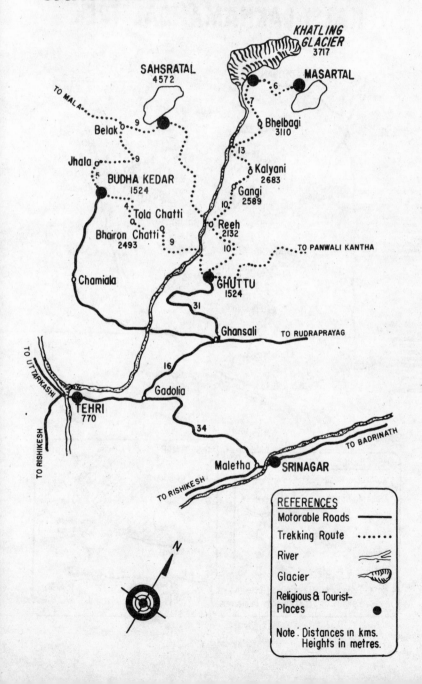

The trek starts from Ghansali (976 m.) or Ghuttu, which is easily approachable from the towns at the foothills of the Garhwal Himalaya, such as Dehradun, Rishikesh, etc. The whole trek passes through very thick forest and lush green meadows. Trekkers have to cross many small streams.

KALSI-LAKHAMANDAL TREK

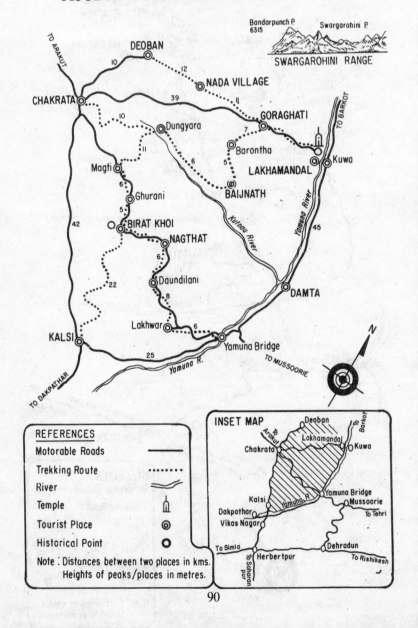

Route	Altitude of Reaching Point (m.)	Distance (kms.)
Ghansali to Ghuttu	1,524	30 (transport)
Ghuttu to Reeh	2,132	10 (trek)
Reeh to Gangi	2,584	10 (trek)
Gangi to Kalyani	2,683	5 (trek)
Kalyani to Bhelbagi	3,110	13 (trek)
Bhelbagi to Khatling	3,717	7 (trek)
Khatling to Masartal	3,675	6 (trek)

Kalsi-Lakhamandal Trek: This is situated through a narrow goat trek, to the pass at an elevation of 4,265 m. ASL in the heart of Chamoli district, on the north-eastern front. It offers a glorious view of the stately eastern peaks of the Garhwal Himalaya, full of charm and grandeur, wearing their white, glossy caps.

The peaks visible from Kauri Pass are Nanda Devi, Dunagiri, Bethartoli, Devsthan etc. Weather permitting, the Nanda Devi Sanctuary is also visible. The trek trails are scenic, especially around Ramni. Lord Curzon had trekked uptó Kauri Pass, and so the road is known as Curzon Road.

Place	Altitude (m.)	Distance (kms.)
Nandprayag	914	
Ghat	1,331	19 (motor)
Ramni	1,982	10 (trek)
Sarkot	2,439	4 (trek)
Jhenjipatni	1,524	9 (trek)
Panarani	2,043	12 (trek)
Sanatoli	2,439	5 (trek)
Domabhiti	2,286	5 (trek)
Kauri Pass	4,268	5 (trek)

Mussoorie-Nag Tibba Trek: Nag Tibba is on the foothills of the Garhwal Himalaya, north-east of Mussoorie. The peak is situated at a height of 3,048 m. ASL. On the top of this peak, local villagers come here to offer their *puja* (prayers) to Nag Devta (Snake God) for the protection of their cattle. The trek starts from Dhanaulti on a forest track and leads to Morina Dhar. This place is situated on a saddle, and sunrise, from behind the mountains, is a beautiful sight to watch from here. From Morina Dhar the trek is on a ridge, most of the time parallel to the Garhwal Himalaya, from Swargarohini to the Nanda Devi ranges. This part of the trek is very

KAURI PASS TREK

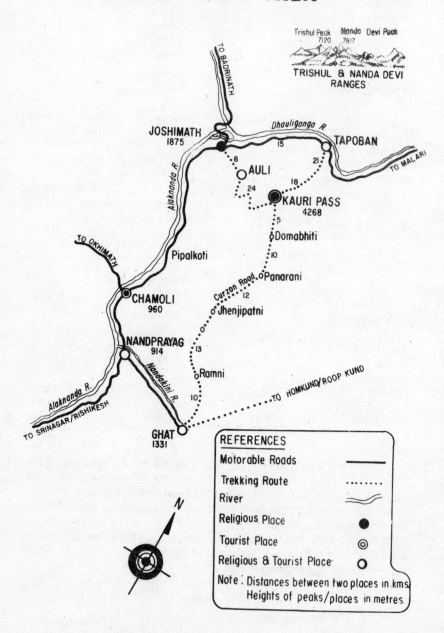

Trishul Peak 7120 Nanda Devi Peak 7817

TRISHUL & NANDA DEVI RANGES

TO BADRINATH

Dhauliganga R.

JOSHIMATH
1875

15

TAPOBAN

TO MALARI

Alaknanda R.

8

AULI

21

24

18

KAURI PASS
4268

5

TO OKHIMATH

Pipalkoti

Domabhiti

10

Panarani

Curzon Road

12

CHAMOLI
960

Jhenjipatni

NANDPRAYAG
914

13

Alaknanda R.

Nandakini R.

Ramni

10

TO HOMKUND/ROOP KUND

TO SRINAGAR/RISHIKESH

GHAT
1331

N

REFERENCES

Motorable Roads	────────
Trekking Route	··········
River	∼∼∼
Religious Place	●
Tourist Place	◎
Religious & Tourist Place	○

Note : Distances between two places in kms.
Heights of peaks/places in metres.

MUSSOORIE - NAG TIBBA TREK

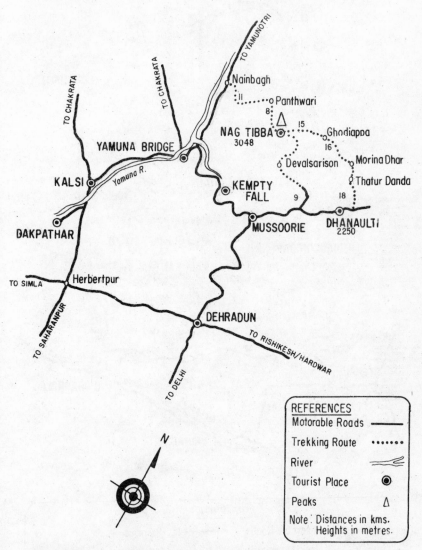

rich in flora and fauna. Only a few villages come en route and even
those are abandoned during the winter months. From Nag Tibba
to Nainbagh is a downhill trek to the picturesque village of
Panthwari, gay with life and presenting the culture of Jaunpur

GANGOTRI-KEDARNATH TREK

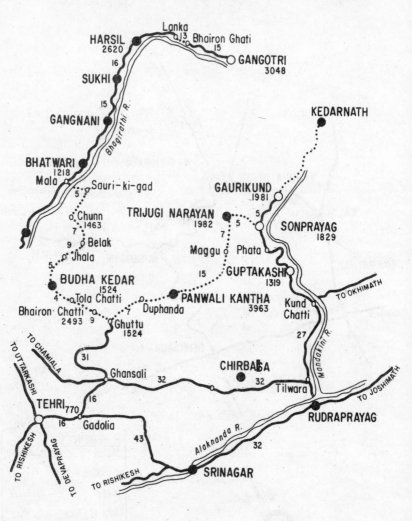

Lanka
13 Bhairon Ghati
HARSIL
2620   15
16   GANGOTRI
SUKHI   3048
15
GANGNANI   KEDARNATH
BHATWARI
1218
Mala   Sauri-ki-gad   GAURIKUND
5   1981
o Chunn   TRIJUGI NARAYAN   5   SONPRAYAG
1463   1982   5   1829
7   7
9 o Belak   Maggu o Phata
o Jhala
5   15   GUPTAKASHI
BUDHA KEDAR   1319
1524   PANWALI KANTHA
4 Tola Chatti   3963   Kund
Bhairon Chatti   Duphanda   Chatti
2493   9   7   TO OKHIMATH
Ghuttu   27
1524
TO CHAMIALA
31
Ghansali   32   CHIRBASA   TO JOSHIMATH
32   Tilwara
TEHRI
770   16
16   Gadolia   RUDRAPRAYAG
43   Alaknanda R.   32
TO RISHIKESH
TO DEVAPRAYAG
TO RISHIKESH   SRINAGAR

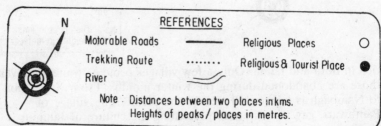

REFERENCES
N
Motorable Roads ———   Religious Places   o
Trekking Route ....   Religious & Tourist Place •
River
Note : Distances between two places in kms.
Heights of peaks / places in metres.

Place	Altitude (m.)	Distance (kms.)
Mussoorie	2,004	
Dhanaulti	2,250	22 (motor)
Morina Dhar	2,350	18 (trek)
Ghodiappa	2,800	16 (trek)
Nag Tibba	3,040	15 (trek)
Panthwari	1,524	8 (trek)
Nainbagh	1,115	11 (trek)

Gangotri-Kedarnath Trek: This trek is along the old pilgrim route from Gangotri to Kedarnath. From Gangotri one has to return to Mal by motor. The actual trek starts from Mal after crossing the River Bhagirathi. Till Sauri-ki-gad the trek is level, and from here the climb to Belak is gradual. From Belak to Budha Kedar it is downhill through very dense forests full of birds and wild life. From Budha Kedar to Panwali it is an uphill climb through terraced fields and villages.

The villages along this trek are picturesque. Though this trek is tiring, along ridges, valleys and dales, it is worth it. The heart-warming panoramic view of the Garhwal Himalaya is most refreshing, which compensates for the efforts of regular ascending and descending.

The Bugyals on this trek are the most beautiful, specially the Kush-Kalyani and the Panwali Bugyals. In the rainy season the mountains are dotted with colourful flowers on the lush green meadows, making it very romantic. Along this trek there are rest houses and dharamshalas. The trek should be well-planned and the services of guides are advisable.

Place	Altitude (m.)	Distance (kms.) point-to-point	Distance (kms.) progressive
Gangotri	3,048		
Mal	1,478	73 (motor)	73
Sauri-ki-gad	1,218	5 (trek)	78
Phyalu	2,286	3 (trek)	81
Chunachatti	1,463	3 (trek)	84
Belak	2,439	4 (trek)	88
Pangrana	2,203	5 (trek)	93
Jhala	2,439	4 (trek)	97
Agund Thatikathur	1,981	3 (trek)	100
Budha Kedar	1,524	2 (trek)	102
Tolachatti	1,311	4 (trek)	106

Bhaironchatti	2,493	3 (trek)	109
Ghuttu	1,524	9 (trek)	118
Gawanachatti	1,677	1 (trek)	119
Gaumanda	2,134	3 (trek)	122
Dhuphanda	2,896	3 (trek)	125
Panwali	3,963	3 (trek)	128
Kyunkholakhal	3,658	4 (trek)	132
Trijuginarayan	1,982	7 (trek)	139
Sonprayag	1,829	3 (trek)	142
Gaurikund	1,981	5 (trek)	147
Kedarnath	3,583	14 (trek)	161

Dodital Trek: Dodital is at an elevation of 3,024 m. east of Uttarkashi (1,150 m.). The clear waters of the lake are surrounded by dense woods of oak, pine, *deodar* and rhododendron.

The trek commences from Uttarkashi to Kalyani, which can be reached by road transport. Kalyani to Agoda is a gradual climb through woods, fields and villages. From Agoda to Dodital the trek lies through thick forests and is steep.

Route	Altitude of Reaching Point (m.)	Distance (kms.)
Uttarkashi to Gangotri	1,219	4 (road)
Gangotri to Kalyani	1,829	7 (jeep)
Kalyani to Agoda	2,286	5 (trek)
Agoda to Dodital	3,024	16 (trek)

Chandrahila Winter Summit: This is a small peak of 3,679 m., good for climbing, skiing and trekking in winter through rich flora and fauna, lakes and meadows.

Route	Altitude of Reaching Point (m.)	Distance (kms.)
Drive to Guptakashi via Deoprayag, Srinagar and Rudraprayag		185
Rudrapayag to Okhimath		14 (road)
Okhimath to Devariatal		8 (trek)
Trek to Dogal-bitta	1,500 to 2,000	16 (trek)
Trek to Chopta	3,000	9
Chandrahila Peak via Tungnath	3,679	7

DODITAL TREK

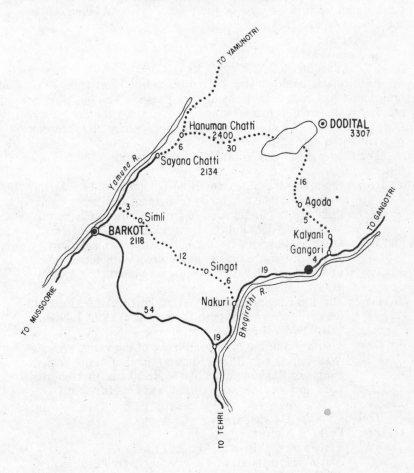

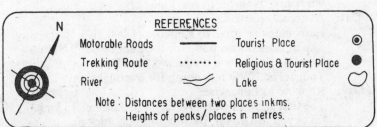

Devi Darshan Trek: This trek is for those who want to see the Garhwal Himalaya and do not have the strength or time for a close view. Three *sidh-peeth* are at the top of a hill, in a triangular form, named after Goddess Durga. From each temple the other is visible, presenting a panoramic view of the mighty Garhwal Himalaya and the Doon Valley. They are:

Kunjapuri	1,645 m.
Surkhanda Devi	3,030 m.
Chandrabadini	2,756 m.

Each trek is approachable by motor and by short treks of an hour and a half each. The treks are not tiresome and one does not require much strength to undertake them. Except for the Chandrabadini, tap water is not available anywhere else; therefore water is to be carried in water bottles.

The Garhwal Mandal Vikas Nigam Ltd. proposes the following itinerary:

1st Day: From Rishikesh drive to Hindolakhal, trek. 22 kms. to Kunjapuri; take two hours off for rest and lunch, then trek back to Hindolakhal (3 kms.). Drive to Dhanaulti — 69 kms. Night halt: Tourist Bungalow, Dhanaulti.

2nd Day: Drive to Kadukhal (9 kms.). Trek to Surkhanda Devi (3 kms.). Leisure time in the afternoon, then trek down to Kadukhal. Drive to Chamba for night halt: Chamba Tourist Bungalow.

3rd Day: Drive to Chandrabadini Devi (63 kms.). After lunch and tea at the temple, drive to Devprayag (32 kms.). Night halt: Tourist Bungalow, Devprayag.

4th Day: After a dip in the holy confluence of the sacred rivers Alakananda and Bhagirathi and the visit to the ancient temple of Raghunathji, drive to Rishikesh. En route visit Laxman Jhula, Swarag Ashram and Gita Bhawan.

Trek to Sunder Dhunga Glacier (4,320 m.)

1st Day: Delhi to Almora
Early morning drive to Almora (1,645 m.) by car or coach. This distance of 446 kms. is covered in about ten hours. Transfer to rest house.

2nd Day: Almora to Kapkote
Early morning drive to Kapkote (1,066 m.); on the way stop at Bageshwar, and visit the famous Bagh Nath temples. Kapkote is on the banks of River Saryu. Transfer to PWD rest house for overnight stay.

3rd Day: Kapkote to Loharkhet
The first stage of trek covering a distance of 16 kms. takes you to Dhakri, passing through thick oak trees.

Descent to rest house presents a lovely view of Nanda Kot.

5th Day: Dhakri to Dwali
Climb down to Dwali (2,590 m.), a distance of 13 kms. On an average it takes you about 5 hours to reach the PWD rest house, which is at the confluence of Rivers Pinder and Kafni. Overnight in PWD rest house.

6th Day: Dwali to Phurkia
A steep climb of 5 kms. takes you to Phurkia (3,265 m.). The trek lies along the bank of River Pinder. Overnight at PWD rest house.

7th Day: Phurkia to Pindari Glacier to Phurkia
The 8 km. trek takes you to the zero point, i.e. right in front of the famous Pindari Glacier. You go as high as 4,270 m. Back to Phurkia for overnight stay.

8th Day: Phurkia to Dwali
Climb down takes one to Dwali. Overnight at the rest house.

9th Day: Dwali to Umila
From Dwali you deviate north-west to Umila (2,285 m.). The distance of 11 kms. is normally covered in about 4 hours. Overnight in tents.

10th Day: Umila to Sona
Further climb to Sona (2,590 m.) which is at a distance of 9 kms. Overnight at tents.

11th Day: Sona to Jatoli
A trek of 12 kms. takes you to Jatoli, which can be covered in about 6 hours. Overnight in tents.

12th Day: Jatoli to Dhungia Dhon
Dhungia Dhon is at a height of 2,743 m. This trek involves steep climbing at a few places and it takes about 5 hours to cover the distance of 13 kms.

13th Day: Dhungia Dhon to Shepherd's Hut
The 11 km. trek takes one to Shepherd's Hut (2,745 m.). Overnight in tents.

14th Day: Sherpherd's Hut to Sukhram Cave
Distance of 10 kms. to Sukhram Cave, which takes about 7 hours as it involves steep climbing. Overnight in tents.

15th Day: Sukhram Cave to Bharoti
Bharoti is at a height of 4,320 m. It has beautiful camping grounds which are at a distance of about 6 kms. Overnight in tents.

16th Day: Bharoti to Sukhram Cave
Downward descent to Sukhram Cave.

17th Day: Sukhram Cave to Shepherd's Hut

Climb down takes one to Shepherd's Hut. Overnight in tents.

18th Day: Shepherd's Hut to Dhungia Dhon
Trek back to Dhungia Dhon. Overnight in tents.

19th Day: Dhungia Dhon to Jatoli
Further on to Jatoli. Overnight in tents.

20th Day Jatoli to Sona
Climb takes one down to Sona. Overnight in rest house.

21st Day: Sona to Dhakri
Trek back to Dhakri rest house; this trail takes about 5 hours. Overnight in forest rest house.

22nd Day: Dhakri to Loharkhet
Further trek down to Loharkhet. Overnight in rest house.

23rd Day: Loharkhet to Kapkote, Almora
Last stage of trek takes one back to Kapkote. Post-lunch drive takes one to Almora. Transfer to rest house for the night.

24th Day: Almora to Delhi
Late evening return to Delhi by coach.

Corbett Park: Corbett Park has the distinction of being the first National Park in India. The park sprawls over an area of 525.8 sq. kms. It was established in the year 1935 under the U.P. National Parks Act and was named the Hailey National Park, after Sir William Malcolm Hailey, an enthusiastic conservationist who was at that time the Governor of U.P. In 1957, the park was rechristened as Corbett National Park in the memory of the late Jim Corbett, legendary sportsman, great naturalist, eminent conservationist and a prolific writer, who spent some of the best and happiest years of his life in the Kumaon Himalayas. It is 118 kms. from Nainital via Kaladhungi and Ramnagar.

Aptly called the "land of roar, trumpet and songs," Corbett Park is a legend come alive. The park embraces the picturesque Patlidun, a broad, flat valley consisting of vast savannahs and surrounded by hills. The Ramganga River, meandering its way through the park, swaying this way and that with some deep pools and foaming rapids forms the main water source. The valley is 400 m. above sea level, while the surrounding hills range between 700 and 1,500 m. ASL. The park is rich in wild life: elephants, tigers, panthers, bears, deer, antelopes, pigs, porcupines, jungle cats, hyenas and jackals. Amongst the birds are the pea fowl, the jungle fowl, kaleege pheasant, grey and black partridge, green and rock pigeon, quail, babbler, bee-eater, bulbul, crow, dove, drongo, fly catcher, hornbull, kingfisher, kite, lark, parakeet and woodpecker. The Ramganga is full of *mahaseer* fish. Amongst the reptiles are python, crocodile, and many species of lizard and snakes in their natural habitat. The park remains closed from June to October owing to the rainy season.

Pindari Glacier: This is one of the most easily accessible of all Himalayan glaciers. Measuring nearly 3 kms. in length, a quarter kilometre in width, Pindari's rugged beauty is a breathtaking sight. Some 69 kms. are to be trekked from Kapkote (Bharari), the bus terminus. The glacier owes its existence to the vast quantities of snow precipitated from Nanda Devi and other lofty mountains above. To reach Pindari, the trekkers' delight, one has to reach Kathgodam by the N.E.R., motor up to Kapkote via Almora and then trek up from Kapkote to the glacier. As one treks along the route surrounded by the majestic Himalayas, every inch becomes a fresh song of nature, and at every curve the eyes embrace a new landscape more beautiful than the one before.

May-June and September-October are the ideal months for this trek.

Stage	Distance (kms.)	Height (m.)	Accommodation	Reservation Authority
Kapkote (bus terminus)		1,082	PWD Dak Bungalow	Executive Engineer, PWD, Almora.
Loharkhet	16	1,753	-do-	-do-
Dhakuri	10	2,621	-do-	-do-
Khati	10	2,210	-do-	-do-
Dwali	11	2,576	-do-	-do-
Phurkia	5	3,261	-do-	-do-
Pindari Glacier	3	3,353	-do-	-do-

Milam Glacier (198 kms.): Over 4,000 m. high, Milam is the biggest glacier in the U.P. Himalayan region. It is about 27 kms. in length. Milam Village, which lies near the glacier, is one of the highest villages in the Himalayan range. The staple food here is potato. The route to Milam Glacier from Nainital is as follows:

Nainital to Bageshwar	156 kms.
Bageshwar to Thal	72 kms.
Thal to Munsyari	77 kms.
Munsyari to Lilam	10 kms.
Lilam to Bogudyar	8 kms.
Bogudyar to Martoli	18 kms.
Martoli to Milam Village	11 kms.
Milam Village to Glacier	5 kms.

The distance from Nainital to Thal can be shortened if one goes via Seraghat. Nainital to Thal via Seraghat is 190 kms. One can also go directly from Pithoragarh via Munsyari.

The glacier, owing to the debris, and surrounded by snow peaks is indeed a sight — seen to be believed. The River Gauri originates from the base of this glacier.

Treks Around Darjeeling

The region of Darjeeling is a veritable paradise for trekkers. Trekking in Darjeeling is an experience which no lover of nature should miss. The treks take you to virginal spots and bring you face to face with the sublime grandeur of the Himalayas.

The region abounds in rhododendrons, primulas and orchids of numerous varieties. About six hundred different species of birds inhabit the forests on the slopes of the mountains.

The pre-monsoon season (February to early May), especially the months of April and May, and the post-monsoon season (September to early December), especially October and November, are ideal for trekking. April and May are the flowering seasons for most of the exotic plants of the area, though there may be occasional showers during this period. December, January and February will be cold and there may be occasional snowfall.

Approximate temperatures in the Darjeeling region range, in summer, from 8.59°C to 14.89°C and in winter, 1.5°C to 6.11°C.

The routes lie through valley depths as low as 2,000 ft. and mountaintops as high as 12,000 ft. Clothes will have to be arranged accordingly. While at lower altitudes a light sweater would be enough, at higher altitudes a heavy pullover topped by a wind-cheater is advisable. Woollen caps and gloves are a must for treks in winter. A muffler may be an added advantage. Good, durable shoes are absolutely necessary. So is a raincoat. A sleeping bag should form an essential part of your equipment. Travellers must carry their own provisions. Food should be such as can be carried easily and will keep in warmer weather. It is essential to carry a packet of salt as this is a rare commodity at higher altitudes. There are small teashops en route to Sandakphu, at places like Meghma, Gairibes, Rimbick, Jhepi, Lodoma and Bijanbari.

A first-aid box should also be carried. Each member of the trekking party should carry a good torch with spare batteries, as well as candles and matches. A stout stick may be helpful when walking. Since trekking routes abound in scenic beauty, a camera and a pair of good field glasses will add to the pleasure of the trip.

There are three leading trekking agents in Darjeeling:

(a) Himal Venture, Indreni Lodge (2nd Floor),
7, Chowrasta Road, Darjeeling.
(b) Summit Tours, Hayden Hall, Darjeeling.
(c) Daku Tenzing Kanchenjunga Tours, Darjeeling.

Porters are available at Manebhanjang and also at Dhotray. Trekking equipment, including sleeping bags, wind-cheaters, blankets, etc. are available at Darjeeling Youth Hostel. Details of routes, maps and charts may also be had from the warden of the Youth Hostel.

Health and medical care: Medical facilities are available at Manebhanjang and Dhotrey Primary Health Centres.

Rescue facilities: There are police camps and B.S.F. posts at Sandakphu and Phalut. Communication facilities are also available with the Hydel Power Construction Project at Ramam. In case of emergencies information may be sent through their channels.

Treks: Some shorter and more popular treks are:

Route I: (a)   Darjeeling — Manebhanjang — Tonglu — Sandakphu — Phalut and return — 160 kms. altogether.

          (b)   Darjeeling — Manebhanjang — Tonglu — Sandakphu and return — 118 kms. altogether.

Route II: Darjeeling — Manebhanjang — Tonglu — Sandakphu — Phalut — Ramam — Rimbik — Jhepi — Darjeeling via Bijanbari — 153 kms. altogether.

Route III: Darjeeling — Manebhanjang — Tonglu — Sandakphu — Phalut — Ramam — Rimbick — Palmajua — Batasi — Manebhanjang — Darjeeling — 178 kms. altogether.

Other longer trails are listed below.

In and around Darjeeling: The following are two treks: a trek of 8 days and another of eleven days.

1st Day: Bagdogra airport to Darjeeling
This is a 90 km. drive, taking three hours. Halt: Darjeeling (2,134 m./7,000 ft.).

2nd Day: Darjeeling
9 A.M. to 12.30 P.M.: Local sightseeing, i.e. Himalayan Mountaineering Institute, Himalayan Zoological Park, Tibetan Refugee Self Help Centre. After lunch, walk around the town and market area in order to acclimatize.

3rd Day: Darjeeling to Manebhanjang (2,134 m./7,000 ft.) to Batasi (2,098 m./6,884 ft.) to Barahatta (1,744 m./5,725 ft.)
7.30 A.M.: Drive from Darjeeling by mini-coach or jeep to Batasi (41 kms., a two and a half hours' journey). Trek begins from Batasi; walk upto Dhotrey (10 kms.) at 2,438 m./8,000 ft. Lunch at Dhotrey; walk downhill all the way through forest and across the stream to Palmajua is another one-hour walk to Barahatta. Approximately four hours of walking is involved altogether. Camp: Barahatta (school compound), which

offers a beautiful view of the surrounding valley.

4th Day: Barahatta to Rimbick (2,280 m./7,500 ft.)
Departure: 8 A:M., after breakfast; road descends to Lodoma Khola and from here there is a steep climb all the way to Rimbick; Barahatta to Rimbick is nearly five hours (approximately 15 kms.). Camp: Rimbick Forest House premises; there is a small market here; on a clear day one sees Darjeeling down from Rimbick.

5th Day: Rimbick to Sandakphu (3,636 m./11,929 ft.)
Departure: 8 A.M.; Rimbick to Sandakphu is a continuous climb through the thick forest. Rimbick to Sandakphu is a nearly eight-hour walk — 16 kms. Camp: Sandakphu.

6th Day: Sandakphu to Tonglu (3,070 m./10,074 ft.)
Sandakphu is the highest point in this trek. It commands a magnificent view of the whole of eastern Nepal and the Sikkim Himalaya, i.e. from the mighty Mt Everest in Nepal to Kanchenjunga in Sikkim to the legendary Chomolhari in Bhutan. Sunrise and sunset over these mountains is not to be missed. Departure: 8 A.M. after breakfast; Sandakphu to Tonglu is nearly 22 kms. through the small Nepalese village. It is slow descent all the way to Tonglu. Camp: Tonglu.

7th Day: Tonglu to Manebhanjang (2,134 m./7,000 ft.)
Tonglu also commands an excellent view of Kanchenjunga. Tonglu to Manebhanjang is a continuous downhill journey. From Manebhanjang take a mini-bus/jeep to Darjeeling; lunch at the hotel; set aside the afternoon for shopping.

8th Day: Drive back to Bagdogra airport early in the morning.
The second trek:

1st Day: Bagdogra airport to Darjeeling (90 kms.)
Takes three hours and a half at Darjeeling (2,134 m./7,000 ft.).

2nd Day: Darjeeling
9 A.M. to 12.30 P.M.: Local sightseeing, i.e. Himalayan Mountaineering Institute, Himalayan Zoological Park, Tibetan Refugee Self Help Centre. After lunch, walk around the town and market area in order to acclimatize. 6 P.M.: Meet at the hotel for briefing on the trek.

3rd Day: Darjeeling to Manebhanjang (2,134 m./7,000 ft.) to Batasi (2,098 m./6,884 ft.) to Barahatta (1,744 m./5,725 ft.)
7.30 A.M.: Drive from Darjeeling by mini-coach or jeep to Batasi (41 kms.) in two and a half hours; the trek

begins from Batasi. Walk upto Dhotrey (10 kms.),
2,438 m./8,000 ft. Lunch at Dhotrey; walk downhill
all the way through forest and across the stream to
Palmajua (2,210 m./7,250 ft.), 11 kms. from Batasi; from
Palmajua another one hour's walk takes you to
Barahatta. The day's walking takes four hours
altogether. Camp: Barahatta (school compound), from
where you get a beautiful view of the surrounding valley.

4th Day: Barahatta to Rimbick (2,280 m./7,500 ft.)
Departure: 8 A.M., after breakfast; road descends to
Lodoma Khola and from here there is a steep climb all
the way to Rimbick; Barahatta to Rimbick is nearly a
five-hour walk (15 kms.). Camp: Rimbick Forest House
premises; there is a small market at Rimbick. On a clear
day one can see Darjeeling town from Rimbick.

5th Day: Rimbick to Ramam (2,453 m./8,000 ft.)
After breakfast leave for Ramam (19 kms.), a six hours'
walk. This trail passes through beautiful forest inhabited
by different varieties of birds. Camp: Ramam Forest rest
house, offering a beautiful view of the western Sikkim
Hills.

6th Day: Ramam to Molle (3,359 m./11,802 ft.)
Ramam to Molle is a nearly four-hour walk. Camp on
the open land.

7th Day: Molle to Phalut (3,600 m./11,811 ft.)
Molle to Phalut takes nearly three hours. Phalut is at
the tri-junction of Sikkim, Nepal and West Bengal.
Excellent view of Kanchenjunga Range can be had from
here. Back to Molle and halt.

8th Day: Molle to Sandakphu (3,636 m./11,929 ft.)
Molle to Sandakphu is nearly 16 kms. or a six-hour
walk. This is a most beautiful trek of this area. All along
the route you will be able to see Mt Everest, towards
your right. Camp: Sandakphu.

9th Day: Sandakphu to Tonglu (3,070 m./10,074 ft.)
Sandakphu is the highest point in this trek. It commands
a magnificent view of the whole of eastern Nepal and
the Sikkim Himalaya, i.e., from the mighty Everest in
Nepal to Kanchenjunga in Sikkim to the legendary
Chomolhari in Bhutan. Sunrise and sunsets over these
mountains are never to be missed. Departure: 8 A.M.
after breakfast; Sandakphu to Gonglu is nearly 22 kms.
through the small Nepalese village; it is a slow descent
all the day to Tonglu. Camp: Tonglu.

10th Day: Tonglu to Manebhanjang (2,134 m./7,000 ft.) to
Darjeeling

Tonglu also commands an excellent view of Kanchenjunga; Tonglu to Manebhanjang is continuous downhill; from Manebhanjang take a mini-bus/jeep to Darjeeling. Lunch at the hotel; afternoon can be set aside for shopping.

11th Day: Bagdogra

9.30 A.M.: Drive back to Bagdogra airport.

Treks in Sikkim

This tiny, remote and mountainous state is bounded by Tibet in the north, Bhutan in the east, Nepal in the west and Bengal in the south. With an area of 2,818 sq. miles (7,325 sq. kms.) its elevation ranges from 8,000 ft. to 28,000 ft. ASL.

Sikkim is a tourist's paradise, with its ice-clad peaks framed by dense tropical vegetation, forested slopes and ridges, fast-flowing rivers and undisturbed peace. Flora and fauna is rich — the rhododendrons are abundant, as also the orchids, magnolias and the primulas. The forests abound with black and brown bear, barking deer, musk deer, *sambhar*, trout, salmon and carp. There are over six hundred varieties of birds and an equal number of varieties of butterflies. The Sikkimese are simple people and deeply religious. The best time to visit Sikkim is mid-February to late May, and then October to December.

The nearest airport is Bagdogra, which is 124 kms. from Gangtok. The journey from Bagdogra to Gangtok takes approximately five hours. Indian Airlines operate regular scheduled flights between Calcutta and Bagdogra and Delhi and Bagdogra. The two closest railway stations to Gangtok are Siliguri, 114 kms. away, and new Jalpaiguri, 125 kms. away. From both these stations one can board trains to Delhi, Calcutta and other important cities.

Gangtok is connected by road with Darjeeling, Kalimpong and Siliguri. Government and private buses are available for to and fro journeys. Foreigners must obtain an Inner Line permit from the Home Ministry at New Delhi, which should be applied for at least six weeks prior to the proposed date of entry into Sikkim. A copy of the application may be endorsed to the Department of Tourism, Sikkim, or to the Sikkim Tourist Office in Delhi or Calcutta to expedite matters. This permit will allow them to stay for four days for purposes of sightseeing and ten days for group trekking, each group not exceeding twenty.

East Sikkim, beyond Rongle, and north Sikkim, beyond Phodong, are restricted areas; they are restricted for Indian citizens also. In west Sikkim, foreigners are allowed to visit Pemayangtse and Tashiding, and, in case of groups, Dzongri. In south Sikkim only Namche and Naya Bazaar can be visited.

The Sikkim state government have notified the following areas to form the Kangchendzonga National Park, with a view to protect, preserve and encourage breeding of rich flora and fauna which is considered of great ecological, geomorphological and biological significance:

On the East: Proceeding from Zedong along the ridge passing through Lama Angdong, along with ridge of Lachen, Benshoi, Latong, Denga, Yugang reserve forests, following the ridges upto Thang R.F.

On the West: Commencing from South Kabur Peak, following the Nepal boundary, passing through Kabur North Peak, Tauling

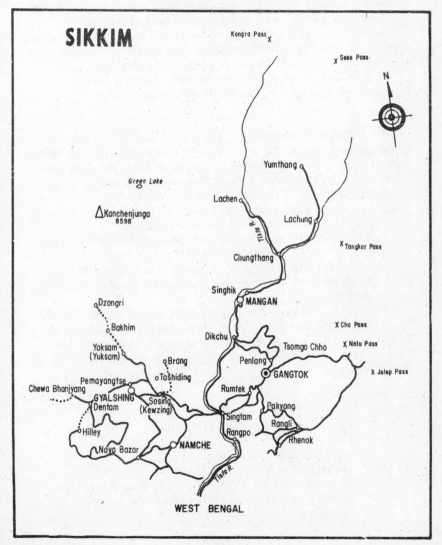

Peak, Mount Kangchendzonga, Nepal Peak and ending at Tent Peak.

On the South: Proceeding from Thang R.F. and passing above Pakal R.F., following the ridge and crossing Ringi Chhu above Tholung Gompa, then following the ridge to a turning point to further South, following the ridges between Umaram Chhu and its tributaries Passaram Chhu, passing through Tsingnok, Pakilho, Mounts Narsing Jho-Punu, Pandim, Geochala, and ending up at Kabur Peak.

On the North: Commencing from Tent Peak, on the Nepal boundary, passing Zemu Glacier along the Zemu Chhu up to the confluence of Zemu Chhu and Lhonak Chhu at Zedong.

A Sikkim Tourist Office has been opened in Siliguri from where Inner Line crossing permits for entry into Sikkim are issued after they have been cleared by the Ministry of Home Affairs at New Delhi. The address of the Sikkim Tourist Office is Sikkim Nationalised Transport Complex, Pradhannagar, Siliguri.

Treks

To Dzongri (West Sikkim): Fly from Delhi or Calcutta to Bagdogra and then a four-hour drive to Gangtok, capital of Sikkim state. Gangtok to Pemayangtse: a five-hour drive the next day takes one to Pemayangtse Village. Overnight in a tourist lodge.

Pemayangtse to Yuksom: A six-hour trek to Yuksom through a plateau of barley and oranges. Yuksom is well-known as a historical spot where the first ruler of Sikkim was crowned.

Yuksom to Bakhim: An easy trek through mountain ranges between 2,500 m. to 3,500 m., passing through dense forest, takes one to Bakhim. This takes approximately five hours. Bakhim to Dzongri: A six-hour strenuous trek to Dzongri through beautiful flower meadows.

Dzongri to Bakhim: An easy six-hour trek down to Bakhim. Night at a forest rest house or in tents. Bakhim to Yuksom to Pemayangtse: Trek back to Yuksom in about four hours. Drive back to Darjeeling, which is an exciting four-hour drive along the River Tista.

Darjeeling-Sikkim Trek:

1st Day: Delhi to Bagdogra to Darjeeling
          From Bagdogra drive to Darjeeling.
2nd Day: Darjeeling
          Sightseeing at Darjeeling.
3rd Day: Darjeeling to Yuksom (1,740 m.)
          Morning leave for Yuksom, a seven-hour drive. Upon
          arrival a very short trek takes you to the tourist-
          bungalow.

108

NORTH-EAST TREKKING ROUTE

SOUTH-WEST TREKKING ROUTE

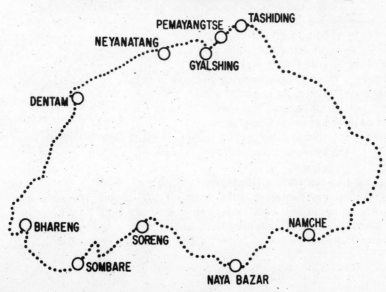

4th Day: Yuksom to Bakhim (2,550 m.)
The trail runs through moss-laden forests of pines, firs, giant magnolias, rhododendrons, spruce and, besides these, 600 varieties of orchids and birds of the Himalaya. A six-hour trek will take you to Bakhim.

5th Day: Bakhim to Jamlingkhang
An easy trek through the dense forest of Jamlingkhang takes you about five hours.

6th Day: Jamlingkhang to Choringkhang (3,800 m.)
A steep trek of seven hours takes you to Choringkhang, which is the base camp for the Himalayan Mountaineering Institute.

7th Day: Choringkhang
Set aside the day to explore the surroundings.

8th Day: Choringkhang to Dzongri (3,880 m.)
A steep climb through Dzongri-La takes 5 hours to Dzongri. At the highest point one can see the massive range of Sikkim mountains presided by the mighty Kanchenjunga.

9th Day: Dzongri to Thangsing (3,780 m.)
Seven hours through meadows and valley lead to one of the most beautiful valleys surrounded by mighty mountains on all sides.

10th Day: Thangsing to Lambi Lake (4,818 m.)
Five hours of trekking brings you to splendid glacial lakes.

11th Day: Lambi Lake to Geocha-La Thangsing (5,336 m.)
An excursion to Geocha-La (pass). The highest point of our trek, starting with a steady climb, the trail climbs up to the pass. From here one gets a splendid view of the glacier rivers flowing down.

12th Day: Thangsing to Dzongri
Trek back to Dzongri.

13th Day: Dzongri to Bakhim
A short downhill trek of two hours takes you to Bakhim.

14th Day: Bakhim to Yuksom
Trek back to Yuksom.

15th Day: Yuksom to Gangtok
Drive to Gangtok via Rabongla takes eight hours; en route visit Pemayangtse Monastery.

Climbing in the Indian Himalaya

The Indian Himalaya offers a variety of climbing possibilities. There are small and easy peaks, and there are high peaks, technically tough. Those interested in the alpine style of climbing, would find an unlimited variety; a list of peaks open for climbing in Kashmir, Himachal Pradesh and Uttar Pradesh will be found at the end of this chapter.

Kashmir: In the Zanskar area, the most popular peaks are Nun (7,135 m.), Kun (7,087 m.), White Needle (6,500 m.), Pinnacle (6,930 m.) and the group of peaks (6,050 m. to 6,270 m.).

In the Ladakh region Stok Kangri (6,153 m.), Parcha Kangri (6,065 m.), Gulap Kangri (5,900 m.), Kanglacha (6,400 m.) and Kang Yishay attract quite a number of expeditions. Except for Kang Yishay, other peaks attract larger groups who climb purely for enjoyment.

In Kishtwar, in the Kiar Nala area, the attractive but technically difficult peaks are Sickle Moon (6,574 m.), Eiger (6,001 m.), Cathedral (5,730 m.) and a host of unnamed peaks. In the Nanth Nala are technically difficult peaks like Brammah I (6,416 m.), Crooked Ginger (5,630 m.), and Flat Top (6,100 m.).

Himachal Pradesh: There are a large number of unnamed peaks in the Kao Rang Valley (numbered as K.R.-1, K.R.-2 and so on) ranging in heights from 6,005 m. to 6,340 m. In the fascinating Mulkila group the peaks vary in heights between 5,730 m. to 6,517 m. In the Chandra Bhaga Valley are the C.B. group of peaks, ranging in heights from between 5,700 m. to 6,254 m. South of the Chandra River in the Bara Shigri Glacier there are beautiful peaks like Devachan (6,200 m.), Papsura (6,451 m.) which is a toughy, and White Sail or Dharam Sura (6,445 m.), a popular peak. South of Chandra River and East of Beas River are peaks like Indrasan (6,221 m.), Deo Tibba (6,001 m.) and Ali Ratri Tibba (5,470 m.). West of Beas River are the Hanuman Tibba peaks, (5,928 m. and 5,516 m.), Ladakhi (5,342 m.), Manali (5,669 m.), Makerbeh (6,069 m.) and Shikerbeh (6,200 m.) — small and beautiful peaks, good for beginners. North of Chenab River are Menthosa (6,443 m.), Phabrang (6,172 m.) and Mainghat Choti (6,094 m.), which is not an easy climb.

Uttar Pradesh: Gangotri region is home of a number of mountain beauties, some of them quite tough technically, which draw the largest number of mountaineers every year: the Gangotri group of peaks (6,577 m. to 6,672 m.), Thalay Sagar (6,904 m.), Bhrigupanth (6,015 m.), Meru (6,660 m.), Kedarnath (6,968 m.), Kharcha Kund (6,632 m.), Shivling (6,543 m.), the Bhagirathi group (6,454 m. to 6,856 m.), Vasuki Parbat (6,792 m.), Satopanth (7,075 m.), and Sudarshan Parbat (6,507 m.), to name a few.

In the Kumaon region, Nanda Devi offered a host of peaks like Nanda Devi West (7,817 m.) and Nanda Devi East (7,434 m.), Trisul (7,120 m.), Changabang (6,864 m.), Dunagiri (7,066 m.), Kalanka (6,931 m.), Devisthan (6,678 m.), Maiktoli (6,803 m.), Mrigthuni (6,856 m.) and so on. The Uttar Pradesh government have, however, declared Nanda Devi Basin a National Park, closing it for climbing and trekking. However, peaks like Trishul, Maiktoli, Mrigthuni, Panwali Devar (6,663 m.) and Nanda Kot (6,611 m.) can be attempted from the outside without entering the Nanda Devi Sanctuary, inner and outer.

Procedure for booking peaks: Under the provisions of the Foreigners' Act, all foreign expeditions have to obtain prior permission of the Government of India for climbing peaks in the Indian Himalaya, on an application made through the Indian Mountaineering Foundation, along with the following booking fee:

(*a*)   Peaks of and above 21,000 ft. in height   Rs 7,500 each
(*b*)   Peaks below 21,000 ft. in height   Rs 5,000 each

Each foreign expedition has to take a liaison officer, provided by the Indian Mountaineering Foundation. A liaison officer is to be treated as a member of the expedition team and provided with the following equipment/clothing, of the same standard as provided to the other members:

(*a*)   a pair of climbing boots along with boot covers;
(*b*)   a pair of crampons;
(*c*)   an ice-axe;
(*d*)   a wind-proof suit;
(*e*)   a down jacket;
(*f*)   a sleeping bag;
(*g*)   an air mattress;
(*h*)   a rucksack;
(*i*)   a pair of socks;
(*j*)   other items that are given to other members, e.g. climbing harness, jumar, water-bottle, knife, cap, etc.

The expedition will also bear transport, food and medicine expenses of the liaison officer from Delhi to the mountains and back.

Training of foreigners in Indian mountaineering institutes: The Himalayan Mountaineering Institute at Darjeeling, which is the oldest in this country, having been established in 1954, offers adventure courses for foreigners interested in training for climbing in the Himalaya.

Four courses, each of 21 days' duration, are held every year. The fee for a foreign student is Rs 1,000.

List of "Open" Peaks in the Kashmir Himalaya

Name	Height (m.)	Longitude	Latitude
ZANSKAR AREA			
Nun	7,135	76° 01'	33° 59'
Kun	7,087	76° 03'	34° 01'
Pinnacle	6,930	76° 05'	34° 01'
White Needle	6,500	76° 02'	33° 59'
Bobang	5,971	76° 08'	33° 25'
Z-2	6,175		
Z-3	6,270		
Z-1	6,181	76° 14'	33° 46'
Z-8	6,050		
D-41	5,813		
Unnamed	5,934		
(North of Gulmatang)			
N-8	6,392	76° 07'	33° 44'
Bien Guapa	6,006		
LADAKH AREA			
Stok Kangri	6,153	76° 08'	33° 26'
Parcha Kangri	6,065	76° 12'	33° 47'
Gulap Kangri	5,900	76° 10'	33° 26'
Kanglacha	6,400	76° 51'	33° 25'
Mashiro Kangri	5,367	77° 24'	33° 59'
Kantaka Kangri	5,275	77° 24'	33° 59'
Kang Yisay	6,400	76° 50'	33° 23'
Cumberland	5,227		
KISHTWAR AREA			
(i) Kiar Nala			
Sickle Moon	6,574	76° 08'	33° 37'
Eiger	6,001	76° 09'	33° 27'
Cathedral	5,370	76° 08'	33° 48'
Unnamed	5,594	76° 06'	33° 50'
Unnamed	5,921	76° 06'	33° 50'
Unnamed	5,817	76° 06'	33° 50'
Unnamed	5,340	76° 06'	33° 51'
Unnamed	5,605	76° 07'	33° 52'
Unnamed	6,045	76° 07'	33° 52'
Unnamed	6,200	76° 08'	33° 52'
Unnamed	6,392	76° 08'	33° 52'

Unnamed	5,560	76° 08'	33° 52'
Unnamed	6,560	76° 09'	33° 54'
Unnamed	6,000	76° 10'	33° 38'
Unnamed	6,225	76° 16'	33° 38'
Unnamed	5,890	76° 09'	33° 48'
Unnamed	5,455	76° 10'	33° 48'
Unnamed	5,645	76° 00'	33° 48'
(South of Cathedral)			
Unnamed	6,520	76° 08'	33° 37'
(North of Sickle Moon)			
Unnamed	6,415	76° 08'	33° 37'
(South of Sickle Moon)			
Unnamed	6,013	76° 07'	33° 37'
(South-west of Sickle Moon)			
Unnamed	5,600	76° 09'	33° 27'

(ii) Nanth Nala

Brammah's wife	5,297	76° 07'	33° 29'
Brammah – I	6,416	76° 03'	33° 30'
Crooked Finger	5,630	76° 10'	33° 34'
Flat Top	6,100	70° 12'	33° 46'
Unnamed	6,001	76° 11'	33° 34'
(East of Flat Top)			
Brammah – II	6,425	76° 08'	33° 36'
Unnamed	6,000	76° 08'	33° 37'
(North of Brammah – II)			
Unnamed	5,630	76° 08'	33° 38'
(Brammah Glacier)			
Unnamed	5,460	76° 08'	33° 38'
(Brammah Glacier)			
Unnamed	5,950	76° 08'	33° 39'
(Brammah Glacier)			
Unnamed	5,830	76° 08'	33° 39'
(Brammah Glacier)			
Dreikant	5,890	76° 09'	33° 39'
Eckpfeiler	5710	75° 59'	33° 35'

(iii) Barnai Nala

Barnaj – I	6,100	76° 23'	33° 35'
Barnaj – II	6,290	76° 22'	33° 35'
Unnamed	6,000	76° 21'	33° 36'
Unnamed	5,640	76° 21'	33° 35'
Unnamed	5,710	76° 21'	33° 33'

Unnamed	5,950	76° 22'	33° 33'

(iv)

Arjuna	6,200	76° 09'	33° 48'
Agyasol	6,200	76° 06'	33° 43'
Shivling	6,000	76° 06'	33° 43'
Chapra (Bhazum Nala)	5,600	76° 10'	33° 36'
Unnamed (Bhazum Nala)	5,415		P.T.O.
Unnamed (Bhazum Nala)	5,890		
Unnamed	6,330		
Chering	6,187		
Unnamed (Durung Drung Glacier)	6,550		
Unnamed (South of Muni-La)	6,220		
Unnamed (South of Muni-La)	6,040		
Unnamed (Keije Nala)	6,250	76° 09'	33° 35'
Unnamed (Haske Nala)	6,225		
Unnamed (Bhut Nadi)	6,139		
Unnamed (Pholachak Nala)	6,070		
Unnamed (Haske Nala)	6,000		
Unnamed (Nanth Nala)	5,950		
Unnamed (Nanth Nala)	5,830		
Unnamed (Bhut Nadi)	5,600		

OTHER SMALL PEAKS (WITHIN KASHMIR VALLEY)

Kolahai	5,425	76° 01'	33° 49'
Harmukh	5,148	76° 01'	33° 48'
Tanak	5,992	76° 05'	33° 43'
Barmal	5,813	76° 20'	33° 36'
Kunirhayan	5,138		

Nichhang	5,444
Cowabal	6,000
Dudal	4,992
Didhnag	4,953
Sun Set	4745
Banbun	4,771
Tatakuti	4,742
Sarbal	5,235
Adventurers	5,222
Challhenmala	4,915
Harbaghwan	4,889
Greater Thajiwas	4,854
Umbrella	4,785
Valshead	4,732
Sekiwas	4,695
Crystal	4,693
Neza	4,661
Mosquito	4,617
Sentinel	4,607

List of "Open" Peaks in Himachal Himalaya

Name	Height (m.)	Latitude	Longitude
KAO RONG RANGE (EAST OF DARCHA)			
T-1	5,669		
T-2	6,035		
Unnamed	5,615		
Kao Rong	6,221	32° 13'	77° 24'
K.R.-1	6,157	32° 37'	77° 58'
K.R.-2	6,187	32° 32'	77° 24'
K.R.-3			
K.R.-4	6,340	32° 41';	77° 22'
K.R.-5	6,258	32° 38'	77° 23'
K.R.-6	6,187	30° 40'	77° 19'
K.R.-7	6,090	32° 35'	77° 25'
Unnamed (near K.R.-7)	6,005		
MULKILA RANGE (EAST OF DARCHA)			
M-1	5,730	32°-41'	77° 05'
M-2	5,832	32° 15'	74° 24'
M-3	5,791	32° 07'	77° 40'

M-4 (Mulkila)	6,517	32° 33'	77° 25'
M-5	6,370	32° 07'	77° 46'
M-6 (Taragiri)	6,279	32° 10'	77° 48'
M-7	6,340	32° 07'	77° 43'
M-8	6,096	32° 37'	77° 24'
M-9	5,679		
Unnamed	5,730		
M-10	5,852	32° 25'	77° 25'

SOUTH OF DARCHA (SISSU NALLAH)
Unnamed	5,560
Unnamed	5,852
Gepang	5,870
Unnamed	5,547
Unnamed	6,113
Unnamed	5,769

CHANDRA BHAGA RANGE (SOUTH-EAST OF DARCHA)
C.B.-9	6,108	32° 34'	77° 27'
C.B.-10 (Tarapahar)	6,227	32° 27'	77° 29'
C.B.-11	6,044	32° 44'	77° 03'
C.B.-12	6,248	32° 20'	77° 33'
C.B.-13	6,254	32° 21'	77° 33'
C.B.-13	6,240	32° 20'	77° 33'
C.B.-14	6,078	32° 23'	77° 34'
C.B.-16	5,822	32° 19'	77° 32'
C.B.-17			
C.B.-18			
C.B.-19			
C.B.-20	5,898	32° 13'	77° 28'
C.B.-21			
C.B.-22	5,700	32° 15'	77° 29'
C.B.-23			
C.B.-24			
C.B.-25			
C.B.-26	5,805		
C.B.-27			
C.B.-28			
C.B.-29			
C.B.-30			
C.B.-31	6,096	32° 26'	77° 28'
C.B.-32	5,639		

C.B.-33 (Minar)	6,172		
C.B.-34	5,913		
C.B.-35			
C.B.-36	5,791		
C.B.-37			
Unnamed	5,890		
(West of CB-18)			
C.B.-38			
C.B.-39			
C.B.-40			
C.B.-41			
C.B.-42 (Ashagiri)			
C.B.-42 a			
C.B.-43			
C.B.-44	5,938		
C.B.-45			
C.B.-46 (Akela Oila)			
C.B.-47			
C.B.-48 (Tombu)			
C.B.-49 (a)			
C.B.-49 (b)	5,964		
C.B.-50	6,096		
C.B.-51			
C.B.-52	5,944		
C.B.-53	6,096		
C.B.-54	6,096		
C.B.-55			
C.B.-56			
C.B.-57 (Tapugiri)	5,791		

SOUTH OF CHANDRA RIVER (BARA SHIGRI GLACIER)

Unnamed	5,645		
Devachan	6,200	32° 06'	77° 42'
Unnamed	6,163		
Unnamed	5,655		
Unnamed	6,250		
Papsura	6,451	32° 04'.	77° 45'
White Sail	6,445	32° 13'	77° 33'
Unnamed	5,953		
Unnamed	6,247		
Unnamed	5,943		
Snow Dome	5,947		

Unnamed	5,943		
Unnamed	6,035		
Pinnacle	5,029		
Tiger Tooth	5,974		
Unnamed	6,100	32° 44'	
Cathedral	6,100	32° 44'	77° 02'

SOUTH OF CHANDRA RIVER and EAST OF BEAS RIVER (TOS GLACIER)

Indrasan	6,221	32° 11'	77° 48'
Deo Tibba	6,001	32° 12'	77° 23'
Consolation	5,661		
Aliratni Tibba	5,470		
Unnamed	5,699		
Unnamed	5,810		
Unnamed	5,647		

WEST OF BEAS RIVER

Hanuman Tibba–I	5,928	32° 21'	77° 02'
Hanuman Tibba–II	5,516		
Manali	5,669	32° 34'	76° 55'
Ladakhi	5,342	32° 11'	77° 28'
Makarbeh	6,069	32° 25'	77° 05'
Shikarbeh	6,200	32° 26'	77° 03'

NORTH OF CHENAB RIVER

Behali Jot	6,279	32° 50'	76° 34'
Behali Jot (North)	6,290		
Behali Jot (South)	6,295		
Menthosa	6,443	32° 55'	76° 43'
Unnamed	6,300		
Dagoi Jot	5,933		
Unnamed	5,956		
Phabrang	6,172	32° 47'	76° 48'
Unnamed	5,800		
Unnamed	5,600		
Unnamed	5,840		
Nainghar Choti	6,094	32° 40'	77° 47'
North	5,901		
Unnamed	6,109		
Unnamed	5,908		
Unnamed	5,977		

Unnamed	6,006		
Unnamed	6,070		

SOUTH OF CHENAB RIVER

Tent	6,113	32° 10'	77° 44'
Unnamed	5,730		
Unnamed	6,020		
Unnamed	6,113		
Alias Jot	5,799		
Sanakdent Jot	6,045		
Laluni Jot	5,973		

List of "Open" Peaks in Garhwal Himalaya

Name	Height (m.)	Longitude	Latitude
GANGOTRI AREA			
Swargarohini	6,252	78° 31'	31° 06'
Unnamed (West of Swagarohini)	6,247	78° 30'	31° 06'
Unnamed (also West of Swargarohini	6,209	78° 30'	31° 06'
Unnamed (East of Swargarohini)	5,654	78° 35'	31° 04'
Unnamed (East of Swargarohini)	5,873	78° 35'	31° 04'
Unnamed (also, East of Swargarohini)	5,736	78° 35'	31° 06'
Unnamed (North of Banderpunch)	5,791	78° 34'	31° 04'
Banderpunch-I (Black)	6,387	78° 34'	31° 02'
Banderpunch–II	6,320	78° 33	31° 00'
Unnamed (West of Banderpunch-II)	61020	78° 31'	31° 00'
Unnamed (West of Banderpunch–II)	5,800	78° 37'	31° 00'
Srikanta	6,133	78° 48'	30° 57'
Unnamed (West of Srikanta)	5,544	78° 47'	30° 57'
Unnamed (South-East of Srikanta)	6,023	78° 49'	30° 57'
Rudugaira	5,819	78° 52'	30° 56'

Gangotri-I	6,672	78° 51'	30° 55'
Gangotri-II	6,590	78° 51'	30° 54'
Gangotri-III	6,577	78° 52'	30° 53'
Joanli	6,632	78° 51'	30° 51'
Unnamed	5,834	78° 50'	30° 52'
Unnamed	6,038	78° 50'	30° 52'

PEAKS IN KEDARGANGA VALLEY

Jogin-II	6,342	78° 56'	30° 54'
Jogin-I	6,465	78° 55'	30° 53'
Jogin-III	6,116	78° 56'	30° 54'
Thaley Sagar or Pathing Pithwara	6,904	78° 59'	30° 52'
Bhrigupanth	6,772	79° 00'	30° 53'
Unnamed (north of Bhrigupanth)	6,529	79° 01'	30° 55'
Unnamed (north of Bhrigupanth)	6,568	79° 00'	30° 57'
Unnamed (also north of Bhrigupanth)	6,008	78° 90'	30° 57'
Manda	6,511	78° 51'	30° 52'
Bhrigu Parbat	6,015	78° 59'	30° 57'
Bhrigu Parbat (west)	5,944	78° 59'	30° 57'
Hanuman Tibba	5,366	78° 59'	30° 58'
Unnamed (Meru Bamak)	6,044	79° 01'	30° 53'
Meru (Meru Bamak)	6,660	79° 02'	30° 52'
Meru North (Meru Bamak)	6,450	79° 02'	30° 53'
Meru East (Meru Bamak)	6,261	79° 01'	30° 53'
Unnamed	6,602	79° 02'	30° 53'

KIRTI BAMAK

Kirit Stambh	6,270	79° 01'	30° 49'
Unnamed (north of Kirti Stambh)	6,124	79° 01'	30° 50'
Unnamed (north of Kirti Stambh)	6,108	79° 01'	30° 50'
Unnamed (north of Kirti Stambh)	6,304	79° 01'	30° 51'
Unnamed (north of Kirti Stambh)	6,112	79° 01'	30° 51'
Kirti Stambh-I	6,274	79° 01'	30° 49'
Kirti Stambh-II	6,259	79° 01'	30° 50'
Bhartikunta	6,578	79° 02'	30° 48'

GANGOTRI GLACIERS

Kedarnath	6,968	79° 04'	30° 48'
Kedarnath Dome	6,830	79° 04'	30° 44'
Unnamed (south-east of Kedarnath)	6,443	79° 04'	30° 47'
Burma Gupha	5,892	79° 05'	30° 48'
Sumeru Parbat	6,350	79° 08'	30° 46'
Kharcha Kund	6,632	79° 08'	30° 47'
Shivling	6,543	79° 04'	30° 53'
Shivling-II	6,505	79° 05'	30° 53'
Bhagirathi—I	6,856	79° 09'	30° 51'
Bhagirathi—II	6,512	79° 08'	30° 53'
Bhagirathi—III	6,454	79° 08'	30° 52'
Unnamed (south-east of Bhagirathi-I)	6,193	79° 09'	30° 51'
Unnamed (south-east of Bhagirathi—I)	6,477	79° 10'	30° 50'
Unnamed (south-east of Bhagirathi—I)	6,792	79° 09'	30° 49'
Basuki Parbat	6,792	79° 10'	30° 53'
Unnamed (south of Basuki Parbat)	6,702	79° 10'	30° 52'
Satopanth	7,075	79° 13'	30° 51'
Unnamed (north of Satopanth)	6,008	79° 13'	30° 52'

SWACHAND BAMAK

Unnamed	6,215	79° 10'	30° 49'
Unnamed	6,464	79° 11'	30° 40'
Unnamed	6,721	79° 12'	30° 49'
Unnamed	6,684	79° 13'	30° 49'
Unnamed	6,668	79° 13'	30° 50'

CHATURANGI BAMAK

Chaturangi	6,304	79° 11'	30° 56'
Unnamed (east of Chaturangi)	6,180	79° 09'	30° 56'
Sudarshan Parbat	6,507	79° 06'	30° 59'
Unnamed (south-west of Sudarshan)	6,002	79° 05'	30° 59'
Unnamed (south of Sudarshan)	6,166	79° 05'	30° 58'

NEPAL

The Country and Its People

More than nine-tenths of the kingdom of Nepal, situated
between India and China, is covered by the Himalayas. Mount
Everest, the tallest mountain in the world, rises 29,028 ft. (8,848 m.)
along Nepal's border with Tibet.

The country has a population of 13.5 million, with an area
of 54,260 sq. miles. Patches of farmland, about 10 per cent of the
country's total area, lie among the mountains of Nepal. Until
1949 Nepal was closed to foreign expeditions and the earliest
foreign visit was a French expedition to Annapurna-I, led by
Maurice Herzeg in June, 1950.

Nepal has a larger number of high peaks than any other area
of the Himalayas, as it includes Everest, Makalu, Lhotse, Cho-oyu,
Annapurna and Dhaulagiri.

The country is divided into three main regions: western Nepal,
central Nepal and eastern Nepal. Western Nepal includes the area
beginning with the Api Nampa group of peaks to Dhaulagiri.
Central Nepal includes the area begining with Dhaulagiri and
Annapurna to Shisha Pangma, and eastern Nepal with Shisha
Pangma to Kanchenjunga.

The temperature, climate and rainfall vary from place to place.
The Terai region has a hot, tropical climate most of the year.
The central hill areas have a cooler sub-tropical climate and the
northern region has an alpine climate.

The natural resources of Nepal are mostly agricultural. Because
of its enormous year-round water resources Nepal has a vast
potential for energy and power. Its isolation and the division
of its area into numerous valleys has favoured the isolation of
different ethnic groups.

There are four major groups: the Tibeto-Nepalis, the
Indo-Nepalis, the Tibetan group and the Indians. The Tibetan-
Nepali group includes the Newaris, Magers, Gurangs and Tomangs.
The Tibetan group includes the Sherpas, the Bhutias and the
Thakalis and the Indo-Nepalese ethnic group comprises the old
Nepalese group such as the Gorkhas, Chhatriyas, Brahmins and
Thakurs. The southern plains are dominated by the ethnic group
of Indian origin because of the climate and surroundings, while

in the north are the people of Tibetan origin, once used to high altitude living.

About two-thirds of the population live in the central valleys and mountains surrounding Kathmandu, Nepal's capital and largest city. Almost all the people live in small villages that consist of two-storeyed houses made of stone or mud brick.

Of all the ethnic groups the Sherpas have won fame as guides and porters for mountain-climbing expeditions. Sherpa men and women carry heavy loads upto high altitudes. Hinduism is the official religion of Nepal; however, Buddhism is practised in the north at higher altitudes. In no other Asian country would the visitor notice the perfect harmony, at every step, of the local people with religious practice and the presence of the deity. Daily life throughout Nepal revolves around the temple: a deep relationship exists between people and priests, both Buddhist and Hindu. Nepal has thousands of temples and monastries. On most trekking trails in mountain passes one finds Buddhist *chortens*, stone steps with Buddhist prayers inscribed on them.

For centuries Nepal was veiled in mystery, as this remote and exotic kingdom remained forbidden to the outside world. The jet age has now brought Nepal close to those who enjoy exploring her timeless landscape and culture. The living forms of her medieval past — rich pagoda architecture, the "living" legends of virgin goddesses, and the mysticism — have to be seen to be believed.

Above the highest villages, at an altitude of 16,000 ft. or more, the Himalayan glaciers begin. Even at these altitudes people herd yaks in the summer months. During the winter trekking season, however, most of these summer villages are deserted, so trekkers are advised to carry their own food and equipment.

Visas and Permits

Travelling above the highest trails into the mountains requires a special permit from His Majesty's government. Trekkers should not consider climbing any peak in Nepal without observing the proper formalities. Information about current mountaineering regulations may be obtained from the Mountaineering Section, Ministry of Tourism, at Kathmandu.

For foreigners the following entry points into the country have been fixed:

Entry Point	Zone	Border
Kakar Bhitte	Mechi	Indian
Rani Sikiyahi (Jogbani)	Kosi	Indian
Jaleswor	Janakpur	Indian
Birgunj	Narayani	Indian
Tribhuvan International Airport	Bagmati	Nepalese (Kathmandu)

Kodar	Bagmati	Chinese
Sunauli	Lumbini	Indian
Kakarhawa	Lumbini	Indian
Nepalgunj	Bheri	Indian
Koilabas	Rapti	Indian
Dhangadi	Seti	Indian
Mahendranagar	Mahakali	Indian

A visa for 30 days may be obtained from the embassies and consulates abroad. Fifteen-day visas, valid for Kathmandu, Pokhara, Chitwan and other areas linked by highway will be issued on arrival at Kathmandu (photo required) for a fee of US $10. Visitors arriving without a regular visa may be issued a visa valid for 7 days at entry point other than Kathmandu, on payment of the visa fee (photo required).

Visa extension fee: For the first month this is US $5.63 per week and for the second US $11.27 per week. If the first visa is issued for less than one month no additional fee is charged for the uncompleted part of the month. The visa may be extended for a period of upto three months, extensions being granted for one month at a time by a branch of the immigration office or a local police office for upto seven days. A tourist applying for an extension must submit proof that he has exchanged US $5 or its equivalent in another convertible currency for each day he intends to stay in Nepal. Extension of the tourist visa beyond the three-month limit by the Central Immigration Office requires a recommendation by the Ministry of Home and Panchayat.

Visits and circuits: The tourist visa is valid for a 30-day period and entitles the traveller to visit Kathmandu Valley, Pokhara and other areas linked by highway.

For tours in areas beyond the places mentioned above, trekking permits are required which will be issued by the Central Immigration Office in Kathmandu together with the visa extension required.

Trekking permit: The new official definition of trekking is as follows: "Trekking is a journey undertaken on foot or in a wagon, for seeing natural and cultural scenes in areas where normally a modern transport system is not available."

Any foreign tourist intending to trek in any part of the country must obtain a trekking permit. This is issued by the Central Immigration Office, to trek in any part of the country except for places where the entry of foreigners is restricted.

Trekking permits are not granted for more than one place at a time, and foreigners who are given this permission can travel only along the route prescribed for them by the Central Immigration Office. Trekkers, when they reach the appointed place, should get

125

their trekking permits endorsed by the immigration office or police office but persons holding diplomatic visas are not obliged to do so. Foreign tourists who visit the place they applied for, should return their permit papers to the Central Immigration Office afterwards.

Domestic Flights

The Royal Nepal Airlines Corporation (RNAC) operates a large network of domestic flights in Nepal. Flights to some of the remote areas are operated by their 19-seat Twin Otters and 6-seater Pilatus Porter. These STOL aircrafts take flights to Jʰomsom, Lukla, Thyangboche, Langtang and other places.

The flights depend a lot on local weather conditions and are subject to cancellation. Trekkers are, therefore, advised to keep a cushion of two to three days if their itineraries involve flights by STOL aircraft.

STOL aircraft can be chartered to several small airstrips in Nepal. One can also charter helicopters for travel to various trekking sites. Helicopters are normally used in Nepal for sight-seeing and rescue operations. Several STOL aircraft are far cheaper than charters.

One of the most exciting aspects of air-travel within Nepal is the opportunity of seeing mountains from close quarters and, thus, enjoying the thrills of spectacular sights and landings. These flights are useful for those who do not have adequate time to carry out some of the longer but more ambitious treks such as the one to Mt Everest base camp.

Trekking in Nepal

Nepal is a land of scenic grandeur and cultural diversity. Trekking on foot is the only way of getting to the people and places intimately. One need not be a mountaineer to trek in the hills of Nepal, where live more than half the total population of the country. A network of tracks and trails marked with shaded rest-places connect numerous villages together. A short trek will reveal picturesque hamlets surrounded by elaborate terraced fields and forested ridges. A longer trek may yield rich contrasts in people and culture from one ecological level to another. The rich variety in flora and fauna within short distances is another rewarding experience. And there is always the prospect of viewing some of the highest mountains in the world.

In the densely populated central hills, there are numerous small shops which serve tea and simple food to travellers at trail junctions, bridge sites and convenient saddles. The track may sometimes be rough because of the mountain terrain but it is a delight to arrive at numerous vantage points that reveal new vistas. In the mountain area, the track may traverse steep slopes with plunging waterfalls. In the high valleys beyond the Himalayas, the villages are set wider apart but here also a traveller can find cattle-sheds and cave-shelters at various stages of the journey. The trans-Himalayan valleys provide magnificent views of grassy slopes, glaciers and snow-peaks.

Whenever one travels, the people are friendly and hospitable and the roads safe. Depending on the season one may meet on the road local people in their distinctive dresses or laden porters, caravans of sheep and goats or Gurkha soldiers on home leave. One can visit simple temples or elaborate gompas along clear mountain streams which provide abundant fishing and swimming opportunity.

Trekkers who choose to travel light may find food and lodging on the more popular routes. Those who find Nepalese food too spicy should take a cook along. Trekking agencies organize treks on individual and group bases with the team of guide, cook and porter, that caters to the needs of the travellers.

A trek to higher mountain regions requires good mountaineering equipment and guides. Trekkers wishing to climb minor peaks along the way can make arrangements with the Nepal Mountaineering Association. There are separate rules for mountaineering expeditions and up-to-date information on climbing regulations that can be obtained from the Ministry of Tourism. The following pages have route descriptions of the major treks, including suggested stopping places. These descriptions will help you choose a trek of particular interest, and make an estimation of the number of days it would take to do it.

Trekking towards Everest

Route		Altitude of	
From	To	Reaching Point (m.)	Time (hrs.)
Kathmandu (1,310 m.)	Lamosangu	792	3 (by car or bus)
Lamosangu	Thulo Pakha	1,820	4 (road under construction)
Thulo Pakha	Serabensi	1,440	7
Serabensi	Kiratichap	1,320	6
Kiratichap	Yarsa	1,974	6
Yarsa	Those	1,799	7
Those	Chyangma (Bhandar)	2,194	6
Chyangma	Sete	2,575	6
Sete	Junbesi	2,675	7
Junbesi	Mandingma	2,194	7
Mandingma	Khari Khola	2,072	6

Khari Khola	Puiyan	2,773	6
Puiyan	Phakding	2,611	7
Phakding	Namche Bazaar	3,440	6
Namche Bazaar	Thyangboche	3,867	5
Thyangboche	Pheriche	4,243	5
Pheriche	Lobuje	4,930	6
Lobuje	Gorakshep	5,150	4
Gorakshep	Everest Base Camp	5,356	4

Trail Description

Lamosangu (792 m.): Porters may be hired at this village before starting on the trek. The new road to Jiri begins near Lamosangu and some parts of the first 5 days will be along sections of this road, which has been partly completed.

Thulo Pakha (1,820 m.): This Tamang village is reached on the first night, after a steep climb. From here it is a 450 m. climb to the pass, then a descent to the river-bed towards Serabensi for the next night's lodging. There are good views of Langtang, Jugal and Rolwaling Himal from the pass.

Serabensi (1,440 m.): This is a Newar village at the trail junction which leads to the region of Rolwaling. From here the route turns south to Namche Bazaar and to the small bazaar of Kiratichap, whose several shops are arranged in a circle around a huge pipal tree.

Yarsa (1,974 m.): The trail descends to the Tama Kosi River at 1,006 m., then climbs through the villages of Namdu and Kabre to Yarsa.

Those (1,799 m.): About 670 m. above Yarsa there is a mountain pass which commands a view of Gauri Shankar and to the left of Gauri Shankar is Choba Bhamare. Ahead, towards, the east, is Numbur (6,954 m.). It is possible to visit Jiri (1,905 m.), the site of a Swiss-aided agricultural station, hospital and airstrip by detouring north from the Sikri Khola and walking uphill for about two hours.

Chyangma (2,194 m.): This village, also known locally as Bhandar, is in a beautifully situated valley of the same name. It is reached after crossing a 2,713 m. pass lined with one of the most extensive arrays of *mani* (prayer) walls along the route. This pass marks the beginning of Sherpa settlements. An alternate halting-place is Thoding (3,091 m.), the site of a cheese factory and a trekkers lodge, about two hours uphill from the pass.

Sete (2,575 m.): From Chyangma the trail descends to the Likhu Khola, and then begins a steep climb to the small monastery of Sete. There is a small hotel just before the monastery, the only accommodation available before crossing the high Lamjura Pass (3,330 m.).

Junbesi (2,675 m.): From Sete is about a four-hour climb to Lamjura Pass (3,530 m.), then a long descent to the large village of Junbesi. Situated amongst pine forests, Junbesi is a beautiful valley.

Mandingma (2,194 m.): From Junbesi the trail climbs over the Solang ridge, from where you can see Everest, then descends to the river and climbs again to Takshindo Pass (3,200 m.). From Takshindo, a short side trip may be made to Takshindo Monastery about half an hour to the north, or to a government cheese factory about half an hour to the south. From the pass it is a step descent through forests to the hamlet of Mandingma, also known as Nuntale.

Khari Khola (7,072 m.): The trail descends to the Dudh Kosi gorge crossing the river on a suspension bridge at 1,493 m., then turns north through the village of Jubing (1,676 m.), inhabited by Rais, to Khari Khola, a mixed settlement of Sherpa and Magars.

Phakding (2,611 m.): After a short climb, the trail descends to the village of Surke (2,348 m.), then continues north through the Dudh Kosi gorge to Chaurikharka (2,713 m.) near Lukla (2,834 m.), and finally Phakding, situated on the bank of the river. Trekkers who fly to Lukla usually spend their first night in Phakding.

Namche Bazaar (3,440 m.): The trail continues up the valley to Jorsale; then begins a steep three-hour climb to Namche Bazaar. The village, well-known to mountaineers as the starting point for Everest expeditions, is situated in a horseshoe-shaped valley. Across the valley is Kwangde Peak (6,187 m.), first climbed in 1975 by a team of Nepalese mountaineers. Namche Bazaar has many shops and lodges to serve trekkers, and is an ideal place to rest and acclimatize before moving on to higher elevations.

Khumjung (3,790 m.): The biggest Sherpa village in the region, it has a gompa that preserves the relic said to be a scalp of a yeti. Khumjung is a two-hour climb from Namche Bazaar. About a half-hour walk west of Khumjung is Kunde (3,841 m.), a similar Sherpa village and the site of a hospital operated by the Himalayan Trust.

Thyangboche (3,867 m.): This is the site of a famous Buddhist monastery presided over by a reincarnate lama. The monastery is set on a wooded ridge completely encircled by snow peaks, dominated by the mountain trio of Everest, Lhotse and Nuptse. Other prominent peaks nearby are Ama Dablam, one of the most beautiful mountains, Thamaserku, Gangtega Kwangde and Khumbila.

Everest Base Camp: Only those with warm clothing and in good physical condition should proceed beyond Thyangboche towards Everest Base Camp at 5,356 m.

The Himalayan Rescue Association recommends that trekkers spend not less than six days from Thyangboche to Everest Base Camp. Among the places which may be visited during this trek are:

Pangboche (3,901 m.)

This is a beautiful Sherpa village situated on the north side of Imja Khola. In the upper portion of the village is a gompa amidst a grove of cedar trees.

Pheriche (4,267 m.)

This is the last summer village on the way to Mount Everest. There are a few lodges here where accommodation is available. Also at Pheriche is the Trekkers Aid-Post run by the Himalayan Rescue Association clinic, where a volunteer physician is stationed during most of the trekking season.

Dingboche (4,343 m.)

This summer settlement is situated east of Pheriche in the Imja Khola Valley. Trekkers who do not wish to visit Everest Base Camp will find it interesting to explore this valley and climb towards the village of Chukhung at 4,734 m. for views of huge vertical ice walls on the north side of Ama Dablam.

Lobuje (4,930 m.)

There are two small stone huts at Lobuje where it is possible to obtain food and lodging. Lobuje offers a spectacular view of Nuptse Peak.

Gorakshep (5,184 m.)

There is only a single, small hut here; nowhere else is food and shelter available. Trekkers planning to spend a night at Gorakshep should bring food, fuel and a tent with them. From Gorakshep it is about a three-hour climb to the summit of Kala Pathar (5,623 m.), from where a panoramic view of Mount Everest, and the entire Khumbu Himalaya, can be had. Everest Base Camp is about a three-hour walk from Gorakshep.

Dudh Kosi and Bhote Kosi: There are two more side valleys worth visiting. One goes up to Dudh Kosi from Khumjung to the pastures and lovely lakes below Cho-oyu (8,153 m.) and Ghyachung Kang (7,753 m.). The trail goes up a ridge (3,883 m.) and then descends to a river (3,643 m.) beyond Phortse (3,840 m.). There are waterfalls on the way and one can see Cho-oyu in the distance. After three hours appear the summer huts of Tongba (4,015 m.), Dole (4,084 m.) and Lhabarma (4,328 m.). Further beyond lie Macherma (4,465 m.) in a tributary valley and the huts of Gyoko (4,791 m.) on the east shore of Dudh Phakri.

Another trek which once used to be the trading route to Tibet across Nangpa-La (5,716 m.), turns north-west of Namche along the Bhote Kosi. The trail passes through Gong Lha (3,476 m.) and Thomde (3,505 m.) with a police check-post. Three hours from Namche is Thami (3,810 m.), where the Mani Rimdu festival of

KHUMBU
(The Mt. Everest Region)

spring is celebrated with great pomp and pageantry. A small ridge north of Thami is the last limit allowed to trekkers, although there is a trek going further west towards Rolwaling across Tashi Lapcha (5,755 m.). The higher valley sections of Bhote Kosi, Dudh Kosi and Imja Khola are included in the Sagarmatha (Mount Everest National Park).

Important Peaks in Khumbu

Name	Height (m.)	Height (ft.)
Mt Everest (Sagarmatha)	8,848	29,028
Lhotse	8,501	27,891
Makalu	8,481	27,825
Cho-oyu	8,153	26,750
Nuptse	7,878	25,850
Ghyachung Kang	7,752	25,434
Pumori	7,415	23,442
Chamlang	7,319	24,012
Numbur	6,954	22,817
Ama Dablam	6,856	22,494
Kangtega	6,809	22,340
Karyolung	6,681	21,920
Thanserku	6,623	21,730
Tawoche	6,543	21,463
Cholatse	6,440	21,130
Kwangde	6,187	20,300
Khumbila	5,883	19,330

Everest Trek (Including Gokyo Lake and Island Peak): This is a 22-day trek.

1st Day· Camp at Phakding (2,500 m.)
Flight to Lukla. Easy walk to Chauri Kharka Village. The route descends to the Dudh Kosi River ghat and follows the right bank of the river till Phakding Bridge. The walk lasts approximately three hours.

2nd Day: Camp at Namche Bazaar (3,440 m.)
Seven-hour trek. Follow the left bank of the river till Benker. Cross the river by a wooden bridge. The route now follows the right bank of the river to Jorsale. An easy walk of half an hour and then a steep climb for about two hours begins from the confluence of the Imja Drangpa and Nangpo Tsanpo to Chautara. Good views of Everest, Lhotse and Nuptse. From Chautara to Namche is a gradual climb of two hours.

3rd Day: Camp at Khumjung (3,790 m.)
You can rest or sightsee around Namche. Ascend for two hours to Thyangboche airport, then descend towards

Kunde. From Kunde it is an easy trek to Khumjung. You can also visit the Khumjung Monastery.

4th Day: Camp at Luza (4,300 m.)
A seven-hour trek. Walk up a steep ascent for half an hour, then climb gradually till Manay Danra. From here the road descends to Phortse. Now climb gradually again till Dole. Steep ascent for half an hour, followed by an easy walk till Luza.

5th Day: Camp at Gokyo Lake (4,750 m.)
Another seven-hour trek; you should walk along the left bank of the Phortse River till you reach Pangka. Easy ascent but it will take two to three hours to reach Gokyo because of the fast gain in altitude. On the way you pass Longpangka Lake.

6th Day: Camp at Na (4,490 m.)
Ascend the top of Gokyo Peak (5,300 m.). This is a steep climb and takes about three hours. Magnificent views from the top of all the eastern mountains. Descend to Gokyo Lake, then walk on to Na. Camp here for the night.

7th Day: Camp at Chugyima (4,690 m.)
Trek begins with a steep climb of two to three hours followed by a gradual climb of two hours till the camping site at Chugyima. The distance is quite short but progress is slow, owing to the rapid gain in altitude.

8th Day: Camp at Dzongla (4,843 m.)
A steep climb to Nima Gawa Pass. A walk on boulders for an hour, then on snow before reaching the top. Ropes may have to be used. Descend to Dzongla again and fix ropes in order to cross the glaciers safely. Once past these, the trek follows an easier trail to Dzongla. Takes seven hours altogether.

9th Day: Camp at Lobuje (4,930 m.)
From Dzongla walk downhill all the way till you reach Duglha. On the way you can get a close view of Jobo Laptshan and Tawoche. From here it is a steep ascent to your camping site at Lobuje, which takes about two to three hours.

10th Day: Camp at Gorakshep (5,100 m.)
Follow the left bank of the Khumbu Glacier till you reach the camping site at Gorakshep. The walk takes about four hours. Although it is an easy walk, it is better to proceed slowly due to the gain in altitude.

11th Day: Camp at Kala Pathar/Gorakshep (5,100 m.)
Ascend towards Kala Pathar. The ascent takes about three hours. Once in Kala Pathar, you can see Pumori

in the north and also panoramic views of Everest, Lhotse and Nuptse. Descend to Gorakshep for rest.

12th Day: Camp at Dingboche (4,243 m.)
From Gorakshep ascend for half an hour to Changri Shar and Nup Glaciers, then descend to Lobuje and Duglha. Descend all the way to your camping site at Dingboche Seven hours altogether.

13th Day: Camp at Chukung (4,730 m.)
Trek begins with an easy walk of two hours followed by a gradual climb (three hours) to Chukung. Due to the gain in altitude it is important to walk in short stages only. Offers close views of Lhotse, Lhotse Shar and Ama Dablam.

14th Day: Camp at Island Peak High Camp (5,300 m.)
An easy walk of three hours to Pareshaya Ghyab. Now begins a steep ascent of about another three hours to Island Peak High Camp.

15th Day: Excursion in the Mountains
Climb Island Peak (6,153 m.).

16th Day: Camp at Dingboche (4,243 m.)
Descend to Pareshaya Ghyab, then walk along an easy track to Chukung (five hours). Now walk for two hours to Dingboche.

17th Day: Camp at Thyangboche (3,867 m.)
Descend till you reach Pangboche. Descend till you reach Imja Bridge. From here starts a gradual climb to Thyangboche Monastery where you camp for the night. Takes seven hours altogether.

18th Day: Camp at Khumjung (3,790 m.)
A five-hour trek. After breakfast, descend to Phunke Bridge. From here you have to ascend till the Namche and Khumjung crossroad. (It is an hour's walk to the camping site at Khumjung.)

19th Day: Camp at Benker (2,700 m.)
A seven-hour trek. Descend to Namche Bazaar. Descend again till you reach the confluence of the Imja Drangpa and Nangpo Tsangpo. From here it is an easy walk. Stop at Jorsale, then walk for another two hours to Benker.

20th Day: Camp at Lukla (2,515 m.)
Follow the river to Thare Kosi. After an easy walk of two to three hours you will reach Lukla. In the evening, you can organize a party for your trekking crew, sit around a camp fire, drink *chang* and join the merry Sherpas dancing.

21st Day: Back to Kathmandu (1,350 m.)
            Back to Kathmandu by air.

Lamosangu to Everest Base Camp via Lukla
1st Day: Pakha (6,500 ft.)
          To reach Lamosangu, drive for three hours along the
Kodari highway which links Nepal's capital with Tibet.
On the way to Lamosangu, you pass through the old
Newar town to Banepa and Dhulikhel, offering an
excellent panoramic view of the eastern Himalayas ·
(including Langtang Peak, Dorji Lakpa and Manaslu)
on a clear day. The road descends to the Sun Kosi River
at Dolalghat, and then follows the river north to
Lamosangu, a bustling bazaar.
From Lamosangu, at about 2,700 ft., the track begins to
climb immediately towards the top of the 9,000 ft. ridge
which forms the watershed between the Sun Kosi
drainage to the west and the Tamba Kosi drainage to
the east. The trek from Lamosangu to the eastern
Himalayas, proceeding as it does from west to east, cuts
across the grain of the country. This is because the rivers
in this region flow from north to south, and are separated
from one another by high ridges jutting down from the
crest of the Himalayas on Nepal's northern border.
Before reaching Namche Bazaar it is necessary to cross
six major ridges, of which this one, involving a climb of
some 5,000 ft., is the first. The ascent is steep,
particularly at the beginning since the slope, as is general
in this region, is convex and passes through small villages
and terraced fields, separated by stretches of scrub
forest. Most of the population in this area consists of
Chhatriyas, Brahmins and Tamangs. After climbing for
the better part of the day, a large village called Pakha
at 6,500 ft. is reached. There is an excellent camping spot
here. Alternatively, you can camp slightly higher up at
Sildhunga (7,000 ft.).
2nd Day: Serabensi (6,500 ft.)
          A six-hour trek. The ascent continues upto Mudi, just
below the top of the ridge, whence the route contours
along the hillside for some distance until Nigale, located
on the top of the pass itself. There are a few shops here.
The nearby settlements are mainly Tamang. From Nigale
there is a moderately steep descent through scrub forest
to Surke. At Surke a tributary stream of the Tamba Kosi
is crossed, after which the route continues along the
other bank, gradually descending through fields and

scrub to Serabensi, where the stream hitherto followed is joined by another to form the Charange River which, lower down, joins the Tamba Kosi. Serabensi is a small bazaar with few shops. You can camp close by on the bank of the river, at about 6,500 ft.

3rd Day: Kiratichap (4,200 ft.)

From Serabensi, the route crosses the Charange River and proceeds along its east bank through villages and paddy fields, after traversing around the side of a spur above the river. The route gradually descends to Kiratichap, another small bazaar, located at about 4,200 ft., on the bit of level ground at the end of the spur above the confluence of the Charange with the Tamba Kosi. At Kiratichap, there are a few shops built in a semi-circle around a pipal tree. It is a small, pleasant market, just beyond where lies a fine camping ground in the forest. The day's trek consists of six walking hours.

4th Day: Yarsa (6,000 ft.)

From Kiratichap, the route descends through pines and then sal forests to the Tamba Kosi River, which it crosses by a cable suspension bridge at an elevation of about 3,000 ft. On the other side of the river the ascent is first steep, but then becomes more gradual as one passes through the villages of Busti, Namdu and finally Kabre. The inhabitants are mostly Chhatriyas, Brahmins and also Newars and Tamangs. Beyond Kabre, the route crosses a stream called Yarsa and then climbs up through scrub forest to a small village of the same name at 6,000 ft. Day's trek: six walking hours.

5th Day: Shivalaya

From Yarsa there is a fairly steep ascent through scrub forest to the watershed between the Tamba Kosi and Khimti Rivers. This is the second major ridge to be crossed on the route, and the pass is at an elevation of 8,200 ft. Like the first ridge, it provides an excellent view of the Himalayan peaks, especially Gauri Shankar. On the other side of the divide the descent is steep, again through forest and scrub valley. The route follows the bed of the Sikri River for some distance, then climbs over a spur and drops to the Khimti River valley. The river is crossed on a chain bridge just below Those. Those is the largest market between Lamosangu and Namche Bazaar where you can buy locally manufactured small items. It is possible to camp near Those but preferably (if there is time), to continue up the river to Shivalaya where the flats by the river afford excellent camping sites. An interesting side trip to Jiri, where there is a hospital and a Swiss-sponsored agricultural station, can be made by detouring up the ridge. Day's trek: six walking hours.

6th Day: Chyangma (Bhandar) (7,200 ft.)

From Shivalaya the route climbs upto the divide between the drainage of the Khimti and Likhu Rivers, the third major ridge to be crossed on the way to Namche Bazaar. For a short distance the ascent is steep, but then eases off, and the remainder of the climb is fairly gradual until just below the top when it again becomes steep. Two villages, Sangbandanda and Buldanda, are passed, but for the most part the route goes through scrub and then forest as one gets higher. On the top of the divide there are long *mani* walls, indicating that the trek is now entering Tibetan Nepal. There is also a tea shop on the very top of the divide, at 8,900 ft. On the other side the route descends into a beautiful valley. Here, at about 6,700 ft., is the village of Chyangma, the first Sherpa settlement with its gompa and chorten. Below the Sherpa village are some houses belonging to members of other ethnic groups, such as Brahmins and Newars. The day's trek: six and a half walking hours.

7th Day: Sete (8,400 ft.)

From the village of Chyangma there is at first a gradual descent through fields and meadows down to the lip of the valley shelf, on which Chyangma is located, then a steeper descent through forest and then scrub down to the bank of the Likhu River. The Likhu River is crossed by a suspension bridge after which the route follows along the east bank upto Kenja; ascent begins towards the high Lamjura Ridge, a major watershed, Sete, a small Sherpa village, is reached where you can camp. At Sete (8,400 ft.) there is a small gompa with a prayer wheel about six ft. in diameter. Trek consists of five walking hours.

8th Day: Junbesi (8,800 ft.)

From Sete it is a long climb (fairly gradual although in spots it gets steep) to the top of the 11,580 ft. pass over the Lamjura Ridge. Although the tops of some of the ridges so far crossed have been forested, for the first time now the trek gets into really good moist mountain forest, with its huge, gnarled moss-covered rhododendrons and giant spruce and fir trees. From here on there are large stretches of forest, a delight for bird lovers. Nepal has 600 species of birds and many of the

137

most colourful birds are found in this zone. The pass over Lamjura Ridge is the highest point reached during the trek between Lamosangu and Namche Bazaar, and affords one of the most magnificent views of the Himalayan peaks, especially Numbur. The route descends through fragrant pine forest to the small Sherpa settlement of Tragdouk and then on down to Junbesi, a splendid Sherpa village located amidst beautiful surroundings just above the river of the same name at 8,800 ft. It is at the north end of the Sherpa region known as Solu. (Walking hours: seven.)

9th Day: Takshindo (3,071 m.)

From Junbesi, the route climbs over a spur between the Junbesi River and the Solu River, passing by the village of Salung. From the top of this ridge is an excellent view of Everest Chamlang and Makalu. After crossing the Solu River there is a climb upto Ringmo, another beautifully situated Sherpa village. This leads to a short ascent to the top of Takshindo Pass, at about 10,500 ft., over the ridge — the fifth major one crossed during the trek, between the watersheds of the Solu and Dudh Kosi Rivers. Just on the other side of the pass is the isolated monastery of Takshindo surrounded by magnificent forests. Built in 1946, Takshindo is a superb example ot Sherpa monastic architecture, certainly the most imposing buildings so far encountered on the trek. Camp will be near the monastery. (Walking hours: six.)

10th Day: Khari Khola (6,800 ft.)

This day's trek involves five walking hours, beginning with a long descent to the bed of the Dudh Kosi — the largest river met since the Sun Kosi — followed by an arduous climb up the other side. From Takshindo one descends through a rhododendron and coniferous forest swarming with birds to the Sherpa hamlet of Mandingma at 7,600 ft. From there the route continues down through more forest, at first gradually and finally steeply to the Dudh Kosi, which is crossed by a steel cable suspension bridge at about 5,200 ft. Up some distance above the river on the other side of the valley is the large, spread-out village of Jubing inhabited by Sherpas and Bais. From Jubing, there is a short but steep climb over a spur to the Sherpa village of Khari Khola, at about 6,800 ft. Camp near the village.

11th Day: Puiyan (9,300 ft.)

From Khari Khola it is necessary to climb for most of the day to reach the top to Buspa Ridge (10,300 ft.), the sixth and last major ridge on the way to Khumbu. Above Khari Khola the route passes through Kharte, another Sherpa village at 9,300 ft., after a stiff climb. From there the ascent continues through pine forests to the top of Buspa Village. There is an inn at the very top which usually has a good supply of local beverages for those who prefer something stronger than tea. On the other side there is a gradual descent of about 1,000 ft. to Puiyan, a Sherpa village near which camp will be made. This small village is completely surrounded by forest. (Walking hours: six.)

12th Day: Phakding (8,700 ft.)

From Puiyan, a short climb followed by a long descent will take you to the hamlet of Suket near the tributary of the Dudh Kosi. Climb again round a spur to reach Chaurikharka from where you will see Lukla situated high above. Stop for lunch at Lukla. Now walk on to Chaurikharka Village. Descend to reach Phakding Bridge. (Walking hours: seven.)

13th Day: Namche (11,300 ft.)

Trek along the left bank of the river till you reach Benker (8,910 ft.) where you cross the river by means of a wooden bridge. The route now follows the right bank of the river till you reach Jorsale (9,405 ft.). Lunch will be served a little above Jorsale. From here an easy walk of half an hour, then a steep climb of 990 ft. begins, from the confluence of Imja Drangpa and Nangpo Tsangpo, to Chautara. The climb takes one to two hours. From this place you can see the world's highest mountains — Sagarmatha, Lhotse and Nuptse. From Chautara to Namche is a gradual climb of another hour or two. At Namche your trekking permits will be checked by H.M.G. Immigration Office. It is principally a settlement of traders as the cultivable area is very small. The houses stand in a semi-circle built against the slopes of a natural amphitheatre. Saturday is a market day. Walk past Namche Bazaar to camping site situated a little above the immigration office. (Walking hours: five.)

14th Day: Khumjung (12,507 ft.)

Ascend for about one to two hours towards Thyangboche air-strip, then descend to Kunde. The village of Kunde is built on flat valley lying high above the level of the Dudh Kosi, as this offers scope for cultivation. There is a small hospital here which is being run with the help of the British government and Sir Edmund Hillary. Now

139

walk on to Khumjung which is the twin village of
Kunde. Visit the monastery here then proceed on to
camp below the Everest View Hotel. For those who have
missed some of the comforts of city life, Everest View
Hotel boasts of a comfortable lounge and a well-stocked
bar. From your camping site at Khumjung, you can get
a close and breathtaking view of Tram Serku, Gangtega
and Ama Dablam. (Walking hours: three.)

15th Day: Thyangboche (12,761 ft.)
From Khumjung, descend towards Phunki (takes two
hours). Ascend towards Thyangboche (about four hours).

16th Day: Thyangboche
Rest day at Thyangboche. Offers a magnificent view of
Gangtega, Tawochem, Ama Dablam, Mt Everest,
Lhotse and Nuptse.

17th Day: Pheriche (13,921 ft.)
Descend to Imja Drangpa Bridge; from here, the route
ascends to Pangboche (takes three hours), from where
it is an easy walk of another three hours to Pheriche.

18th Day: Lobuje (16,175 ft.)
From Pheriche is an easy walk of an hour followed by
an hour-long steep climb to Diglha. Ascend to Lobuje
(this takes two to three hours).

19th Day: Gorakshep (17,300 ft.)
Follow the left bank of the Khumbu Glacier for about
four hours to camping site at Gorakshep.

20th, 21st
and 22nd
Days: Gorakshep
After breakfast, ascend to Kala Pathar (18,265 ft.) to
get a better view of the great peaks of the world. Return
to Gorakshep camp for the night.
On the second day, visit Everest Base Camp area
(18,000 ft.).(The third day is kept as rest day.)

23rd Day: Pheriche (13,921 ft.)
Ascend for half an hour to Changri Shar and Nup Glacier
and then descend to Lobuje and Diglha, then all the
way to Pheriche (takes over five hours).

24th Day: Thyangboche (12,761 ft.)
From Pheriche, descend to Pangboche. Then descend
further down to Imja Bridge. Now climb gradually to
Thyangboche. Walking time: four hours.

25th Day: Khumjung (12,507 ft.)
Descend to Phunki Bridge (10,665 ft.), then ascend till
you reach the crossroads to Namche and Khumjung.
Walk for an hour to Khumjung.

26th Day: **Benker (8,910 ft.)**
Descend to Namche Bazaar, then further down till you
reach the confluence of Imja Drangpa and Nangpo
Tsangpo (takes about five hours). From here it is an
easy walk. Walk for another two hours to Benker.

27th Day: **Lukla (9,200 ft.)**
Follow the river till Thare Kosi (this will take you over
three hours). After an easy walk of two to three hours
you will reach Lukla — your last night's halt.

28th Day: **Kathmandu**
After an early breakfast, pack and wait at the airport
for your flight to Kathmandu.

Everest Base Camp — Alpine Trail: This would take you 18
nights and 19 days.

1st Day: **Ghat (8,173 ft.**
Fly to Kathmandu.

2nd Day: **Camp at Jorsale (9,331 ft.)**
This is a busy trail, also offering tantalising glimpses of
the peaks. (Takes four hours.)

3rd Day: **Namche Bazaar (11,300 ft.)**
A hard pull up to Namche (four hours). On the way,
first views of Everest (29,028 ft.), Nuptse (25,850 ft.) and
Lhotse (27,923 ft.).

4th Day: **Namche Bazaar (11,300 ft.)**
A rest day to aid acclimatisation before moving towards
Gokyo Valley. Visit the Sagarmatha National Park
Headquarters.

5th Day: **Phortse (12,617 ft.).**
Steep climb out of Namche Bazaar. Cross the small
Thyangboche airstrip and proceed to Khumjung
(12,400 ft.). Ascend the lower slopes of Khumbila just
below Phortse and the peak of Taboche (20,889 ft.),
taking 5 hours altogether.

6th Day: **Luza (14,108 ft.)**
A steady climb through rhododendron forest up the deep
Gokyo Valley. Eventually the trail flattens, and passes
through some small fields of the yak herders' huts at
Luza. Excellent views of Taboche and Ama Dablam
(22,494 ft.) (Six hours altogether.)

7th Day: **Gokyo (15,583 ft.)**
A four-hour trek. Heading north towards the Nhozumpa
Glacier, the source of the Dudh Kosi, we pass the first
of the valley's three main lakes. The trail then levels out
and brings us to the small settlement of Gokyo on the
banks of the lake. An idyllic campsite.

8th and
9th Days: Gokyo
Spend the next two days resting and exploring the Gokyo area. Be prepared to cross the Chola Pass. Various exploratory trips can be made from the base at Gokyo. The steep climb to Gokyo Ridge (18,000 ft.) rewards you with stunning views of the upper Gokyo Valley, the huge Ngozumpa Glacier and an incredible 360° panorama of the entire Nuptse, Makalu (27,826 ft.), Cho-oyu (26,750 ft.) and Ghyachung Kang (25,990 ft.). If you wish, make exploratory trips to Ngozumpa Lake, across the glacial moraine; the Gokyo trips are equally rewarding.

10th Day: Choa-La (16,700 ft.)
A four-hour trek. Leave Gokyo and cross the Ngozumpa Glacier, spreading across the valley floor, to reach the yak huts at Dragnac. After Dragnac the trail is very steep. Camp at the foot of the pass.

11th Day: Dzongla (15,800 ft.)
Steep ascent on loose moraine. Near the top of the pass (17,785 ft.) a large snowfield is reached before descending steeply on loose rock to the yak pastures of Dzongla. Carry ropes, crampons and icepicks. Takes five hours.

12th Day: Lobuje (16,175 ft.)
A comparatively easy day contouring round to Diglha and Lobuje. Takes four hours altogether.

13th Day: Lobuje (16,175 ft.)
Walk slowly over the moraine before a hard climb to Kala Pathar (18,250 ft.). Takes five hours altogether.

14th Day: Thyangboche (12,715 ft.)
Takes six hours. Retrace your steps and follow the valley to Pheriche. Pass through Pangboche and camp at Thyangboche Monastery.

15th Day: Thyangboche Camp
A day to relax.

16th Day: Namche Bazaar (11,300 ft.)
Descend to the Imja Khola and then to Namche Bazaar (five hours).

17th Day: Phakding (8,700 ft.)
Rejoin the Dudh Kosi again (four hours).

18th Day: Lukla (9,175 ft.)
Follow the trail to Lukla (three hours). A small farewell party to thank your trekking crew.

19th Day: Back to Kathmandu.

142

Everest Area: This trek would take you 11 days.

1st Day: Lukla
             Fly to Lukla from Kathmandu. Proceed through
             picturesque villages with grand views of Kwangde (three
             hours altogether).

2nd Day: Namche Bazaar
             Walk to Jorsale. A steep climb will take you to Namche
             Bazaar. Magnificent views of Everest, Lhotse, Nuptse,
             Kanglepa etc. (takes five hours). There is a police
             checkpost at Namche where all trekking permits
             will be checked.

3rd Day: Thyangboche
             Walk along straight path with views of Ama Dablam,
             Langtega, Everest etc. for about one and a half hours,
             after which descend downhill for about half an hour next
             to Dudh Khola River at Phingutenga. Walk steeply uphill
             for about one and a half hours to Thyangboche (takes
             altogether five hours).

4th Day: Khonar
             A walk through a small rhododendron forest to
             Dingboche, the village of nuns, after which you go
             steeply downhill to the river. Cross the bridge and climb
             up to Phortse. Proceed gradually towards Khonar where
             camp will be set up. Views of Khumbuta etc. (six hours).

5th Day: Nala
             Walk towards Nala with Bumori and Choogu. Lunch will
             be served at Nala and you can also camp there (four
             hours).

6th Day: **Chuguwa Pass**
             Climb towards your right to a meadow just below the
             Pass (15,000 ft.) (takes five hours altogether).

7th Day: Lobuche
             Cross the Chuguwa Pass and proceed toward Dzongla,
             then proceed downhill to Lobuje.

8th Day: Kala Pathar
             Climb down towards Gorakshep, climb Kala Pathar at
             a height of 19,800 ft. where magnificent views of nearly
             all the Himalayan mountains of east Nepal can be
             viewed (takes seven hours).

9th Day: Thyangboche
             Walk downhill towards Pangboche, crossing the village
             of Pheriche and Showare. Visit the monastery there
             where you can see the "Yeti Scalp". Go downhill towards
             Thyangboche (six hours).

10th Day: Khumjung
             Proceed towards Khumjung. Walk downhill to

Thyangboche. Option of staying at the Hotel Everest
View or camping.
11th Day: Kathmandu
Flight to Kathmandu.

To Thyangboche

1st Day: Phakding
Fly from Kathmandu to Lukla (9,200 ft.) which takes
35 mins. Trekking starts from Lukla gradually downhill
towards the valley of Dudh Kosi River flowing from
Mount Everest area. A three hour walk from Lukla
takes to Phakding (8,700 ft.).

2nd Day: Namche
Trekking commences along the Dudh Kosi River crossing
at the two places, Benker and Jorsale, by wooden
bridges. Thereafter two hours' ascent to Namche Bazaar
(11,300 ft.) the gateway to all famous expeditions to
Khumbu Himal peaks. It is also the trading centre of the
Sherpas of the region.

3rd Day: Thyangboche
The walk from Namche to Thyangboche is one of the
most beautiful from the scenic point of view. The track
follows the western spur of Dudh Kosi River till it
descends to **Phungitengma Bridge** (10,665 ft.). After two
hours' gradual ascent through beautiful rhododendron
forest, Thyangboche Monastery will be reached.
Thyangboche is one of the biggest Buddhist monasteries
in the Khumbu region. The views of the gigantic
mountains are at very close range.

4th Day: Thyangboche
Make small excursions to the village of nuns.

5th Day: Khumjung
Trek back by the same route to Khumjung.

6th Day: Everest View Hotel
Ascend gradually to Everest View Hotel.

7th Day: Kathmandu
After an early breakfast, descend to Thyangboche STOL
strip for flight to Kathmandu.

Treks to Helambu, Gosainkund and Langtang

There are interesting places north of Kathmandu for those who
have only a short time for trekking. Helambu, lying north-east of
Kathmandu, and Gosainkund and Langtang to its north, provide
glimpses of Tamang and Sherpa life, temperate forests with varieties
of rhododendron, lakes, glaciers and snow mountains.

144

Helambu: About 72 kms. north-east of Kathmandu Helambu is noted for its scenic grandeur and pleasant climate. The Helambu region extending from the north of Talamarang to the tree-limit of the Gosainkund Lekh and lower slopes of Jugal Himal has several highland Tamang and Sherpa villages, scattered around and on both sides of the Malemchi Khola.

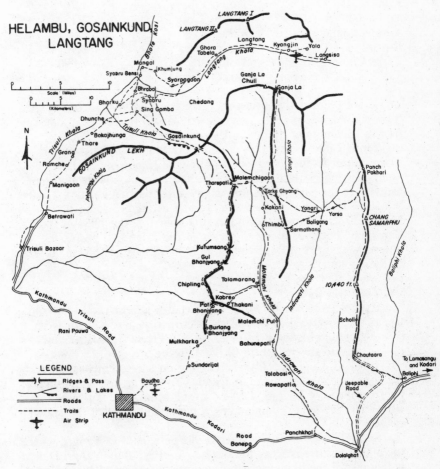

Route		Distance	
From	To	m.	kms.
Kathmandu	Sundarijal	1,585	11
Sundarijal	Mulharka	1,786	5
Mulkharka	Chyaubas	2,286	3
Chyaubas	Borlang Bhanjyang	2,438	2

Borlang Bhanjyang	Chisapani	2,194	2
Chisapani	Pati Bhanjyang	1,737	6
Pati Bhanjyang	Thana Bhanjyang	2,130	3
Thana Bhanjyang	Taramarang	960	8
Taramarang	Mahankal	1,150	5
Mahankal	Kiul	1,460	6
Kiul	Timbu Village	1,761	6
Timbu Village	Yembu Lama	2,130	3
Yembu Lama	Kakani	2,058	3
Kakani	Tarka Chasa	2,160	5
Tarka Chasa	Tashithang	2,590	3
Tashithang	Tarke Ghyang	2,560	3

There is an alternative route to Talamarang. A regular bus service from Kathmandu reaches Panchkhal (945 m.), from where one can trek to Talamarang by the valley of Indravati Khola.

From Talamarang, after crossing the Malemchi Khola, there is a direct trail to the village of Sarmathang (2,664 m.) in Helmu. After crossing the Malemchi Khola the trail, which is steep at first, ascends up the east side of the valley. After passing Palchok Village (1,615 m.), one has to gain the crest of a ridge dividing the Malemchi Khola from the Indravati Khola at about 1,980 m. The trail then continues along the crest of the ridge and passes the Sherpa settlement of Raithane, and the monastery at 2,550 m. as well as Sarmathang is reached.

Trail Description

Kakani (2,160 m.): Quiet scenic charm amidst rhododendron forests and overlooked by the snow-capped peaks, Kakani is one of the most interesting villages of Helmu. From Timbu, Kakani lies on the way to the village of Tarke Ghyang.

Tarke Ghyang (2,560 m.): Nestling on a crescent base under the towering slopes of Yangri Danda, Tarke Ghyang is the biggest Sherpa village of Helmu. Tarke Ghyang Monastery is situated in a very attractive spot, commanding a panoramic view of the snowy ranges.

From Tarke Ghyang, a steep bridle path leads to Yangri, where the alpine pasture reaches up to a height of 3,770 m. Yangri Danda is famous for the immense panoramic view it offers of Jugal Himal.

Malemchi (2,560 m.): Perched on a high shelf on the precipices of Thare in Yurin Danda, Malemchi is a small and very pleasant Sherpa village. From Tarke Ghyang, the trail to Malemchi Village descends to the Malemchi stream at about 1,820 m. and ascends steeply to the village. The track to Tharepati Pass, which lies on the main trail to Gosainkund, climbs steeply up from the villages through thick rhododendron forest From Tharepati Pass (3,505 m.)

the trek continues to Gosainkund.

Sarmathang (8,678 m.): About 10 kms. south-east of Tarke Ghyang, with high mountains towering above, Sarmathang is a pleasant Sherpa village. The natural beauty of Sarmathang is greatly enhanced by the surrounding hills. Close by is a government horticulture farm.

From Tarke Ghyang one can head north and a four-hour climb through a forested ridge brings one to Dukpu (4,023 m.). In another three hours appear the huts of Kelchung and then the huts of Yangri Khola (4,389 m.). Then there is a steep ascent to the Ganja-La (5,122 m.), across which one can reach Kyangjin Gompa (3,749 m.) in Langtang Valley (in six hours).

The track to Panch Pokhari turns east of Tarke Ghyang via Sarmathang and Yangri at the confluence of Larke Khola and Indravati Khola. The other hamlets on the path are Yarsa and Kukang. The lakes of Panch Pokhari (4,084 m.) can be reached in two days.

Gosainkund: Situated at an altitude of 4,380 m. and cradled amidst the craggy peaks, Gosainkund Lake is one of the famous pilgrimages of Nepal. Thousands of people trek annually in the month of August on a pilgrimage to this glacial lake. The trek to Gosainkund passes through varied landscape ranging from evergreen forest, cascading waterfalls and turbulent streams to alpine grass and barren country. Besides the famous Gosainkund Lake the other lakes in the neighbourhood are Nag Kund, Bhairab Kund, Saraswati Kund and Suraj Kund.

Gosainkund lies to the north-west of Helmu beyond a pass at 4,602 m. However, the best approach to Gosainkund is through Trisuli Valley, 71 kms. north west of Kathmandu. Trisuli Valley is linked with Kathmandu by a motorable road.

Route		Altitude	Distance
From	To	(m.)	
Kathmandu	Trisuli Bazaar	548	71 kms. (bus or car)
Trisuli	Betrawati	320	8 kms. (motor)
Betrawati	Manigaon	1,196	4 hrs. (trek)
Manigaon	Ramche	1,780	3 hrs. (trek)
Ramche	Thare	1,889	3 hrs. (trek)
Thare	Bokajhunda	1,920	2 hrs. (trek)
Bokajhunda	Dhunche	1,950	2 hrs. (trek)
Dhunche	Chandanbari	3,353	5 hrs. (trek)
Chandanbari	Lauribina	3,932	5 hrs. (trek)
Lauribina	Gosainkund	4,380	2 hrs. (trek)

After crossing a long bridge over Trisuli Khola beyond

Dhunche, the track to Gosainkund leaves the main trail to Rasua Garhi and the Langtang Valley. The track to Gosainkund turns right (east) up a dense forest ridge. Langtang (7,246 m.), the highest peak in the Langtang Valley, is seen from Dhunche Village.

You can return to Kathmandu from Gosainkund via Helmu or directly to Pati Bhanjyang. These routes provide a worthwhile alternative, for the fine landscape and the Sherpa settlements of Helmu cannot be seen from the route via Trisul Valley. From Helmu the track to Gosainkund begins from Malemchi Village.

The track from Malemchi Village climbs steeply up through rhododendron forest to Tharepati Pass. This pass, which lies on the main trail to Gosainkund, passes through Ghopte (3,216 m.), eastern Lauribina (4,608 m.), Suraj Kund and Gosainkund.

From Tharepati one can return directly to Pati Bhanjyang without making the detour to Helmu. The route is as follows: Tharepati (3,486 m.), Mangegothe (3,285 m.), Kutumsang (2,471 m.). Pati Bhanjyang lies on the main trail between Helmu from Sundarijal.

Langtang Valley: Surrounded with many peaks and glaciers; Langtang Valley is a delightful valley north of Gosainkund. Above an altitude of 3,000 m., Langtang Valley opens out beyond Ghora Tabela. In the Langtang Valley there are beautiful camping sites on yak pastures and spectacular mountain and glacier landscapes. From Langtang Village the track continues to Kyangjin Gompa (3,749 m.). This is the site of the Langtang cheese factory established with Swiss help. There is a STOL airstrip at Chhaldang, a short distance east of Kyangjin.

A visit to the Yala cheese factory (4,633 m.) and the small lakes beyond Yala is worthwhile. Yala can be reached within half a day from Kyangjin Gompa.

From Kyangjin Gompa, a continuation to the pastures of Langsisa (4,084 m.) provides good views of numerous glaciers. There are some huts in Langsisa, which can be reached within a day from Kyangjin Gompa.

Trek to Gosainkund: This is a ten-day trek.

1st Day: Kathmandu to Betrawati
The 50-mile drive to Betrawati (2,000 ft.) takes about three hours from Kathmandu. The road passes the beautiful hill of Kakani and descends to Trisuli Valley without losing the view of Ganesh Himal. Trisuli is the site for a hydro-electric project for power supply to Kathmandu.

2nd Day: Betrawati to Ramche
The track steadily gains height on the eastern bank of Trisuli River, passing through well-maintained fields and

148

villages to Manigaon (4,000 ft.). After ascending about 2,000 ft. Ramche Village (6,000 ft.) is reached (takes six hours).

3rd Day: Ramche to Dhunche
A pleasant walk on shady track to Grang and Thare Villages (6,800 ft.). Descend a little to Bokajhunda (6,500 ft.) and then ascend another 500 ft. before descending gradually to Dhunche (6,500 ft.), a large village with a school, clinic, and some government offices. Langtang and Lirung can be seen from here. (Takes six hours.)

4th Day: Dhunche to Khumjung
Descend to the stream from Gosainkund and ascend for about two hours before reaching the villages of Bhargu and Munga. Descend to the confluence of Bhote Kosi and Langtang Khola at Syabru Bensi. (Takes six hours.)

5th Day: Syabru Bensi
Descend for about one hour. Trek to the confluence of Bhote Kosi and Langtang Khola at Syabru Bensi.

6th Day: Syabru Bensi to Gosainkund
Descend through undulating country for one hour and then ascend to Gosainkund (14,373 ft.).

7th Day: Khumjung
Return by the same route.

8th Day: Dhunche
Return by the same route.

9th Day: Ramche
Return by the same route.

10th Day: Betrawati
Trek to Betrawati and drive back to Kathmandu.

Trek from Kathmandu to Langtang Valley: This trek takes 12 days.

1st Day: Kathmandu to Betrawati
The drive to Betrawati (2,000 ft.) of 31 kms. takes about three hours from Kathmandu. The road passes the beautiful hills of Kakani and descends to Trisuli Valley without losing the view of Ganesh Himal. Trisuli is the site for a hydro-electric project for power supply to Kathmandu. Camp above Betrawati in the mango grove.

2nd Day: Betrawati to Ramche
The track steadily gains height on the eastern bank of Trisuli River, passing through well-maintained fields and villages. After Manigaon (4,000 ft.) an ascent of about

149

2,000 ft. takes you to Ramche Village (6,000 ft.). Takes six hours.

3rd Day: Ramche to Dhunche
A pleasant walk on shady track to the villages of Grang and Thare (6,800 ft.). Descend a little to Bokajhunda (6,500 ft.) and then ascend another 500 ft. before descending gradually to Dhunche (6,500 ft.). (Takes six hours altogether.)

4th Day: Dhunche to Khumjung
Descend to the stream from Gosainkund and ascend for about two hours before reaching the villages of Bhargu and Munga. Descend to the confluence of Bhote Kosi and Langtang Khola at Syabru Bensi. The trek now ascends to a small village before getting into the thin pine forest and to Khumjung Village. Takes six hours. (7,300 ft.).

5th Day: Khumjung to Ghora
After gaining an altitude of about 500 ft., the track passes through thin pine forest and windy spurs to a Sherpa *gaon*, a small Sherpa hamlet. Follow the western bank of the Langtang stream through the narrow gorge of bamboo and pine forest to Ghora Tabela (10,000 ft.), an old horse-breeding ground. Takes six hours.

6th Day: Ghora Tabela to Shingdum
Beyond Ghora Tabela, Langtang Valley opens up. The track passes through villages, yak pastures and a Tibetan refugee camp. After Mundrung Village, head towards Shingdum (11,000 ft.), near the Swiss Dairy Farm to camp. A typical Sherpa-Tibetan tribe lives in this beautiful valley, surrounded by the majestic peaks of Langtang, Lirung and Dorje Lhakpa. Takes five hours.

7th Day: Shingdum
Set aside the day for local excursions.

8th, 9th,
10th and
11th Days: Follow trail back to Ramche.

12th Day: Trek up to Betrawati and drive to Kathmandu.

Trek to Helambu Valley via Panchkhal: A trek of 8 days.

1st Day: Kathmandu to Bhawani Patti (848 m.)
By car or coach you reach Panchkhal in about two hours. The trek begins here. First descend to Chak Khola. An easy two-hour walk takes you to Madan Danra and a further walk of about three hours along the left bank of the Indrawati River to Bhawani Patti.

150

2nd Day: Kiul Phyaudi (970 m.)

Follow the left bank of the Indrawati River for two hours till the confluence of the Indrawati and the Malemchi Khola. Then follow the left bank of the Malemchi Khola for one to two hours till Tarang Marang; now cross a suspension bridge and follow the right bank (for about three hours) of the Malemchi Khola till you reach Kiul Phyaudi.

3rd Day: Tarke Ghyang (2,545 m.)

A steep climb of about one and a half hours to Timbu (1,666 m.). The route continues in a gradual climb of one hour to Tarke Ghyang. The day's trek involves a total number of five walking hours.

4th Day: Malemchi (2,456 m.)

A two-hour steep descent to Malemchi Khola and then a climb up a steep trail for about three hours to Malemchigaon, a Sherpa village which has a thriving orchard.

5th Day: Kutumsang (2,456 m.)

A descent to the stream, then a steep ascent for two hours to Ghotkharka. A gradual climb of an hour and then an easy walk of three to four hours through a rhododendron forest to Kutumsang. The trek offers good views of the eastern Himalayas.

6th Day: Golbhanjyang Danra (2,212 m.)

A walk through a forest for an hour, then a descent for another two hours to Golbhanjyang. From here a steep climb for two to three hours to Golbhanjyang Danra.

7th Day: Chisapani Chaur (1,758 m.)

After an hour's easy walk, you reach a pass. A steep descent of two to three hours takes you to Patti Bhanjyang. A steep climb of about two hours to Chisapani Danra. Panoramic views of Everest, Gauri Shankar, Ganesh Himal and other eastern mountains.

8th Day: Back to Kathmandu via Sundarijal

A gradual climb to Mulharka for an hour. From here the route descends all the way to Sundarijal. Back to Kathmandu in a car/coach.

The route from Kathmandu (1,310 m.) to Langtang is as follows:

Route		Height	Distance
From	To	(m.)	
Kathmandu	Trisuli Bazaar	548	71 kms. (bus or car)
Trisuli	Betrawati	320	8 kms. (motor)

151

Betrawati	Manigaon	1,196	4 hrs. (trek)
Manigaon	Ramche	1,780	3 hrs. (trek)
Ramche	Thare	1,899	3 hrs. (trek)
Thare	Bokajhunda	1,920	2½ hrs. (trek)
Bokajhunda	Dhunche	1,950	2½ hrs. (trek)
Dhunche	Barku	1,920	2 hrs. (trek)
Barku	Syabru Bensi	1,249	2½ hrs. (trek)
Syabru Bensi	Khumjung	2,210	3 hrs. (trek)
Khumjung	Syabru Bensi	2,590	4 hrs. (trek)
Syarpagaon	Ghora Tabela	3,048	6 hrs. (trek)
Ghora Tabela	Langtang	3,350	3 hrs. (trek)
Langtang	Kyangjin	3,749	3 hrs. (trek)

Besides the route mentioned above, there is an alternative route from Barku to Ghora Tabela connecting Barku-Syabru Villages. Ghora Tabela is four hours closer than the former route.

There is a trek from Langtang Valley to Helmu over a hard stretch. The pass of Ganja-La (5,122 m.) is open only during the monsoon months and early autumn. The route is as follows: Kyangjin Gompa (3,74C m.), Ganja-La Pass (5,122 m.), Yangri Khola (4,389 m.), Chamungthang (3,169 m.), and Tarke Ghyang (2,560 m.).

Langtang National Park (1,243 sq. km.): The alpine Langtang Valley is the home of the Himalayan thar and musk deer. Scenically this is a spectacular region, including Gosainkund with its lakes and the headwaters of a number of streams flowing across steep slopes of extensive temperate forests.

Around Pokhara

Pokhara Valley, connected by a 200 km. highway with Kathmandu, is ideal for good views of some high mountains and a convenient starting-point for treks. The town of Pokhara (910 m.) is located in an intermount plain and close by are the deep gorges carved by the Seti River. Four kms. south-west of the town is Phewa Tal, with a temple on an island. A 12 km. motorable road leads east to Pachbhaiya Ridge (850 m.) with good views of Begnas Tal and Rupa Tal on its either side. From the Pokhara airfield you can have a superb view of the entire Annapurna range.

For a fuller view of the mountain range, you can trek 18 kms. south to Nuwakot (1,535 m.). Here there is an old fort and the view towards the northern horizon emcompasses snow ranges from Dhaulagiri to Ganesh Himal. One can trek eastwards of Nuwakot along a low ridge that confines Pokhara Valley from the south. The ridge track along Phoksing Danda (91,134 m.) provides an excellent panaromic view of the whole Pokhara Valley with its

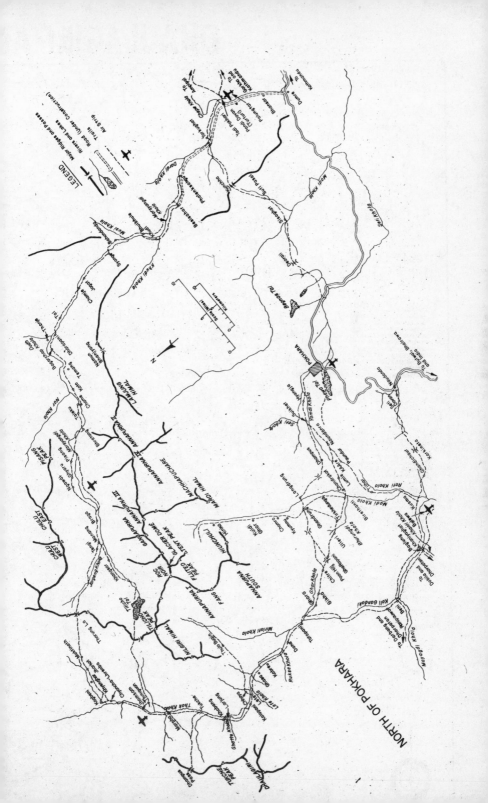

lakes and mountains beyond. The array of snow peaks visible from Phoksing are Dhaulagiri, the Annapurna range, Manaslu and Himalchuli and Ganesh Himal. For a more direct approach, Phoksing is about a two-hour walk south of the Pokhara airfield across Seti River.

There are short treks north of Pokhara into the valleys of Madi, Seti and Modi Rivers. The trek to Madi River turns east of the town through the Gurung villages of Antighar (1,751 m.) and Mauja (1,371 m.) to Thak (1,554 m.). Another alternative route is to approach Thak from further south along Sijaypur Khola. From Thak, one can reach Siklis (1,981 m.), one of the largest Gurung villages in upper Madi Valley that provides close views of Annapurna-II, Annapurna-IV and Lamjung Himal. The return trek can be made by a high trail along the villages of Khilang and Chipli. The track then climbs a forested ridge from where one turns due south to Armala (1,430 m.) and Batulechaur (975 m.) and the other descends west to Seti Valley to Bhurjung (1,219 m.) and Ghachok (1,219 m.). Above Ghachok are some high alpine meadows from where Machhapuchare can be viewed at close range. You can return to Pokhara from Ghachok in a day, passing the villages of Lahachok (1,158 m.) and Hyangja (1,041 m.) along the high terraces of River Seti.

Another interesting trek is towards north-west of Pokhara to Ghandruk and Annapurna Sanctuary. Ghandruk, another large Gurung village in upper Modi Valley, is a two-day walk from Pokhara. The trek begins at Hyangja, north of Pokhara town. The route beyond Suikhet (1,127 m.) and after crossing the Modi River, climbs steeply to Ghandruk. The houses are all slate-roofed and the village provides good views of Machhapuchare and Annapurna South. You can trek further to the Annapurna Sanctuary, a high valley enclosed by snow ranges. Since there are no settlements beyond Chomrong (1,691 m.), you must carry food and tents. The recommended return trip from Ghandruk is through the villages of Mohariya (1,820 m.) and Dansing (1,730 m.) on the west side of the Modi River. The river is crossed at Birethanti (1,188 m.). The track then climbs through Chandrakot (1,500 m.) and Lumle (1,520 m.) to Kande Pass (1,700 m.) near the British agricultural farm. A camp at Nag Danda (1,443 m.) on Kaski Ridge provides good views of the mountains to the north and Phewa Tal to the south. From Nag Danda, it is a pleasant walk along the Kaski Ridge to Pokhara town.

Trekking in the Pokhara Region: The trek will take you about five days.

1st Day: Pokhara to Hyangja

Fly to Pokhara from Kathmandu. Trek to Hyangja through the old Pokhara town and by the bank of River Seti.

2nd Day: Hyangja to Khara
Trek through the village of Hyangja and the paddy fields
of Suikhet Valley to the ford (3,800 ft.) at the foot of
Naundanra (4,782 ft.). Ascend to Khara along the
Naundanra Ridge for about three hours and then
descend for about one hour to the camping place.

3rd Day: Khara to Khapauti
The trek back from Khara to Naundanra is very
picturesque, with views of Annapurna massif on the
left and Phewa Lake green valley on the right. Trek
down to Khapauti for camping at night.

4th Day: Khapauti to Pokhara
Proceed to Hotel Fishtail Lodge for a day's stay.

5th Day: Pokhara to Kathmandu
Fly to Kathmandu by scheduled flight.

Five- to Six-day Trek in Pokhara

1st Day: Naundanra
A flight will take you from Kathmandu to Pokhara
airport in 45 minutes. Then proceed to Phewa Lake from
where trek begins. From there, a walk of about three
hours through terraced and cultivated fields and villages,
will bring you to Naundanra (4,782 ft.).

2nd Day: Naundanra to Chandrakot
A trek to Khare. The trail is a gradual climb and gives
panoramic views of the Annapurna massif. Khare is
reached after two hours. A descent, passing the village
of Lunle at 5,000 ft., and a walk will bring you to
Chandrakot (5,124 ft.) — view-point for high mountains
overlooking the Modi Khola Valley. Takes four hours
altogether.

3rd Day: Longdrung
A walk towards Longdrung Village (6,300 ft.) along the
right bank of Modi Khola. The trail passes through
Tamlejing, offering views of Annapurna South. On the
left side of Modi Khola is a large Gurung village, the home of
the famous Gorkha soldiers. Takes five hours altogether.

4th Day: Dhampus Pass
From Longdrung, Dhampus Pass (6,800 ft.). For those
interested in flora, this is indeed an enjoyable walk as
orchids are in view along the trail. Throughout you get
an unending view of cultivated fields, small villages,
forests and flowers. Takes four hours altogether.

5th Day: Dhampus Pass to Hyangja
From Dhampus Pass, descend gradually. The trek
passes through the villages of Dhampus and Hyangja

Kot. A further descent brings you to the Suikhet Village.
From here the trail passes through picturesque rice fields.
A walk of a little over two hours brings you to the
Hyangja Tibetan refugee camp (3,600 ft.). Takes four
hours altogether.

6th Day: Back to Pokhara
Proceed back to Pokhara in time for return flight to
Kathmandu. The walk goes along the bank of Seti River,
and through the old town and shopping centre of
Pokhara.

Eleven-to Twelve-Day Trek Around Pokhara

1st Day: Pokhara to Suikhet
Having flown from Kathmandu to Pokhara, start your
trek along the Mardi Khola River passing all manner of
colourful locals with their strings of pack donkeys, goats.
sheep, all ambling past with bells tinkling. All along the
track you will get good views of Annapurna and
Machhapuchare. Then you drive in the village of
Hengha. Continue along the Yangdi Khola through
paddy fields to the tumbling waterfall near Suikhet; you
can bathe in the many pools found here.

2nd Day: Around Suikhet
Start climbing steeply up a rough track. Continue
climbing up for the rest of the day, but less steeply,
through terraced fields and a little collection of houses,
then to the rhododendron lines.

3rd Day: Longdrung
Continue on up through the winding rhododendron path
where you cross a ridge at approximately 7,100 ft., from
where you wander down, and continue down through the
lovely terraced hillsided village of Longdrung.

4th Day: Gandrung
Trek to the fascinating village of Gandrung. From here,
Annapurna South seems very close.

5th Day: Gandrung
Climb through the green moss-hanging rhododendron
forests.

6th Day: Ghorapani
Continue climbing steeply up and finally out on the
top of the Deorali Pass. From here, you can enjoy
endless wonderful snowy mountain views. Continue
along the Deorali Pass. By now Annapurna-I, II, III
south plus the sacred Machhapuchare have been
joined by the great Dhaulagiri which is slightly in the
west of the others. You climb till about 10,000 ft. before
arriving at Ghorapani.

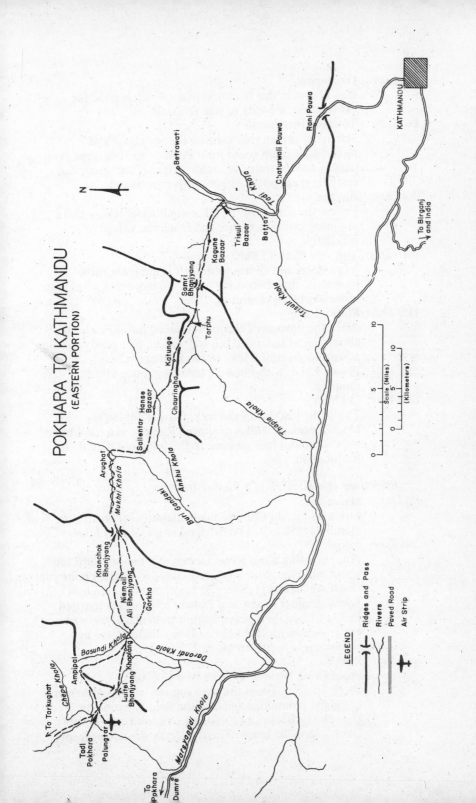

POKHARA TO KATHMANDU
(EASTERN PORTION)

N

LEGEND

Ridges and Pass

Rivers

Paved Road

Air Strip

Scale (Miles)

0   5   10

0   5   10

(Kilometers)

To Tarkughat

Chepe Khola

Tadi Pokhara

Palungtar

To Pokhara

Dumre

Marsyangdi Khola

Ampipal

Basundi Khola

Luitel
Bhaniyang Khoplang

Darondi Khola

Niemail
Ali Bhaniyang

Gorkha

Khanchok Bhaniyang

Arughat

Mukhi Khola

Sallentar Hanse Bazaar

Buri Gandaki Khola

Ankhu Khola

Katunge

Chauringha

Thople Khola

Tarphu

Samri Bhaniyang

Kagune Bazaar

Trisuli Bazaar

Battar

Tadi Khola

Betrawati

Chaturwali Pauwa

Trisuli Khola

Rani Pauwa

KATHMANDU

To Birganj
and India

7th Day: Ghorapani

Day of rest in this beautiful place which is good for exploration, viewing or just relaxing.

8th Day: Towards Birethanti

Start your return trek viewing the very busy and picturesque main route from Pokhara to Jhomsom. You pass masses of trains of mules, donkeys and ponies all carrying great packs either north or south.

9th Day: Birethanti

Follow the course of the Bharungdi River where there are many pools to bathe, and reach the village of Birethanti.

10th Day: Towards Phewa Lake

Very steep, hot climb; to the left is the great snow mountain, now becoming more and more distant as your homeward trek continues.

11th Day: Phewa Lake

After the down trek through terraced hilisides, climb aboard great hollowed out tree canoe, and gently paddle across the beautiful lake to the final camp besides the Phewa Lake, with Phewa Island containing Hindu temple.

12th Day: Pokhara

This is the last day of the trek; leaving behind the Machhapuchare and Annapurna Ranges, you have to walk for about half an hour to Pokhara and then fly to Kathmandu.

Rolwaling Himal: This is a 22-day trek.

1st Day: Barabise

Drive by bus on Chinese-made highway for 86 kms. to Barabise (950 m.). The drive takes about four hours.

2nd Day: Jalijale

After crossing Kose River ascend to Dhungey Patti for about an hour. With a gradual ascent of over an hour you reach Aklaigaon (1,500 m.). Another one and a half hours' gradual ascent and Piskar (1,760 m.) is reached. Piskar to Jalijale is very pleasant trekking. If the day is early, ascend for one hour to Dong Jhale (2,450 m.). (Total: eight hours' trekking.)

3rd Day: Boncha

From Dong Jhale to Chotke Pass (2,670 m.) it takes about an hour. From the pass you can see Gosaithan and Langtang mountains and also the Solu Khumbu areas. Descend to Burkosir (2,480 m.). After passing Dorey Dunga, stop for lunch. The track now descends steeply

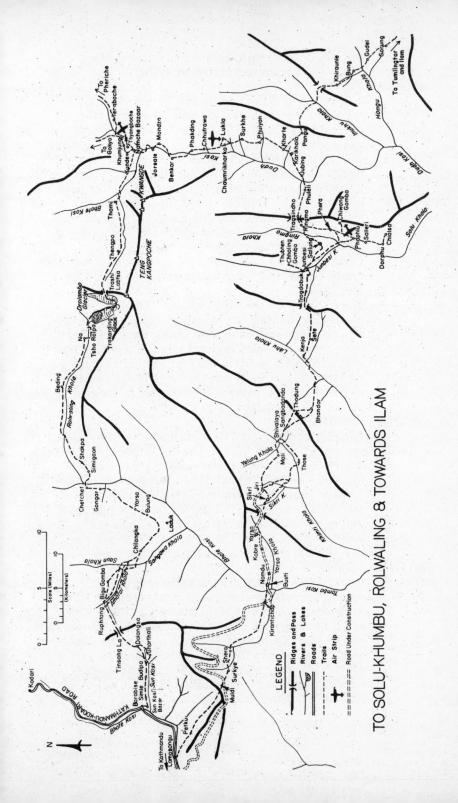

TO SOLU-KHUMBU, ROLWALING & TOWARDS ILAM

towards Boncha, passing through a Tamang village.
Takes seven hours of trekking altogether.

4th Day: Domban

After crossing the stream, ascend for ten minutes. The track now maintains a steady height and passes through the scattered village of Makai Bari. You reach Tarmans stupa near the track junction from Lamosangu, and pass well-cultivated fields till Charikot. From Charikot the track to Solu Khumbu bifurcates. Charikot is a large village with a number of government offices. The track now descends to Dolkha—1,800 m., another large settlement of Newars. The Bhimsenthan, a Hindu temple, is a famous place for pilgrimage. The track now descends steeply along the crest of a ridge down to Doban off Bhote Kosi. There is a good campsite near the bridge. Takes eight hours altogether.

5th Day: Suri Doban

The track follows the western bank of Bhote Kosi, maintaining a steady height through terraced fields and thin pine forest for about three hours. Trek to Pekuti. From there to Bareley suspension bridge is a three-hour walk and after crossing it, walk for another hour along the right bank to reach Suri Doban. The day's unpleasant trek in the narrow valley is compensated by the cool breeze of Bhote Kosi.

6th Day: Jashinam

After walking along the right bank for about two hours, you reach Tatopani Village. The hot spring is on the other side of the river. It takes another hour to reach Mandali Village (1,245 m.). Now a steep ascent of about 1,000 m. starts from here, through lovely pine and rhododendron forests. The last few kms. are pleasant walking to Tashinam, a Sherpa village. There is a Buddhist temple here. This village is the last place to buy eggs and chicken. Takes eight hours altogether.

7th Day: Shakba

After climbing a little, the track descends gradually round a spur and reaches a *patti* (rest place) at 2,310 m., from where you can see the confluence of Bhote Kosi and Rolwaling Kosi. Lambagar (Choksom in Sherpa) can also be seen. There is a police post and wireless station here. From the *patti* the track becomes quite dangerous while crossing the big rocky hill and then descends through a thin forest to Senbigaon (21 ft./50 m.). A six-hour trek altogether.

8th Day:	Ramding
	From Shakba the track passes through rhododendron and bamboo, and some portions of burnt forest. You can see Gauri Shankar (7,145 m.) and many smaller peaks. Stop by the stream at Dongkhang Dzong (3,100 m.) for lunch. The track climbs gradually upto a new bridge; and after crossing follows the western bank, passes Nimerey cattle-houses to Ramding. The people of Rolwaling move down to these settlements from Nangaon and Beding for the winter. In summer these houses are empty. A seven-hour trek altogether.
9th Day:	Nangaon
	After passing Jomojunjo, you will reach Beding (3,800 m.) in an hour's time. Beding is the biggest village and the centre of Rolwaling Valley. There is a fine Buddhist temple here. The houses are built on the hillside. *Chang* (local beer) and *raksi* are sold in Sherpa houses. It is now a steady ascent of about three hours along the left bank of the stream to Nangaon. This is the last settlement of Yak and sheep rearing. All the houses are made of stone. (You have to stock food supplies here before going further.)
10th to	
14th Days:	You can take these days off for excursions in the region.
15th Day:	Tsobuk Lake Area
	From Nangaon the track leads to Ramding Himal and Tashi Lapcha. After gradual ascent through the valley you reach Tsobuk Lake in about three hours. The track beyond has to cross a dangerous stony area. There is a pass here leading towards Phaphlu to the right via Ahhjamo Pass. Mountain scenery is beautiful throughout the day. A six-hour trek for the day.
16th Day:	Drolum Bau
	Cross the moraine to the right and climb on ice and snow for about 300 m. to be on the flat Drolum Bau Glacier. Walk for about three hours, steadily gaining an altitude of 100 m. on the glacier and climb to the camping area at 350 m. short of Tashi Lapcha Pass (5,750 m.).
17th Day:	Tashi Lapcha
	Climbing to Tashi Lapcha and descending towards Khumbu area involves technical gear and skill. The view from Tashi Lapcha is beyond description. You can see Mt Everest with its satellites, the Kunde Range. Also, Thamserku, Ama Dablam and numerous peaks surrounding Drolum Bau Glacier. A four-hour trek altogether.

18th Day: Thami

Descend all along on steep slopes upto the yak pasture at Thengpo (4,320 m.) and stop for lunch. The track now descends very pleasantly to Thami Village. Above the village you will pass the Thami Monastery, beautifully built on the rocky feature. Thami is a large Sherpa village, where you can buy *raksi, chang,* vegetables, meat, butter etc. A six-hour trek altogether.

19th Day: Namche Bazaar

A very pleasant walk of about three hours from Thami to Namche. The police post en route may check your trekking permits. During the entire walk you are in view of Kunde Range on the right and Thamserku in front. At Namche, the campsite is preferable above the bazaar in the flat grazing ground. Your trekking permits are checked here by the Immigration Office. Medical and wireless facilities are available. The weekly market day on Saturday is quite interesting — there is a gathering of Sherpas, local Tibetans and Tamang from the lower region. Good *chang/raksi* are available for buying. Visitors to Sherpa houses are quite welcome, though their trip may prove rather expensive; there are also numerous shops to buy souvenirs and stock your supplies. Takes five hours altogether.

20th Day: Thyangboche

Those who are interested to visit the Thyangboche Monastery, should take a packed lunch and proceed with the guide to Thyangboche. It takes about four hours going and four hours coming. The others could conveniently visit Khumjung, Kunde and Hotel Everest View at Thyangboche and return to camp. Total trekking time: eight hours.

21st Day: Ghat

After breakfast, descend to Hillary bridges and then follow Dudh Kosi to Jorsale. The walk along the stream through lovely pine forests and scattered Sherpa settlements is very pleasant. (Six hours of trekking for the day.)

22nd Day: Lukla

After breakfast, ascend gradually to Lukla camp near the landing strip (a four-hour trek)

23rd Day: Kathmandu

It is advisable to be at Lukla one day earlier to make sure that your further programme is not upset by delays in flights due to weather conditions.

Previous page: Annapurna, South (Frank Hoppe).
This page, above: The Everest range from Phalut, near
Darjeeling. Below: The Kanchenjunga range from Darjeelin.

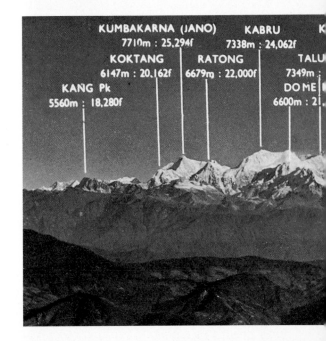

EVEREST
8848m:29,028f
LHOTSE
8500m:27,890f
MAKALU
8470m:27,790f
TSE   NUPTSE   SOUTH COL   CHOMOLONZO
3,688f 7879m:25,726f 7986m:26,200f   7815m:25,640f

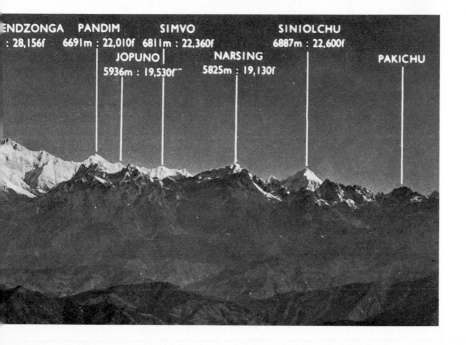

ENDZONGA   PANDIM   SIMVO   SINIOLCHU
:28,156f   6691m:22,010f 6811m:22,360f   6887m:22,600f
                 JOPUNO | NARSING   PAKICHU
                 5936m:19,530f   5825m:19,130f

Leh panorama, with the palace in the background.   Frank Hoppe.

The Salang Pass, Afghanistan.

Mt. Pumouri, Nepal.

Thyangboche, with Mt. Amadablam in the background.

Peaks on the Tibet border beyond Mustang.   Frank Hoppe.

Opposite: Machu Puchare (Frank Hoppe).

The Buddhist Monastery, Ghoom, near Darjeeling, and its richly decorated interior, below.

Kinner Kailash, Himachal Pradesh.

The monastery of Lamayuru in Ladakh.

A view of Nanga Parbat.

Balahisar Fort, Kabul.

A group of northern people, Afghanistan.

Overleaf: Camp at Dabush, Nepal (Frank Hoppe).

Porters at Dhaulagiri.   Frank Hoppe.

Annapurna Base Camp: This is a fifteen-day trek.

1st Day: Hyangja

After breakfast, fly to Pokhara in the morning. After a 30-minute flight you will be at the Pokhara airport, from where the trek starts. You will pass through Pokhara Bazaar area and along the Seti River bank to reach the village of Hyangja (36,000 ft.), your camping site. Takes three hours.

2nd Day: Trek through Hyangja Village, and the Suikhet paddy fields, to a ford at the foot of Naundanra (3,800 m.). Stop by the stream for lunch. It is a steep climb of over an hour to Naundanra. The ascent to Khare (5,600 ft.) is now more gradual and it takes about two hours. The trek from Naundanra to Khare is very picturesque, with a view of Annapurna massif on the right and Phewa Lake green valley on the left. Seven hours of trekking altogether.

3rd Day: Gandrung Bensi

After breakfast, trek through the villages of Lumle (5,000 ft.) and Chandrakot (5,124 ft.) to Tamlejung. Descend to Modi Khola and after crossing the improvised wooden bridge, trek through paddy fields to Gandrung Bensi (4,000 ft.). Chandrakot is a good viewpoint overlooking the entire Modi Khola Valley, Annapurna (South) and Machhapuchare.

4th Day: Kimru Khola

From Bensi, the ascent is quite steep and passes through terraced rice fields and a few scattered villages. After about three hours' ascent you reach Gandrung Village. You can have magnificent views of Modi Himal, Machhapuchare and other Annapurna ranges from here. The track passes through the village, and gains height steadily till it reaches a saddle where a few houses stand on either side of the track. Tea and liquor are available here. From here to Kimru Khola (5,900 ft.) is a steep descent of an hour.

5th Day: Khuildi

From Kimru Khola ascend for an hour. Now the track is around a spur passing through a village before it descends to Chamru Village (6,700 ft.). Descend to Chamru Khola and ascend again after passing through. The track now leads through thick forest and follows the western bank of Modi Khola. Takes eight hours altogether, before you reach Khuildi (7,000 ft.)

6th Day: Hinko

From Khuildi, the track follows the western bank of

Modi Khola and through the thick bamboo and bushes reaches Doban (8,000 ft.) after three hours' trek. The bushy forest in this area is well stocked with leeches. From Doban to Hinko (10,000 ft.) is a steady ascent of about three hours. Now the forest disappears and the valley opens up and becomes very picturesque. You will be right at the foot of Modi Himal and Machhapuchare. (Total trekking time: six hours.)

7th Day: Annapurna Base Camp
The track steadily gains altitude and after about three hours along the bank of Modi Khola, amidst awe-inspiring mountain scenery, you will reach Annapurna Base Camp area (12,000 ft.). This area is the main base camp for the expeditions to most of the Annapurna ranges. It is a short stage day to overcome altitude effects. Takes three hours of trekking time altogether.

8th Day: Annapurna Base Camp
Ascend steadily for about 1,000 ft. to reach the campsite right at the foot of Modi Himal, facing all the peaks of Machhapuchare, Gangapurna, the Annapurna series, Glacier Dome, Tent Peak etc. Immediately on the right is the Annapurna Glacier moraine. Takes two hours.

9th and
10th Days. Hyangja Base Camp
Set aside these two days for excursions in the area (around 13,200 ft.).

11th Day: Hinko
Return by the same route (takes three hours) to Hinko (10;000 ft.).

12th Day: Chamru Village
Return by the same route (takes eight hours) to reach Chamru Village (6,700 ft.).

13th Day: Gandrung
Return by the same route (takes seven hours) to Gandrung (6,200 ft.).

14th Day: Dhampus
Descend to Modi Khola and after crossing ascend to Landrung Village. The track now passes through picturesque terraced fields, village houses, orchid fields and thin forests towards Dhampus (6,400 ft.). Takes eight hours.

15th Day: Pokhara
Descend to Suikhet by passing through the village of Dhampus, Hyangjakot. Now follow the same route to Pokhara town (2,900 ft.) and drive to Phewa Tal lake for camping. Takes eight hours altogether.

16th Day: Kathmandu
Drive by car to Pokhara airport to catch your flight to
Kathmandu (4,450 ft.).

Around Annapurna: This trek would take about 21 days.
1st Day: Hyangja
Fly to Pokhara from Kathmandu. Trek to Hyangja
(3,600 ft.) through the old Pokhara town and by the bank
of River Seti.
2nd Day: Khare
Trek through the village of Hyangja and the paddy
fields of Suikhet Valley to the ford, 3,800 ft. at the foot
of Naundanra (4,782 ft.). Stop for lunch. Ascend to
Khare (5,600 ft.) along the Naundanra Ridge for about
three hours.
3rd Day: Tirkhedunga
After having a pleasant walk through the village of
Lumle (5,000 ft.) and Chandrakot (5,134 ft.) for about
two hours, descend to Modi Khola. Now follow
Bhurungdi River to ascend to Tirkhedunga (900 ft.).
4th Day: Ghorapani
After crossing Bhurungdi River ascend to Ulleri Village
for lunch. Ascend again for another three hours to
Ghorapani (4,000 ft.). From Ghorapani you can have
good views of both Annapurna and Dhaulagiri.
5th Day: Tatopani
Descend all day to Tatopani passing through the villages
of Chire (7,700 ft.), Sikha (6,600 ft.) and Ghasa. After
crossing Ghar Khola and Kaligandaki, trek along the
western bank of Kaligandaki River for about an hour
to reach Tatopani (3,900 ft.).
6th Day: Ghasa
Trek along the gorge of Kaligandaki River, crossing
two bridges at points. At Dana (4,800 ft.) your permits
will be checked by the police. After crossing the
beautiful waterfall, you have to ascend to 9,200 ft. and
then descend again to 6,000 ft. Another one hour's walk
along the bank of Kali River and you will reach Ghasa
Village (6,600 ft.).
7th Day: Sirkung
After three hours of pleasant trekking along the western
bank of Kaligandaki River, cross Lete Khola by a
wooden bridge and pass through Lete (7,500 ft.). Stop
for lunch near the school. Pass through the pine trees
along the bank of Kalapani (9,000 ft.) and cross at Depa.

After walking another five miles you will reach Sirkung.
There is a small Buddhist temple here and a few houses.

8th Day: Jhomsom
After passing the village of Khanti (8,500 ft.) and Tukche (8,485 ft.) you will reach Marga (8,760 ft.). Pass Syand (9,000 ft.) and Jhomsom airstrip to reach the main Jhomsom Village on the eastern bank of Kaligandaki River. There are government offices, police and military posts, a wireless station and a number of local shops.

9th Day: Kagbeni
After a sight-seeing tour of Jhomsom Village, trek to Kagbeni.

10th Day: Muktinath
There is a gradual gain in altitude of about 1,000; Muktinath is a sacred Hindu pilgrimage centre. There is a Buddhist temple also. The place has a typical landscape beauty overlooked by Damodar Hills.

11th Day: Through Pass
Ascend through a pass, about 5,400 m. It will take about seven hours to reach the pass.

12th Day: Ghusang
The track follows Jargung Khola in Manang Bhot Valley, just north-east of Annapurna Range.

13th Day: Pisang
The valley becomes wider and more beautiful. The inhabitants are all Buddhist Gurungs, known locally as Manage.

14th Day: Chane
This is the biggest village with a number of government offices, and a police checkpost with wireless contracts to Kathmandu.

15th Day: Thonge
This is at the confluence of Marsyangdi and Dudh Khola. From this the track to Barkya Pass starts eastward.

16th Day: Jagat
A steep descent starts into Marsyangdi Valley. Jagat is a small Gurung village.

17th Day: Khadi
This lies at the confluence of Khadi Khola and Marsyangdi Rivers. Khadi is a bigger village. It is a Newar settlement.

18th Day: Naina
After following a track along paddy fields ascend to Baghung Pani. Descend steeply towards Nalima for about three hours.

19th Day: Korbe Tar
    The track is all through lowland along the river bed of
    Midam Khola.
20th Day: Begnas Tal
    The track enters a small forest and reaches Begnas Tal.
21st Day: Pokhara
    Trek to Danrarange near police post. Checking of the
    Trekking permit is done at the post. Reach Pokhara by
    bus.

Kaligandaki Valley: This is a 14-15 day trek.
1st Day: Hyangja
    Fly to Pokhara from Kathmandu. Trek to Hyangja
    through the old Pokhara town and by the bank of River
    Seti, in the evening (three hours).
2nd Day: Khare
    Trek through the village of Hyangja and the paddy
    fields of Suikhet Valley to the ford 3,800 ft. at the foot
    of Naundanra (4,782 ft.). Ascend to Khare along the
    Naundanra Ridge for about three hours and then
    descend for about one hour (seven hours).
3rd Day: Tirkhedunga
    After having a pleasant walk through the village of
    Lumle (5,000 ft.) and Chandrakot (5,134 ft.) for about
    two hours, descend to Modi Khola. Cross the Bhurungdi
    River to ascend to Tirkhedunga (seven hours).
4th Day: Ghorapani
    After crossing Bhurungdi River ascend to Ulleri Village.
    Ascend again for another three hours through forest area
    to Ghorapani. From Ghorapani you can get a good view
    of both Annapurna and Dhaulagiri (six hours).
5th Day: Tatopani
    Descend all day to Tatopani, passing through the villages
    of Chire (7,700 ft.), Sikha (6,600 ft.) and Ghasa. After
    crossing Ghar Khola and Kaligandaki, trek along the
    western bank of Kaligandaki River for about an hour
    to reach Tatopani (seven hours).
6th Day: Ghasa
    Trek along the gorge of Kaligandaki River, crossing
    two bridges at points. At Dana (4,800 ft.) your permits
    will be checked by the police. After crossing the
    beautiful waterfall, ascend to an altitude of 9,200 ft. and
    then descend again to 6,000 ft. It is another one hour's
    walk along the bank of Kali River to Ghasa Village
    (takes six hours altogether).

7th Day: Sirkung

After two hours of pleasant trekking along the western bank of Kaligandaki River, cross Lete Khola by a wooden bridge and pass through Lete (7,500 ft.). Pass through the pine trees along the bank of Kalapani (8,000 ft.) and cross at Depa. After walking another three miles you will reach Sirkung. There is a small Buddhist temple here and a few village houses (six hours).

8th Day: Jhomsom

After passing the villages of Khanti (8,500 ft.) and Tukche (8,485 ft.) you will reach Marga (8,760 ft.), Pass Syang (9,000 ft.) and Jhomsom airstrip to reach the main Jhomsom Village on the eastern bank of Kaligandaki River. There are government offices, police and military posts, a wireless station and a number of local shops (takes seven hours altogether).

9th Day: Lete

Lete by the same route (seven hours).

10th Day: Dana

Dana by the same route (seven hours).

11th Day: Sikha

Sikha by the same route (seven hours).

12th Day: Deorali

You can reach Deorali (9,000 ft.) by the same route (six hours). After Chire Village, follow the left track to Deorali by passing Ghorapani. This is a fine place to enjoy the mountain scenery.

13th Day: Gandrung

Descend all day to Gandrung Village (5,600 ft.). This is one of the biggest Gurung villages (five hours altogether).

14th Day: Dhampus Pass

Descend to Modi Khola. After crossing ascend to Longdrung Village. Trek through fine forest, and fields with numerous orchids. Camp at Dhampus Pass (6,200 ft.); you will get a good viewpoint of the mountains from here. Takes eight hours altogether.

15th Day: Pokhara

Descend through the villages of Dhampus and Hyangja to Suikhet. Follow the same route to Hyangja and Pokhara old town. From there drive to Phewa Tal. Next morning, drive to the airport.

Pokhara/ Ghorapani

1st Day: Hyangja

Fly from Kathmandu to Pokhara, where the hike begins.

Hyangja (1,060 m.) can be reached in about two hours.

2nd Day: Modi Khola

The hike (six hours) includes magnificent views of the snow-covered (8,000 m.) peak. A three-hour hike will take you to Dhampus Pass. The path descends gradually through beautiful rhododendron woods to **Longdrung** (1,610 m.) and onwards to Modi Khola (1,250 m.).

3rd Day: Gandrung

Steep ascent to the typical Gurung village, **Gandrung** (2,070 m.). The hike will take approximately four hours from where you can get a beautiful view of the Annapurna mountain chain.

4th Day: Thante

Narrow paths lead through a fantastic jungle steeply downwards to the upper Bhurungdi Khol River. After four to five hours' hike the Thante clearing (2,740 m.) can be reached.

5th Day: Ghorapani

Ascend to Deorali Pass (3,130 m.); this will take two to three hours. From here, hike for approximately four hours near the ridge to the Ghorapani Pass (2,895 m.). In front lies the Kaligandaki Valley, the Dhaulagiri and the Annapurna group.

6th Day: Birethanti

A steep descent (of two to three hours) leads through a cool jungle to the Magar village, Ulleri (2,000 m.) and over many steps downwards to the Modi Khola. After another two to three hours Birethanti (1,060 m.) is reached.

7th Day: Naundanra

Roughly 650 m. must be climbed to the 1,710 m. Khare Pass. The path leads downwards all the way along the valley with rice fields to Naundanra. From here, a beautiful view of the Annapurna chains and **Dhaulagiri** can be had.

8th Day: Sarankot

A leisurely hike, past a beautiful village, to Sarankot (1,000 m.).

9th Day: Pokhara

After a hike of approximately two hours, you reach Phewa Lake.

10th Day: Kathmandu

Take the flight to Kathmandu from Pokhara.

Treks to Jhomsom and Muktinath

Jhomsom or Jomosom lies in the upper Kaligandaki, beyond Annapurna and Dhaulagiri Himal. Pokhara (910 m.) is the starting-point for a trek to Jhomsom and it takes over six days. The track passes first through Magar villages on the ridge between Modi Khola and Kaligandaki, and then up the Kaligandaki Valley inhabited by Thakalis. The trek provides sharp changes in landscape, vegetation and culture within a short distance. Beyond Tukche (2,586 m.) it is dry and bare, reminiscent of the Tibetan landscape. Food and lodging are available all along this trek.

Route		Height	Distance
From	To	(m.)	(kms.)
Pokhara	Hyangja	1,067	7
Hyangja	Suikhet	1,127	5
Suikhet	Nag Danda	1,443	2
Nag Danda	Khare	1,646	5
Khare	Tikhedhunga	1,439	15
Tikhedhunga	Ghorapani	2,835	8
Ghorapani	Tatopani	1,180	15
Tatopani	Dana	1,490	6
Dana	Ghasa	2,010	9
Ghasa	Larjung	2,560	14
Larjung	Tukche	2,586	6
Tukche	Jhomsom	2,710	11
Jhomsom	Muktinath	3,749	18

Nag Danda (1,443 m.): On Kaski Ridge, is climbed from Suikhet. It can also be reached by climbing north of the Bindubasini temple in Pokhara town towards Sarankot (1,591 m.), and then along the high Kaski Ridge. Nag Danda gives good views of the Annapurna Range and Phewa Tal.

Route		Height	Distance
From	To	(m.)	(kms.)
Kathmandu or			by bus
Pokhara	Dumre	420	or car
Dumre	Tarkughat	488	18
Tarkughat	Phalesangu (Dalal)	632	14
Phalesangu (Dalal)	Khudi or Bhulbule	790	15
Khudi or Bhulbhule	Bahundanda	1,310	10
Bahundanda	Jagat	1,341	11
Jagat	Thonje	1,920	12
Thonje	Chame	2,651	14
Chame	Pisang	3,333	14
Pisang	Manang	3,505	15

Dumre (420 m.): The trek begins at Dumre, that can be reached by a three-hour car ride from Kathmandu or a two-hour drive from Pokhara. Here porters can be hired. During winter, vehicles can be driven up to Turture, about 10 kms. north of Dumre.

Tarkughat (488 m.): This is reached by a gentle track amidst rice fields along the west bank of the Marsyangdi. Tarkughat is a small bazaar on a bridge-site that leads east to Palungtar airfield and Gorkha.

Phalesangu (632 m.): This is another bridge site on the Marsyangdi River. From here, there are two tracks going north. West of the river, the track continues to Besidahar (792 m.), district headquarter of Lamjung, and then Khudi (822 m.) at the confluence of the Marsyangdi and Khudi Khola Rivers. The east side route reaches Bhulbule (853 m.), another bridge site beyond Khudi. There are good views of Himalchuli from Bhulbule and Taranche Village.

Bahundanda (1,310 m.): A hill promontory above the confluence of the Marsyangdi and Nagadi Khola Rivers, this is the last limit of paddy fields and Hindu population. The Marsyangdi Valley turns into a narrow gorge beyond Bahundanda.

Thonje (1,950 m.): This town, at the confluence of the Marsyangdi and Dudh Khola has some tea shops at Dharapani. On the higher slopes around Thonje are numerous Gurung villages. The track turning east of Thonje along the Dudh Khola is presently restricted to trekkers.

Ghame (2,651 m.): Here lies the headquarter of Manang district, with a police post and radio communication. Ghame is located in a deep gorge immediately below Annapurna-II.

Pisang (3,352 m.): This is the first Tibetan-type village in upper Marsyangdi and from here the valley widens. *Mani* walls, gompas and yaks appear on the scene with pine forests and rings of snow ranges on all sides.

Ulleri (2,073 m.): This is a large Magar village which appears after climbing a steep trail west of Tikhedhunga. The road beyond Ulleri ascends to Ghorapani through a dense forest.

Ghorapani (2,835 m.): On a high ridge, with good views of Dhaulagiri and Nilgiri, lies Ghorapani. There are lodges and camping sites near the pass and also a view-tower made by the local people. The track descends through oak and rhododendron forest to Sikha (2,012 m.), a delightful Magar village.

Tatopani (1,180 m.): Lies on the right back of Kaligandaki and has a hot-water spring. Several lodges here offer good accommodation and food.

Ghasa (2,012 m.): Ghasa, reached through a narrow gorge after Rupse Chahara (a waterfall on the trail), is a Thakali village amidst pine forests.

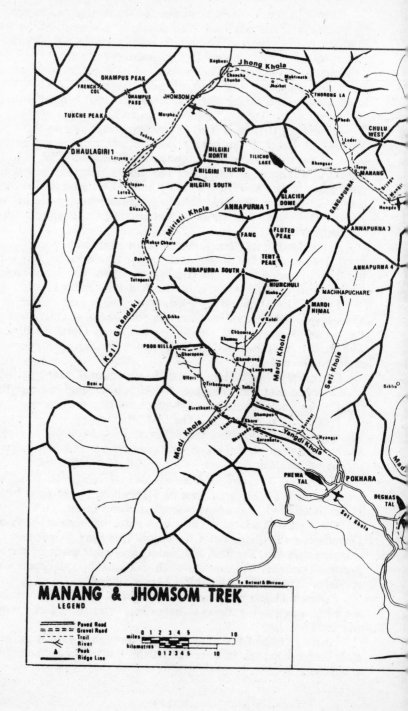

MANANG & JHOMSOM TREK
LEGEND

▬▬▬▬	Paved Road
▭▭▭▭	Gravel Road
⌁⌁⌁⌁	Trail
⌇	River
▲	Peak
▬▬▬	Ridge Line

miles 0 1 2 3 4 5   10
kilometres 0 1 2 3 4 5   10

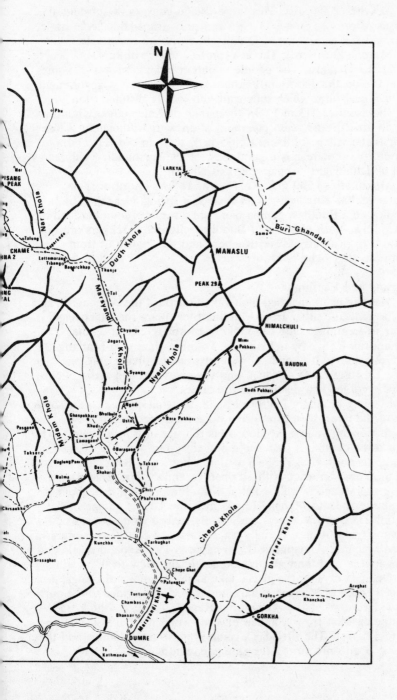

Tukche (2,590 m.): This large village consists of substantial houses of dressed stone. Once a centre of trans-Himalayan trade, it provides a good view of Dhaulagiri from the north side.

Marpha (2,670 m.): This is a compact village of Punels, a people similar to Thakalis. The people maintain large caravans of ponies for trade on the Jhomsom-Pokhara trail. Nearby is a government horticultural farm which sells fruit and locally distilled brandy.

Jhomsom (2,713 m.): On the banks of Kaligandaki, Jhomsom has an airstrip and radio communication with Kathmandu. Close by it is the village of Thini (2,895 m.), with an old fort and a gompa, that commands a good view of the surrounding villages as well as Dhaulagiri, Annapurna and Nilgiri.

Muktinath (3,749 m.): This town, 18 kms. north-east of Jhomsom, has a natural gas jet close to a spring. Near the Hindu temple and a Buddhist gompa there are a series of fountains and the place draws both Hindu and Buddhist pilgrims. Trekkers are not allowed to proceed beyond Kagbeni and the high trail from Jhomsom to Tilicho is also restricted.

Manang and Lamjung

Manang is an enclosed high valley north of the Annapurna and can be reached either from Muktinath or along the Marsyangdi River in Lamjung. One can make a complete circuit of the Annapurna Range by trekking the Pokhara-Jhomsom-Manang-Lamjung route. It is one of the best treks involving only one high pass, Thorung La (5,416 m.), and traverses through some of the deepest gorges and diverse culture zones.

Manang (3,505 m.): From Pisang, the trail crosses to the south side of the river, then climbs to a ridge for a spectacular view of the upper Manang valley. At Hongde is the site of a new airstrip. The main track continues past Sabje and the Marsyangdi is crossed at Mungji to reach Braga (3,505 m.). The houses of Braga are stacked one atop another, each with an open verandah. The large gompa above the village is well worth a visit. From Braga it is about a 45-minute walk to Manang (3,505 m.), the largest village in the region. The narrow streets and closely-spaced stone houses of Manang make it an especially interesting and picturesque place. From Manang, Annapurna-II, Annapurna-IV, Annapurna-III and Gangapurna and their glaciers dominate the view to the south.

One can explore the glacial lake at the terminus of Gangapurna Glacier south of Manang Village and also climb a ridge to the north for wider views of the Annapurna Range. There is a high trail continuing west from Manang towards Muktinath across Thorung La (5,416 m.). The first day's camp is at about 4,400 m. and the pass is open only during the summer months.

Jumla and Rara

Jumla is a trans-Himalayan valley with high ridges covered with forests and alpine pastures. The town of Jumla has an airstrip and radio communication facilities. The one and a half hour flight from Kathmandu to Jumla that passes south of Dhaulagiri Range is

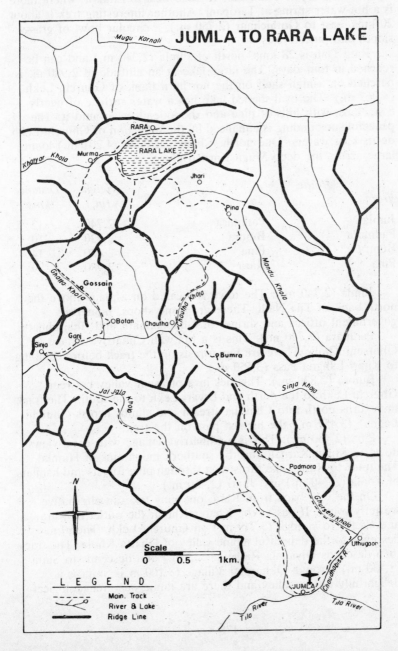

JUMLA TO RARA LAKE

Mugu Karnali

RARA

RARA LAKE

Khatyar Khola

Murma

Jhari

Pina

Ghata Khola

Gossain

Mandu Khola

Chautha Khola

Botan

Chautha

Gani

Sinja

Bumra

Jal Jala Khola

Sinja Khola

Padmora

Ghurseni Khola

N

Uthugaon

Scale

0   0.5   1km.

Chaudhabise R.

JUMLA

Tila River

Tila River

L E G E N D

- - - - -   Main. Track

River & Lake

Ridge Line

itself the revelation of a large section of the landscape of west Nepal. Jumla town (2,340 m.) is in a delightful valley and at the upper limit of paddy fields. The villages nearby have archaeological monuments from medieval times. From Jumla one can track along the broad valley of Tila Nadi, 18 kms. west to Litakot, where there is a hot-water spring at Tatopani. Another interesting trek is about 20 kms. east to Gothichaur (2,750 m.), a circular bowl of grassy slopes and pine forests.

Rara Dah is 28 kms. north of Jumla (2,340 m.) and can be reached in four days. The large lake at an altitude of 2,980 m. is perched on a high shelf on the northern flank of Ghurchi Lekh (4,067 m.). The oval-shaped lake has a water surface of nearly 8 sq. kms. with hills of pine and rhododendron around it. The peaceful surrounding is enhanced by the reflection of Ghurchi Lekh on its blue waters. Due north, Chankheli Peak (4,201 m.) looms large across the deep Mugu Karnali Gorge.

Route		Height	Distance
From	To	(m.)	(kms.)
Jumla	Padmara	2,740	12
Padmara	Bumra	2,830	10
Bumra	Pina	2,430	14
Pina	Rara	2,980	9

Jumla (2,340 m.): The town is located on a plain above the north bank of Tila Nadi. There are some shops, numerous government offices and shrines of Ghandannath and Bhairabnath.

Padmara (2,740 m.): This is a Matwali Chhatriya village in Ghurseni Khola. There are fine forests on the track before climbing to Khari Langna Pass (3,550 m.).

Bumra (2,830 m.): This lies in a pleasant valley between Ghurchi Lekh to the north and Dwari Lekh to the south. The track then turns north into Chautha stream and climbs across Ghurchi Lagna (3,457 m.), the highest pass on the trek.

Pina (2,430 m.): This is a Chhatriya village with good views down to Mugu Karnali and the southern mountains of Humla. The track to Rara Lake turns west through pine forests and hamlets of Topla (2,740 m.) and Jhari (2,460 m.).

On the way back from Rara, one may take an alternative westerly route. It passes the Khater Khola, the outlet of Rara, and climbs to a ridge (3,749 m.) on Ghurchi Lekh. Then one descends to the delightful alpine valley of Ghatta Khola. The track then descends Diyabala Ridge (3,522 m.) and descends to Sinja (2,430 m.) through Okharpeti Village (3,100 m.). Sinja is a delightfully fertile valley and there are numerous archaeological remnants from the Malla empire of the fourteenth century. There is a direct road to Jumla from Sinja across the forested pass of Jaljala (3,300 m.).

Trek to Lake Rara: This famous lake with its incomparable waters, surrounded by forested foothills of pine, spruce and juniper and formed in the background by a breathtaking succession of Himalayan snowpeaks, lies in a green valley north of the remote Mugu district and Karvali zone of Nepal, situated at an altitude of 9,780 ft. Oval in shape, with an east-west axis, this peaceful stretch of water has an area of 5 sq. miles.

There is a magnificent meadow at the southern bank of the lake. Across the meadow to the south, there lies the high mountain of Ghurchi Lagna (13,346 ft.). The summit of Ghurchi Lagna is a magnificent view. The beautiful lakeside village of Rara stands in an ideal position at the northern extremity of the lake, decked with the small stone- and mud-built houses of peasants, with the Chankheli Danda (13,787 ft.) in the background airstrip (linked with Kathmandu by air). Blessed with an enchanting Himalayan backdrop, the landscape of Jumla Valley (7,600 ft.) is one of the most beautiful and remote regions of Nepal. From Jumla, the trail continues along the crest of Dovi Leka, passing through Khali Lagna, Ghurchi Lagna, Pima and Thakurigaon Village situated at the western extremity of the lake.

Lake Rara can also be reached from Dhorpatan, north-west of Pokhara Valley and entails a difficult 15-day trek across passes, just under 15,000 ft. After a trek of six to eight days from Dhorpatan, across Jangla Bharijyang, you reach Tara or Ba. The trail follows the right bank of the Suli God, which follows into the Bheri from the north. From here lie the routes of Ringmo·Lake (north) via Dunli and Rara Lake, Jumla (north-west).

Climbing in Nepal

Climbing in Nepal is the dream of mountaineers all over the world. Mount Everest lies here, which is the ultimate goal. Everest is so popular that one has to wait in a long queue for five to six years to book the peak.

Besides the lofty Himalayan summits, there are 18 minor peaks called trekking summits, which can be climbed by trekkers. For this a proper permit is required from the Nepalese authorities. Some of these trekking peaks are reasonably difficult and provide a good degree of adventure.

Apart from Everest, other mountaineering peaks in Nepal have also to be booked in advance. Applications in this regard are to be addressed to the Nepal Mountaineering Association (GPO Box 1435, Ram Shah Path, Kathmandu). Permission for trekking the peaks is usually granted for a period of two weeks, and this can

179

be extended for an additional two weeks.

According to regulations a registered guide from Nepal must accompany each party. According to current rates he must be paid Rs 30 a day along with food and tent accommodation, and if he is required above base camp, he must be furnished with climbing equipment and clothing as well as insured for Rs 75,000. At present the Nepalese government charges Rs 315 for each member of the party attempting a trekking peak. The minimum fee is Rs 1,260 for peaks higher than 20,014 ft. (6,100 m.) and Rs 630 for lower peaks. The charge for time extension is Rs 25 per person.

Parties are also required to submit a report of the Nepal Mountaineering Association on their return. According to rules applications to the Nepal Mountaineering Association for booking peaks should include the climbing fee and the following information:

(a) Name of the peak.
(b) Period of time for which the permit is requested.
(c) The route.
(d) The name and nationality of each member of the party.
(e) The name, nationality, passport number and home address of the leader.
(f) The name of the organization or address of the guide or *sirdar*.

The trekking groups, according to area, are as follows:

Khimbu Himal
Island Peak (6,189 m.)
Kwangde (6,187 m.)
Kusum Kangru (6,369 m.)
Lobache East (6,119 m.)
Mehra Peak (5,820 m.)
Mera Peak (6,437 m.)
Pokalde (5,806 m.)

Rolwaling Himal
Pharchamo (6,318 m.)
Ramdung (6,060 m.)

Langtang Himal
Ganja-La Chuli (5,846 m.)

Ganesh Himal
Paldor Peak (5,928 m.)

Manang Himal
Chulu East (6,059 m.)

Chulu West (6,583 m.)
Pisang (6,091 m.)

Annapurna Himal
Fluted Peak (6,390 m.)
Himalchuli (6,441 m.)
Mardi Himal (5,586 m.)
Tent Peak (5,500 m.)

With regard to expeditions there are detailed rules and regulations available with the Ministry of Tourism in Kathmandu. In general an application for booking a peak has to be made to the ministry with the recommendation of a reputed and recognised mountaineering institution of the country, or through the embassy of that country in Nepal.

A royalty of Rs 10,000 to Rs 15,000 is required to be paid and the party is required to take a liaison officer chosen by the government. The liaison officer has to be given full equipment and payment according to rules. The Nepalese government is particular about these rules and anyone showing disregard is not allowed to climb in Nepal for a period of three to five years. In serious cases the disqualification may extend to ten years. Certain peaks are open to climbers and others only to the Nepalese. There are a few peaks open to joint expeditions. These peaks are listed below.

Peaks open for Nepalese expeditions or joint Nepalese-foreign expeditions with at least three Nepalese members

Name	*Height (m.)*	*Location*	*Administrative Zone*
Bhrikuti	6,720	Damodar Himal	Dhaulagiri
Big White Peak	7,083	Langtang Himal	Bagmati
Chamar	7,177	Sringi Himal	Gandaki
Changla	6,715	Gorakh Himal	Karnali
Dorje Lakpa	6,990	Jugal Himal	Bagmati
Gurza Himal	7,193	Dhaulagiri Himal	Dhaulagiri
Gyachung Kang	7,922	Khumbu Himal	Sagarmatha
Gyalzen Peak	6,705	Langtang Himal	Bagmati
Jongsang Peak	7,473	Janak Himal	Mechi
Karyolung	6,681	Khumbu Himal	Sagarmatha
Langtang Ri	7,230	Langtang Himal	Bagmati
Madiya Peak	6,800	Jugal Himal	Bagmati
Nala Kankar	6,935	Chandi Himal	Karnali
Nepal Peak	7,168	Janak Himal	Mechi
Omi Kangri	7,922	Janak Himal	Mechi
Phurbi Chhyachu	6,658	Jugal Himal	Bagmati
Tent Peak (K)	7,365	Kanchenjunga Himal	Mechi

Peaks open for foreign expeditions only after they are climbed by a Nepalese or joint Nepalese-foreign expedition

Bobaye Himal	6,808	Byasrikshi Himal	Mahakali
Chamlang	7,319	Khumbu Himal	Sagarmatha
Cheo Himal	6,812	Gorkha Himal	Gandaki
Cho-oyu	8,153	Khumbu Himal	Sagarmatha
Ganesh Himal-I	7,406	Ganesh Himal	Bagmati
Ganesh Himal-III	7,132	Ganesh Himal	Bagmati
Ganesh Himal-V	6,950	Ganesh Himal	Bagmati
Himlung Himal	7,128	Gorkha Himal	Gandaki
Jethi Bahurani	6,849	Byasrikshi Himal	Mahakali
Kanchenjunga Central	8,496	Kanchenjunga Himal	Mechi
Kanchenjunga South	8,490	Kanchenjunga Himal	Mechi
Lhotse Shar	8,383	Khumbu Himal	Sagarmatha
Ngozumba Kang	7,806	Khumbu Himal	Sagarmatha
Roc Noir	7,485	Annapurna Himal	Gandaki
Shartse Himal	7,502	Khumbu Himal	Sagarmatha

Peaks open for foreign expeditions

Ama Dablam	6,856	Khumbu Himal	Sagarmatha
Annapurna-I	8,091	Annapurna Himal	Gandaki
Annapurna-II	7,937	Annapurna Himal	Gandaki
Annapurna-III	7,555	Annapurna Himal	Gandaki

Peaks open for trekking expeditions

Name	Height (m.)	Region
Chulu West	6,630	Manang district, Gandaki
Chulu East	6,200	Manang district, Gandaki
Fluted Peak	6,390	Annapurna Himal, Gandaki
Himalchuli	6,331	Annapurna Himal, Gandaki
Island Peak	6,153	Khumbu Himal, Sagarmatha
Kwangde	6,194	Khumbu Himal, Sagarmatha
Kusum Kangru	6,369	Khumbu Himal, Sagarmatha
Lobuje	6,119	Khumbu Himal, Sagarmatha
Mera Peak	6,431	Khumbu Himal, Sagarmatha
Pharchamo	6,282	Rolwaling Himal, Janakpur
Ganja-La Chuli	5,800	Langtang Himal, Bagmati
Mardi Himal	5,555	Annapurna Himal, Gandaki
Mehra Peak	5,820	Khumbu Himal, Sagarmatha
Paldor	5,894	Langtang Himal, Bagmati
Pisang	6,091	Manang district, Gandaki
Pokhalde	5,806	Khumbu Himal, Sagarmatha
Ramdung	6,021	Rolwaling Himal, Janakpur
Tent Peak	5,500	Annapurna Himal, Gandaki

Pakistan

The Country and the People

Pakistan is a Muslim nation in South Asia. It is a fascinating land which has withstood countless invasions from its north-west, and has preserved the culture of its conquerors in its monuments and archaeological heritage such as Mohenjodaro and Taxilla — seats of the ancient Indus Valley and Gandhara civilisations. It possesses the architectural monuments of the Mughals, the Khyber Pass and the ancient unchanging traditions of the Kafir Kailash in the Chitral Valley.

Pakistan has towering snow-capped mountains, high plateaux, fertile plains, sandy deserts, and an inviting coastline. The population of Pakistan consists of a number of cultural groups, each with its own language. The official language of Pakistan is Urdu, but large parts of the population speak Baluchi, Punjabi, Pushto and Sindhi.

About three-fourths of the people of Pakistan live in villages and farm. Traditional customs and beliefs have a strong influence on life in rural Pakistan. Most of the rural villages consist of clusters of two or three-room houses made of clay or sun-dried mud. A typical home may have a few pieces of simple furniture, with straw mats covering the bare earth floor.

The most common garment of both men and women is the *shalwar-kamiz*, which consists of loose trousers and a long overblouse. Women may wear a *dupatta* (scarf) over their shoulders. Turbans or various types of woollen or fur caps are popular head coverings amongst Pakistani men.

Most of Pakistan has a dry climate, with hot summers and cool winters and an average rainfall of about ten inches a year. Long, dry spells may be broken by severe rainstorms that cause rivers to overflow and flood the countryside. Like in India, monsoon prevails from July to September.

Having spent the first sixteen years of my life in the northern mountain ranges of Pakistan, I had the opportunity to take in their beauty and charm, their gentle folds of mountains, range after range, their lovely meadows and hill stations. The subsequent three and a half decades have not been able to erase from memory the imprint of those years. I can never forget early morning walks along fields of hundreds and thousands of lillies, all along Haripur and the surrounding villages. In 1981, and again in 1982, I visited Haripur in the Hazara district of N.W.F.P. The recently built Tarbela Dam has brought the Indus close to the town. Beyond the river, as far as the eye can see, there are ranges after ranges of mountains, extending far beyond to the Kaghan Valley — a paradise for trekkers and nature lovers.

The northern mountain ranges of Pakistan are amongst the most fascinating.

Visas and Permits for Nationals

(*a*)   United Kingdom (or British subjects, being "Citizens of the United Kingdom and Colonies" or "British-Protected Persons"): Valid passport without visa, for unlimited stay.

(*b*)   For nationals of Australia, Bahamas, Barbados, Botswana, Canada, Cyprus, Fiji, Gambia, Grenada, Guyana, Ireland, Jamaica, Japan, Kenya, Lesotho, Malaysia, Malawi, Malta, Morocco, Nauru, Nigeria, New Zealand, Papua New Guinea, Samoa, Seychelles, Sierra Leone, Singapore, Sri Lanka, Swaziland, Tanzania, Tonga, Trinidad and Tobago, Tunisia, Turkey, Uganda, Zambia: Valid passport without visa for a stay of upto three months.

(*c*)   For nationals of the Philippines: Valid passport without visa for a stay of upto 59 days.

(*d*)   For Romanians and Yugoslavians: Valid passport without visa for a stay of upto one month.

(*e*)   For South Africans: Nationals not of Indo-Pakistani origin require a permit, in addition to a valid passport and visa, under the South African Reciprocity Act. This permit is issued by the immigration authorities at the point of entry.

(*f*)   For nationals of other countries: Valid passport with visa.

(i)   Diplomats: Algeria, Austria, Belgium, Denmark, Finland, Federal Republic of Germany, Iran: diplomatic passport only; Luxembourg, Netherlands, Norway, Spain, Sweden, Turkey: diplomatic or official passport without visa, for a stay of upto three months; Austria, Iran: diplomatic passport without visa for a stay of upto three months.

(ii)   For personnel of the United Nations or the International Court of Justice at The Hague, travelling on duty with a *laissez-passer*: no visa required.

The facility of entry without visa is not available to a foreigner who intends to take up employment, etc. (with or without remuneration in Pakistan).

Visas are issued free of charge on a reciprocal basis to nationals of Afghanistan; People's Republic of China, Czechoslovakia,.

Denmark, Iceland, Iran, Iraq, Japan, Norway, Sweden, United States and the USSR.

Validity of visas:

(*a*) A single journey entry visa is valid for a stay of three months.

(*b*) Multiple journey visas are also valid for a three-month's stay at a time. Any number of journeys (normally six) during a specified period not exceeding one year, may be allowed on such visas.

(*c*) Visas once issued can be utilised within six months from the date of issue.

(*d*) Foreigners entering any province of Pakistan do not have to obtain a fresh visa for entering another province.

(*e*) No visa is required by a bona fide tourist, i.e. foreigners coming to Pakistan for sightseeing and recreation, except the nationals of India, Bangladesh, Afghanistan and South Africa, stateless persons and nationals of the countries recognised by Pakistan, who are in possession of valid passport and intend to stay in Pakistan for a period not exceeding 30 days.

(*f*) Requirement of transit for 15 days has been waived for all foreigners transiting through Pakistan (other than the nationals of countries mentioned in sub-paragraph (*e*) above), irrespective of whether or not they are tourists, provided their onward journey is assured.

(*g*) Foreign tourists (other than nationals of India, British passport holders ordinarily residing in Kenya or Uganda, Afghanistan and countries not recognised by Pakistan), are exempted from the requirements of police registration, if their stay in Pakistan exceeds 30 days.

Foreign tourists entering Pakistan through regular checkposts are not required to obtain road permits if tourist stamps are affixed on their passports.

(*a*) "Entry visa" and "police registration" are two different things. Therefore, the foreigners not eligible for exemption under note 3(*e*) above should get themselves registered with the nearest Foreigners Registration Office, in addition to obtaining a visa, where necessary.

(*b*) Foreigners entering Pakistan as tourists without a visa, under note 3(*e*) above are not granted a visa or extension of stay beyond the prescribed period of 30 days. Therefore, persons desiring to stay in Pakistan for more than 30 days (and also those not falling under the category of tourists as defined in note 3(*e*) must obtain visa before coming to Pakistan.

Taxes: Foreigners leaving Pakistan by land routes are expected to pay a tax of Rs 2. Similarly foreigners leaving Pakistan by air are expected to pay an airport tax of Rs 100 or Rs 5 on domestic

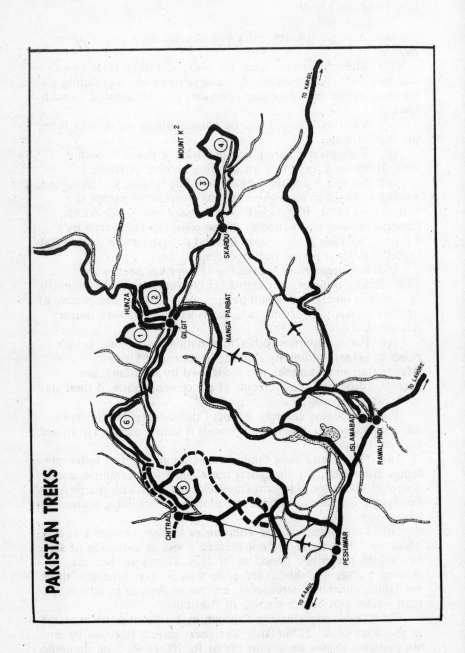

PAKISTAN TREKS

flights. Children below two are exempt from embarkation fees.

Treks in Baltistan, Hunza and Gilgit[1]

Baltistan: Baltistan extends more than a 100 kms. along either side of the Indus Valley. The Indus has its headwaters in the Kailash Range near the holy lakes of Manasarovar and Rakas Tal in western Tibet, from where it flows in a north-westerly direction.

Set amidst the Karakorams it is a land of many splendours and contrasts. Barren and desolate, it still has several oases of fruit orchards containing apricots, grapes and apples.

The mountain ranges in Baltistan are known as the "Third Pole." They contain the largest glaciers outside sub-polar latitudes and many of the highest peaks in the world. Here lies K-2 (8,610 m.), the second highest peak in the world.

The flight to Skardu is one of the most spectacular in the world. Skardu, the main town of Baltistan, is situated at 2,286 m. It is on the bank of the Indus and sustains a 600-year-old fortress commanding both the town and the river.

Skardu is the staging post for most of the climbing and trekking expeditions to the Greater Karakorams.

Skardu-Baltistan Trek: This is a strenuous 17-day trek. From Skardu to Kondus and back you cover 150 miles (241 kms.); the altitude ranges from 2,590 to 4,267 m. (8,500 to 14,000 ft.). The best time for the trek is between June and the end of August.

SKARDU-BALTISTAN-KONDUS

[1]All three are under the illegal occupation of Pakistan.

187

1st Day:	Islamabad to Skardu
	This is one of the most beautiful flights (PIA).
2nd Day:	Skardu to Khaplu
	This has to be covered by jeep. Khaplu is on the mighty Shyok River and its apples enjoy the reputation of being the best in Pakistan.
3rd Day:	Khaplu to Machlu
	Cross the River Shyok to Machlu, then on to Halde.
4th Day:	Halde to Sinu
5th Day:	Sinu to Thang
6th Day:	Thang to Lachit (Kondus)
7th Day:	Lachit to Summer Pasture
	This lies above Karamading Village.
8th Day:	Summer pasture to Base Camp of K-6
9th Day:	Khaplu
	Begin return journey to Khaplu, following the above trek with camps at the same places.
10th to	
16th Days:	Khaplu to Skardu
17th Day:	Skardu to Islamabad
	Take the PIA flight to Islamabad.

Skardu-Baltistan Trek: From Baltoro to Karakoram, this is another strenuous trek of 30 days. The total distance covered is 402 kms. (250 miles), and the altitude ranges are 2,438 to 4,976 m. (8,000 to 16,000 ft.). The best time of the year for this trek is June to the end of August.

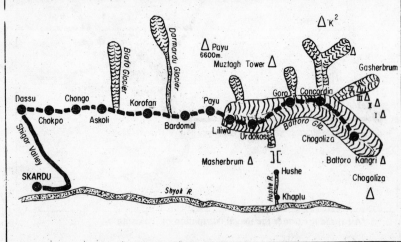

SKARDU-BALTISTAN-BALTORO-KARAKORAM

1st Day:	Islamabad to Skardu to Dassu
	The one-hour PIA flight is said to be the most beautiful in the world, flying at 6,400 m. (21,000 ft.) with Nanga Parbat, Haramosh and Rakaposhi above and the Indus River flowing below. Skardu to Dassu can be covered by jeep.
2nd Day:	Dassu to Chakpo
3rd Day:	Chakpo to Chongo
4th Day:	Chongo to Askoli
5th Day:	Askoli to Korofan
6th Day:	Korofan to Bardomal
7th Day:	Bardomal to Payu
	Payu lies at the foot of the Baltoro Glacier.
8th Day:	Payu to Liliwa
9th Day:	Liliwa to Urdokoss
	The camps at Liliwa and Urdokoss are located on Baltoro's southern edge and provide excellent views of Payu Peak and Trango Towers.
10th Day:	Urdokoss to Goro
	Camp at Goro, perched on a ridge in the middle of a glacier. This offers splendid views of Masherbrum (7,821 m./25,660 ft.) and the Mustagh Tower (7,273 m./23,863 ft.).
11th Day:	Goro to Concordia
12th Day:	Concordia to Chogoliza
13th Day:	Towards Skardu
30th Day:	Skardu to Islamabad

Arriving at Skardu, you can take the PIA flight to Islamabad.

The climax of the Baltoro trek is the spectacular conjunction of the Godwin-Austin and Baltoro Glaciers, called Concordia, lying at the heart of the most heavily glaciated region outside the Polar areas. Within a radius of about 19 kms. (12 miles) rise six peaks (over 7,925 m./26,000 ft.): Broad Peak (8,047 m./26,400 ft.); Gasherbrum-II (8,035 m./26,360 ft.); Gasherbrum-III (7,952 m./26,090 ft.) and Gasherbrum-IV (7,925 m./26,000 ft.). This is the centre of the densest concentration of lofty peaks on earth.

Hunza: Hunza Valley, situated at an elevation of 2,438 m. has become famous all over the world. The Hunza River, fed by glacier and mountain streams, sustains rich orchards of apricots, apples, plums, cherries, peaches and grapes. The people of Hunza are noted for their longevity. They attribute this to their diet, the main ingredients of which are fruit, specially apricots, vegetables and Hunza water which, the locals say, apart from its high iron content carries traces of gold.

The local people of Hunza are comparable to the Sherpas of Nepal. Their way of life and the mountains surrounding their homes make them strong and hardy.

The women of Hunza, too, in their baggy trousers, their heads covered with embroidered caps, work hard and carry heavy loads. The main town is Karimabad, which offers an awe-inspiring view of Rakaposhi (25,551 ft.)

Gilgit: Gilgit (4,770 ft.) is a small, exciting town with exceptional scenic beauty and splendour. Six miles from Gilgit town there is a beautiful engraving of Buddha out of the rugged mountainside at the mouth of the Kargahnullah. A victory monument of Taj Mughal, built 700 years ago, is a 20-miles jeep drive from the town of Gilgit. The bridge over the fast-flowing Gilgit River is the largest suspension bridge in Asia (600 ft. long and 6 ft. wide, permitting enough room for one jeep at a time to cross)

GILGIT-NALTAR-PAKHOR-BALTAR

Naltar to Pakhor (Gilgit): This is a medium trek, neither too strenuous nor too easy. It takes six days, covering a distance of 80 kms. (50 miles) altogether. The altitude ranges between 3,048 to 4,267 m. (10,000 to 14,000 ft.). The best time of the year for this trek is between June to the end of August.

1st Day: Islamabad to Gilgit

190

Karakoram Highway

A new all-weather road, the Karakoram Highway connects Rawalpindi with China's Sinkiang province. It touches Haripur, Abbottabad, Manshehra, Thakot, Beesham, Pattan, Sazin, Chilas, Gilgit and Hunza before moving on to the Chinese Frontier across the Khunjerab Pass (15,100 ft.).

The Karakoram Highway is a magnificent achievement and is considered one of the great engineering feats of the world. The road passes through the Himalayas, Karakoram, Hindu Kush and the Pamirs. For part of the way it follows a branch of the old Silk Route. From Rawalpindi, it takes about 12-14 hours to reach Gilgit and from there it winds up on a very picturesque route to Hunza, passing through green cart terraces and the popular avenues. It is almost incredible to see enchanting fertile areas in the midst of granite rocks soaring up to the sky. Beyond, the road continues to Shishkut Bridge revealing a startling view of the Gugal peaks, and then onward to Batura, the final point.

Treks in Chitral

The Chitral Valley, at an elevation of 1,127.76 m. (3,700 ft.) is a favourite with mountaineers, anglers, hunters, hikers, naturalists and anthropologists. The 7787.64 m. (25,550 ft.) Tirich Mir, the highest peak of the Hindu Kush Range, dominates this 321.87 km. (200 mile) long exotic valley.

Chitral district has Afghanistan on its north, south and west. A narrow strip of Afghan territory, Wakhan, separates it from the Soviet Union. The tourist season in Chitral is from June to September. The maximum temperature in June is 35°C (95°F) and the minimum 19.44°C (67°F). In September, the maximum is 23.89°C (75°F) and the minimum 7.78°C (46°F).

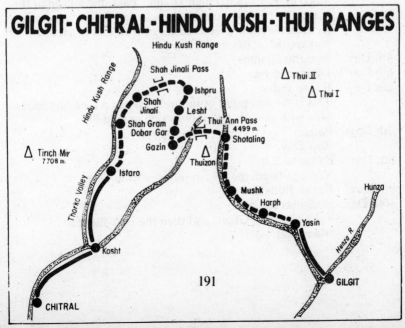

GILGIT-CHITRAL-HINDU KUSH-THUI RANGES

191

This one-hour PIA flight provides a panoramic view of the Karakoram and passes close to the 8,125 m. (26,660 ft.) high Nanga Parbat. From Gilgit to Naltar by jeep.

2nd Day: Naltar to Naltar Lake
Naltar, thickly forested, is surrounded by the high peaks of the Karakoram Range. It is rich with wild life: ibex, *chikor*, *ram chikor*, *markhor* and snow leopards.

3rd Day: Naltar to Naltar Lake
4th Day: Shani to Naltar Pass and Koribort
5th Day: Koribort to Pakhor
6th Day: Pakhor to Gilgit
The drive is through scenic valleys of Ishokman and Punial. Gilgit-Rawalpindi to Islamabad by PIA.

Naltar to Baltar (Gilgit): Another medium trek, it takes 10 days, covering a distance of 129 kms. (80 miles) altogether. The altitude ranges between 3,048 to 4,267 m. (10,000 to 14,000 ft.). The best time of the year for the trek is between June and the end of August.

1st Day: Islamabad to Gilgit
Take the PIA flight to Gilgit, and move on to Naltar by jeep. The jeep drive winds its way along the Hunza River up to Nomal Village, from where a jeep road climbs up to Naltar and offers spectacular views of the Rakaposhi chain.

2nd Day: Naltar to Naltar Lake
3rd Day: Naltar Lake to Shani
There is a lovely campsite here. After crossing the 4,800 m. (15,748 ft.) high Dianter Pass, the village of the same name is the most fertile valley in Gilgit, famous for its unspoilt beauty, abundance of fruit and its views of Rakaposhi (7,788 m./25,552 ft.).

4th Day: Shani to Dianter
5th Day: Dianter to Bar
6th Day: Bar to Baltar
This is the last point of the trek. Baltar is a mountainous area with glaciers and forests rich in wild life.

7th Day: Baltar
Rest Day.

8th Day: Baltar to Bar
You can begin the return journey from here.

9th Day: Bar to Budalas
10th Day: Budaldas to Gilgit
Take a jeep to Gilgit, and then the PIA flight to Islamabad.

Chitral Trek: This is a strenuous trek, from Shah Jinali to Hindu Kush, taking between 15 to 18 days. The total distance covered is 160 kms. (100 miles), and the altitude ranges from 1,707 to 4,267 m. (5,600 to 14,000 ft.). The best time of year for this trek is between June and August.

1st Day: Peshawar to Chitral
             This is to be covered by PIA.

2nd Day: Chitral to Istaro
             You can take a jeep to Istaro.

3rd Day: Istaro to Shah Gram
4th Day: Shah Gram to Uzhnu
5th Day: Uzhnu to Phurgram
6th Day: Phurgram to Shah Jinali Village
7th Day: Shah Jinali Village to Ishpru
8th Day: Ishpru to Shost
9th Day: Shost to Lesht
10th Day: Lesht to Dobargar
11th Day: Dobar Gar to Gazin
12th Day: Gazin to Brep
13th Day: Brep to Mastuj
14th Day: Mastuj to Chitral
15th Day: Chitral to Peshawar
             From Chitral take the PIA flight to Peshawar.

Thorko and Yurkhun Valleys are in an area of magnificent scenic beauty, offering awe-inspiring views of Tirich Mir, the highest peak of the Hindu Kush Range.

Gilgit to Chitral: A strenuous trek, it takes you through the Hindu Kush and Thui Ranges, passing through some of the isolated parts of Chitral and Gilgit. You can cover the distance in 23 to 27 days, totalling 241 kms. (150 miles) altogether. The altitude ranges from 2,438 to 267 m. (8,000 to 14,000 ft.). The best time of year for this trek is June to the end of August.

1st Day: Islamabad to Gilgit
             Take the PIA flight.

2nd Day: Gilgit to Yasin
             This is covered by jeep. The drive is through the scenic
             Punial Valley, which is full of orchards and varied
             landscape, and Gupis, which is surrounded by
             mountains.

3rd Day: Yasin to Harph
4th Day: Harph to Mushk
5th Day: Mushk to Shotaling
6th Day: Shotaling to Thui Ann Pass
7th Day: Through Thui Ann Pass
8th Day: Gazin

193

9th to
13th Days: Gazin to Dobar Gar
14th Day: Dobar Gar to Lesht
15th Day: Lesht to Shost
16th Day: Shost to Ishpru
17th Day: Ishpru to Shah Jinali
18th Day: Across Jinali Pass
19th Day: Shah Jinali to Shah Jinali Village
20th Day: Shah Jinali Village to Shah Gram
21st Day: Shah Gram to Istaro
22nd Day: Istaro to Chitral
23rd Day: Chitral to Islamabad
Take the PIA flight.

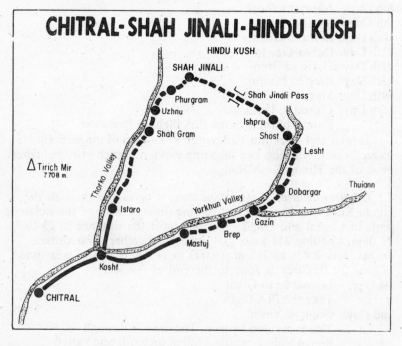

CHITRAL-SHAH JINALI-HINDU KUSH

HINDU KUSH
SHAH JINALI
Phurgram
Shah Jinali Pass
Uzhnu
Ishpru
Shah Gram
Shost
Lesht
△ Tirich Mir
7708 m.
Thuiann
Dobargar
Yarkhun Valley
Istaro
Gazin
Brep
Mastuj
Kosht
CHITRAL
Thorko Valley

Swat

The lush-green valley of Swat, with its rushing torrents, icy-cold lakes, fruit-laden orchards and flower-decked slopes is ideal for holiday-makers intent on relaxation. It has a rich historical past, too.

This is the "Udayana" (the "Garden") of the ancient Hindu epics, "the land of enthralling beauty" where Alexander of Macedonia fought and won some of his major battles before crossing over to the plains of Pakistan. This is "the valley of the

194

hanging chains" described by the famous Chinese pilgrim-chroniclers Huain Tsang and Fa-Hian in the fifth and sixth centuries.

Swat was once the cradle of Buddhism and all its schools — Little Vehicle, Great Vehicle and the Esoteric sects where once 1,400 monasteries flourished. It was the home of the famous Gandhara school of sculpture. which was an expression of Graeco-Roman form in the local Buddhist tradition.

Mingora, 3.21 kms. (two miles) from Saidu Sharif, has yielded magnificent pieces of Buddhist sculpture and the ruins of great stupas.

Other beauty spots worth visiting are Marghzar, 12.87 kms. (8 miles) from Saidu Sharif, famous for its "Sufed Mahal," the white marble palace of the former *wali* (ruler) of Swat; Kabal, 16.09 kms. (10 miles) from Saidu Sharif with its excellent golf course and Madyan, 54.74 kms. (34 miles) from Saidu Sharif, Bahrain and Kalam.

Malam Jabba, at 2651.76 m. (8,700 ft.) ASL and 38.62 kms. (24 miles) north-east of Saidu Sharif is being developed as a ski-cum-summer resort. Swat is linked by road and air to Islamabad/Rawalpindi and by road to Peshawar. Cars from Rawalpindi and Peshawar are charged Rs 2.75 per mile plus Rs 75.00 for each overnight halt.

Kaghan

A holiday in the Kaghan Valley, the Himalayan hideaway north-east of the Hazara district of Pakistan's North West Frontier Province, is an unforgettable experience. Its mountains, dales, lakes, waterfalls, streams and glaciers are still in an unbelievably pristine state, an unspoilt paradise. That is why it can be such a deeply satisfying experience to spend a few days here.

The Valley extends for 154.50 kms. (96 miles), rising from an elevation of 2133.60 m. (7,000 ft.) to its highest point, the Babusar Pass, at 4145.28 m. (13,600 ft.). Kaghan is at its best in the summer months (May to September). In May the temperature is a maximum of 10.55°C (51°F) and a minimum of 2.78°C (37°F). From the middle of July till the end of September, the road beyond Naran, snow-bound throughout the winter, is open right upto Babusar Pass. Movement is restricted during the monsoon season also.

The Kaghan Valey is accessible by road from Rawalpindi, Islamabad and Peshawar. You can drive in your own or in a rented car, taxi, station-wagon or bus to Abbottabad, which is 115.87 kms. (72 miles) from Rawalpindi and 217.26 kms. (135 miles) from Peshawar. Abbottabad is a charming town spread out over several low, refreshingly green hills. From here you drive 72.42 kms. (45 miles) to Balakot, the gateway to the Kaghan Valley. Balakot has the shrines of Syed Ahmed Shaheed and Ismail Shaheed Brelvi, the subcontinent's great freedom fighters. For the drive to Kaghan switch over at Balakot to a jeep. Your first stop is 33.80 kms. (21 miles) away, at Shogran (2362.20 m./7,750 ft.) ASL. At Kaghan, the little village that gives the valley its name (61.16 kms., 38 miles from Balakot) — you can stop the jeep and stretch your legs awhile.

Lake Saiful Muluk has a touch of the unreal about it, nestling 3,200.40 m. (10,500 ft.) high in the shadow of the Malika Parbat (Queen of the mountains) at 5,291.33 m. (17,360 ft.). You can go boating on the lake and hear the boatmen narrate the local legend about Prince Saiful Muluk, who fell in love with a fairy. Further up are quaint woodland villages: Battakundi, Burawani, Besal Gittidas and Lalazar.

The Kaghan Valley is blocked at the end by high mountains but a pass lets the jeepable road snake over into the Gilgit Valley. This is the 4,145.28 m. (13,600 ft.) high Babusar Pass, which commands the entire Kaghan panorama as well as gives you, on a clear day, glimpses of the Nanga Parbat (Naked Mountain), glistening at 8,125.97 m. (26,660 ft.).

Rules and Regulations for Trekkers and Climbers

Rules and regulations for trekkers and climbers have been divided into two groups: open zones and regulated zones. Applications are to be forwarded through Pakistani travel agents or tour operators to the Tourism Division (Government of Pakistan, 13-T/U, Commercial Area, F-7/2, Islamabad), who will issue permits for treks in the open zones. In case of treks in the regulated zones, prior permission will have to be obtained from the Tourism Division, Government of Pakistan.

It takes about 30 days for the case to be processed and permits to be issued. Permission for trekking in the open and regulated zones are issued by the Tourism Division, Government of Pakistan for Rs 100 per person per trek, irrespective of the duration.

Trekking guides or liaison officers provided by the Pakistan Tourism Development Corporation Ltd., or licensed Parkistani travel agencies/tour operators accompany trekking groups in the open and regulated zones.

Pakistan Tourism Development Corporation Ltd. briefs trekkers before their departure for the treks, and also after their arrival. Photography, at places where notice boards prohibiting photography are displayed, shall render the holder of a trekking permit liable to prosecution and result in the automatic invalidation of the permit itself.

As far as climbing in Pakistan is concerned, application forms for allotment of peaks, excepting K-2, are to be sent to the nearest

Pakistan Embassy during the period from January to October, a year in advance. In case of K-2 a team has to apply two years in advance.

The mountaineering teams are required to take with them a liaison officer, to be detailed by the Pakistan government. Expeditions to Pakistan are also required to be equipped with walkie-talkie and radio transmitter sets including high power transmitters for communication with district headquarters. Equipment and non-consumable stores are permitted free of customs duty subject to an undertaking, furnished by the leader of the expedition, to the effect that the equipment will be re-exported out of Pakistan on completion of the mission. Similarly the consumable stores and medicines are also permitted (duty free) on providing an undertaking that these items will be used for the purpose for which they have been imported and will not be sold or otherwise disposed of in Pakistan.

Aerial photography is permitted with respect to mountains en route to the northern areas and Chitral, after notifying the pilot of the aircraft or the accompanying liasion officer. Still, photography is not permitted regarding military installations, aerodromes and tribal ladies. Low altitude porters are required to carry a maximum of 25 kgs. and to cover a maximum distance of 13 kms. per day with a few suitable stoppages. High altitude porters carry weights according to scales: 20 kgs. from 5,000 to 6,000 m., 17 kgs. upto 7,000 m., 14 kgs. upto 8,000 m. and 12 kgs. beyond this height.

The rates of royalty for attempting peaks range from Rs 7,000 to Rs 30,000. A party is required to deposit the full amount of royalty as prescribed above with the concerned Embassy of Pakistan at the time of making an application for allotment of a peak.

The Alpine Club of Pakistan and the Adventure Foundation of Pakistan, which have been looking after the trekking and climbing activities in Pakistan, have been in existence now for quite some time. Their activities, however, have been on a very limited scale. The Adventure Foundation of Pakistan with its headquarters in Abbottabad has done some pioneering work in organising indigenous production of special tents, sleeping bags and personal clothing required for trekkers. The Alpine Club operates a mountaineering school in Nilt, not far from Gilgit, where about 300 young boys and girls have so far been trained in mountaineering. No efforts have been made to train high-altitude porters who receive their training only with foreign expeditions. The Pakistan government is now keen to establish a full-fledged mountaineering institute.

The government has announced simplification of various procedures for trekking. The ceiling of heights for trekking has been raised from 5,000 m. to 6,000 m. All trekking areas have now been divided into "open" and "restricted" zones. No permits will be required henceforth for trekking in the open zone, which comprises the districts of Rawalpindi, Abbottabad, Mansehra, Kohistan, Dir, Swat and Diamir. However, a permit would be necessary for approved treks in the "restricted" zones (districts of Chitral, Gilgit and Skardu), which would be issued *within 24 hours* of the receipt of application instead of 60 days required earlier. The tourism division of PTDC and the concerned deputy commissioner would issue these permits.

Like the trekking sector, all peaks/routes in the mountaineering sector have been divided into the "open" and "restricted" zones. Permits for climbing peaks in the "open zone" would be issued within 24 hours of the receipt of application as against 90 days in the past. However, for peaks/routes in the "restricted zones," a permit would be issued within a period of 14 days from the receipt of application as against a time schedule of 90 days at present. Pakistani liaison officers would accompany all mountaineering expeditions. Whereas, in the past, ten copies of application forms had to be submitted in order to secure a permit, the number has now been reduced to two only. Royalty for peaks upto 6,000 m. has now been abolished. Royalty for peaks above 6,000 m. has been rationalised and fixed as follows:

6,001 to 7,000 m.	Rs 7,000
7,001 to 7,500 m.	Rs 12,000
7,501 to 8,000 m.	Rs 15,000
8,001 and above m. (except K-2)	Rs 20,000
K-2	Rs 30,000

Availability of allied facilities for mountaineering expeditions such as emergency helicopter service and high-altitude porters have also been streamlined. Funds have been made available for construction of four steel rope bridges to especially make certain areas accessible to trekkers and mountaineers. At present, all mountaineering and trekking parties can bring with them food and equipment as per their requirement, duty free. In order to further facilitate these expeditions, it has been decided to allow them to make duty-free purchases of edible items as per requirement from bonded warehouses in Islamabad.

BHUTAN

The Country and the People

From as early as the seventh century, the tiny kingdom Dreek Yul — Land of the Thunder Dragon — known to the world as Bhutan, has existed as an independent nation. Surrounded by awesome natural barriers, imposing mountain ranges separate it from the hill districts of India in the east and west; towering in the north-east the stark mountains of the Chomolhari Range provide the frontier with the Chumbi Valley of Tibet. In the infinite wastes of ice and snow of the savage snow peaks of the great Himalaya lies the border with the Tibetan region of China.

Secluded from its neighbours by some of the highest mountain ranges in the world, Bhutan has only recently emerged from self-imposed isolation. This country of strange customs, of stranger legends and scenery of breathtaking beauty remained a mythical Shangri-La for a long time. Early travellers marvelled at its inaccessibility, for they could reach the heart of the country only after days or weeks of arduous trekking. Now, however, from an isolated feudal state, Bhutan is slowly developing into a member of the world community; but for all the outward signs of modernity — new roads, schools, hospitals — it remains a profoundly traditional and religious society, retaining firmly its rich and valued heritage of the past.

Occupying an area of 18,000 sq. miles, the far north of Bhutan lies in the Great Himalayas, a sparsely inhabited area of giant snow peaks and glacial lakes. The bulk of the 1,200,000 population lives in the Inner Himalayas at an altitude of 3,500 to 10,000 ft. The land here is extensively cultivated, and the high annual rainfall breeds luxurious vegetation and dense forest.

The Bhutanese are a handy, well-built people, skilled archers and industrious farmers. Despite their strong martial spirit they are peaceful and funloving. The people fall into three broad ethnic groups — the Scharchops, the Ngalops and the Nepalese. The first of these, the Scharchops, are believed to have been the earliest inhabitants of the country and live largely in the eastern regions. Apparently Indo-Mongolian, their actual origin and ancestry remains a mystery. The Ngalops, descendents of Tibetan immigrants who came to Bhutan from about the ninth century, settled primarily in the west. The third section of the population, the Nepalese, settled in the southern region towards the end of the eighteenth century.

Bhutan has never had a rigid class system and social and educational opportunities are unaffected by rank or birth. The women enjoy equal rights with men, including the right to vote, active participation in the affairs of the country, and freedom to chose or leave their marriage partners.

Though English has been the medium of instruction in secular schools since the 1960s, the official language is Dzongkha, a dialect similar to Tibetan, and written in classical Ucan script. Monastic and traditional schools use Cheokay; classical Dzongkha and Nepali is spoken in the South. In addition there are a number of dialects, including Scharchopka and Khen Kha; in eastern Bhutan alone there are as many as eleven vernaculars.

For women, the ankle-length robe called *kira* — usually made from beautifully coloured, finely woven fabrics in traditional patterns, is fastened at the waist with a wide sash and at the shoulders by silver brooches. Though the robes are almost always worn, the knee-length boots of embroidered cloth with soft leather soles have been largely replaced by modern shoes and are now only seen at festivals. Corals, pearls, precious agate and eyestones are used to fashion necklaces.

Tourists, however, will find that light woollens and cottons are sufficient for day wear, with warmer clothing for the evenings, except during the winter from December to February.

The State religion of Bhutan is Mahayana Buddhism of the Drukpa Kagyupa Sect. Buddhism was introduced in the seventh century by the saint Padma Sambhava in the early ninth century. Legend says that he was born of the Lotus Lake, situated in the north-eastern Indian region of Himachal Pradesh.

Today pilgrims still visit the original temple which stands on the site called Tsho Rema. From the twelfth century onwards the influence of this sect, the Nyugmapa, gave way gradually to the Kagyupa sect, which after long periods of internal rivalry was united into the present Drukpa Kagyupa sect by a lama named Ngawang Namgyal. This happened in the early seventeenth century. During his 35 years' rule Namgyal not only consolidated the authority of the Drukpa sect throughout most of the country, but also set up an administrative system that endured until the establishment of the present hereditary monarchy.

Buddhism has played a vital part in the life of the Bhutanese people. Religious monuments and symbols are scattered throughout the country, even in remote mountain passes. Every home has a chapel where the family prayers are held. Monasteries and temples are the focal point of each village and all shrines are erected by voluntary labour. Monks are held in great respect and play an active part in community life.

Discovering Bhutan can be a delightful experience. The countryside is beautiful, much of which can be seen by tourists during the drive from the border town of Phuntsholing to Thimphu, the capital. Originating from enormous glaciers in the north, the rivers of Bhutan have carved labyrinthine valleys through the land. The variety of flora and fauna is truly overwhelming. In the narrow valleys at the foot of the glaciers there are dwarf rhododendrons, irises, poppies, miniature azaleas and many kinds of herbs. This is also the terrain of the Himalayan bear, and the rare and beautiful snow leopard. Musk deer, *gharal*, *busket* and *trakhim* roam the steppes and in the summer pheasant species migrate to this alpine zone.

In the Inner Himalaya, differences in altitude (from 3,500 to 10,000 ft.) and heavy monsoon rains give this region an enormous variety of vegetation: oaks and rhododendrons, dark forests of blue pine, and spruce and cypress on the higher slopes. In the west there is extensive cultivation and terraced fields of rice, wheat and maize lie in the sun.

In the southern foothills, with their tropical climate and dense vegetation, the evergreen magnolias and wild orchids splash the hills with a rainbow of colours. The hot, steamy jungles are home to elephants, tigers, buffaloes, bison, many species of deer and especially the golden *langur*, a monkey found nowhere else in the world. The Manas Game Sanctuary, situated in the southeast on the banks of the River Manas, is famous for the countless varieties of migratory birds that rest there, and a must for the tourist.

Bhutan has an abundance of monasteries; large fortress monasteries called *dzongs* dominate the valleys. The oldest *dzong*, the Scintokha, stands at the entrance to the Thimphu Valley and was bulit by Ngawang Namgyal, the first Shabdrung (literally meaning "at whose feet one submits"), in 1627.

Thimphu is dominated by the newly rebuilt Tashichho Dzong, a beautiful monastery constructed on ancient, traditional lines. The *dzongs* have all been built to a general pattern; no plans are drawn and no nails used. This ancient pattern provides what in architectural terms is called harmonasis, a classic example of Bhutanese architecture. The buildings have gently tapering walls, shingle roofs, large courtyards with tall towers called "uchi" in the centre and lovely galleries.

Perhaps the most spectacular *dzong* is the Tongsa Dzong, the ancestral seat of the royal family in Tongsa. Other places of interest are the Phajoding Monastery in the west, which commands a splendid view of the whole area, and Paro, the most beautiful of Bhutan's valleys where the Ta Dzong, now the National Museum, contains a treasurehouse of sacred scrolls, religious manuscripts and ancestral weapons. Taktsang, also known as "tiger's nest" — for legend has it that the Saint Padma Sambhava flew here from Tibet on a tiger's back — is another must for the tourist. This gem-like monastery clings to a sheer 3,000 ft. rock-face. The monks here welcome visitors and will readily act as guides.

Punakha the old capital of Bhutan, contains the sacred Punakha Dzong, a superb example of Bhutanese architecture. Fire, earthquake and floods have inflicted their devastating influence on this *dzong*, which, under the direction of the present king, has been restored completely. The remains of the Shabdrung are extomed here in the Chapel of Machin Lhakhang.

The road from Thimphu to Punakha is a magnificent canvas of colour, a profusion of multi-coloured blossoms amongst the soft green of wild herbs and forest trees. The Punakha River, with its abundance of trout, is also a paradise.

The visitor to Bhutan has a unique chance to see some of the spectacular ancient dances and music of the Himalayan region. The extraordinary grace and colour of these energetic, dramatic dances become a vivid memory. The tales and legends of Buddhist history and mythology are choreographed and dancing is at the centre of all religious festivals.

Bhutanese art is primarily spiritual, whether in painting, sculpture or architecture. Artistic creations are not solely for aesthetic pleasure but aids to devotion and an understanding of Buddhist tenets. Mandalas are mystic patterns usually found adorning walls and ceilings of temples and shrines. They are also painted, embroidered or appliqued on scrolls of cotton or canvas, known as *thangkas*. Weaving, woodcarving, bamboo and canvas work are also special crafts. Craftsmanship in bronze, silver and other fine metals is painstakingly executed.

Sports lovers may find it well worth their while to watch practice sessions of archery, the much-loved national sport of Bhutan. Targets are made of wood splashed with colourful patterns and arrows are tipped with steel. Other traditional sports include *keshey* or wrestling, and *pung-do* or shotput. Soccer is avidly pursued, a legacy of Bhutan's early contact with the British in India. Golf, tennis, basketball and horse-racing are the popular imports.

The local cuisine is rich in meat and cereals, and pork and beef dishes are often hot and spicy. A favourite accompaniment is *chang*, the local beer. Salted butter tea is served on all occasions. In some places Indian, Chinese and Tibetan food is also available.

Bhutan is ideal for visiting in all seasons except winter, from December to February. From June to August the monsoons inhibit travel. All places of tourist interest are linked by buses. Jeeps are required on some smaller side roads and vehicles are also available for private hire.

The Department of Tourism of Bhutan offers package and trekking tours. Certain conditions are laid down, such as the minimum and maximum number for groups (six and 30 respectively) and the number of days (a maximum of twelve). Charges per person are fixed but different rates are offered for students and for the particular tour or trek outlined. Some treks are tough and meant for the physically fit but several "cultural treks," which are easier, can be chosen. Detailed information on the various types of tours is supplied by the Department of Tourism.

Entry and Permits

Entry is mostly effected by the overland route. Till now the best way was by air from Calcutta to Bangladesh on Indian Airlines, which has a weekly flight on this route. Thereafter a further 10 kms. by train to Siliguri, from where transport buses of the Royal Government of Bhutan ply twice daily to Phuntsholing.

Recently, however, Druk Air has been inaugurated by the Government of Bhutan; at present the frequency is twice every week between Paro and Calcutta. More flights are under consideration. The German aircraft, a Dornier, with a seating capacity of 18 people, is an all-economy configuration and the air fare is approximately 240 US dollars.

Tourists in groups of six or more can visit Bhutan. Visa applications should be made at least two to three months in advance at the Department of Tourism in Thimphu, the Permanent Mission of Bhutan to the United Nations, or the Embassy of Bhutan in Delhi, India, Dacca or Bangladesh. Travel agents can also process the requisite visa and transit permits for tourists.

Bumthang Cultural Trek

This trek is an easy 21-day trek in and around the legendary Bumthang Valley.

1st Day: Bagdogra to Phuntsholing (175 kms.)
From Bagdogra Airport drive to Phuntsholing. The drive lasts approximately three hours before you enter Phuntsholing, the gateway of Bhutan. This small town is Bhutan's commercial centre and holds most of Bhutan's commercial organisations. Overnight at Kharbandi Hotel 4 kms. away from the town. Before you settle in for your first night in Bhutan do not forget to

adjust your time to Bhutan Standard Time, which is half an hour ahead of IST.

2nd Day: Phuntsholing to Paro (168 kms.)

This is your first experience on Bhutan's highway. The twisting road takes you high into the mountains to give a breathtaking view of Phuntsholing and the bordering plains of India. The scenery and vegetation changes. En route you pass Chukha Hydel Project and the small town of Chimokothi. Lunch at Bunakha Jakhang, a three-hour drive from Phuntsholing. After a further two and a half hours you reach Paro, one of Bhutan's most beautiful valleys, and if there is time and you are not too tired from the journey a stroll in Paro town can be arranged. Overnight at Hotel Olathang, 3 kms. away from Paro town.

3rd Day: Paro

A full day sightseeing programme in Paro. After breakfast drive to Drugyel Dzong (a ruined fortress 18 kms. away from the hotel). Although now in ruins this *dzong* is of historical importance. From here too the peak of Chomolhari— "Mountain of the Goddess," 7,329 m./2,429 ft. — can be viewed on a clear day. On the way back you visit one of the holiest *lhakhang* of Bhutan. The Kyichu built in the seventh century A.D. dates back to the time of the Tibetan King Songtsen Gampo. After lunch at the hotel visit Ta Dzong Museum and the Paro Rimpung Dzong (centre of the district administration and monk body). Overnight at Olathang Hotel.

4th Day: Paro

Excursion to the famous "Taktsang" (Tiger's den), 3,000 m./9,480 ft. This will no doubt be one of the highlights of your stay in Bhutan. According to legend the "Precious teacher" Guru Rimpoche came from Tibet on the back of a flying tigress and landed at the spot where now the Taktsang Monastery is situated. Virtually clinging to the cliff, the monastery is a place of pilgrimage which all Bhutanese try to visit at least once in their lifetime. Lunch at Taktsang Kakhang. Overnight at hotel.

5th Day: Paro to Thimphu (66 kms.)

Today you drive further to Thimphu, the present-day capital of Bhutan. Just before Thimphu stands the Simtokha Dzong. Built in the year 1627, it is the first *dzong* built by Shabdrung Ngawang Namgyal and now

204

houses the Dzongkha University, teaching language and religion. Lunch at hotel. In the afternoon visit the great Tashichho Dzong, "Fortress of the Glorious Religion," was built in the year 1641 by the first Shabdrung and reconstructed in 1961 under the late king Jigme Dorji Wangchuk. Overnight at Motithang/Bhutan Hotel.

6th Day: Thimphu
An excellent opportunity to see the mask and folk dances of Bhutan. You can also visit the Memorial Chorten and the Handicrafts Emporium. Overnight at hotel.

7th Day: Thimphu to Nobding/Khelekha (122 kms.)
Your journey to Central Bhutan begins here. After a two and a half hour drive you reach Punakha, the old capital. Here the religious head of Bhutan, "Je Khempo," resides in winter and during this time the *dzong* of Punakha holds more than 500 monks. The *dzong* of Wangdiphodrang south of Punakha is also very interesting. Overnight in camp at Nobding/Khelekha.

8th Day: Nobding/Khelekha to Tongsa (88 kms.)
The drive to Tongsa takes approximately five hours. In the afternoon you can visit Ta Dzong, and the town of Tongsa. Overnight at Tongsa Guest House or camp.

9th Day: Tongsa to Jakar
In the morning visit Tongsa Dzong. The foundations of this *dzong* were laid by the grandfather of the Shabdrung in 1543 and the real *dzong* was completed in 1648 by Shabdrung Ngawang Namgyal. Here began the roots of the present dynasty. The first king, Sir Ugyen Wangchuk, was Tongsa Penlop before he was unanimously appointed hereditary monarch of Bhutan on December 17, 1907. It is now a tradition that the crown prince, before being crowned king, must first become the Tongsa Penlop. Besides this historical importance Tongsa Dzong is also the largest fortress in Bhutan. Altogether there are 22 temples here. After lunch drive to Jakar. Overnight at guest house or camp.

10th Day: Jakar
You can plan a whole day's walking tour in the valley and visit some of the holy temples that Bumthang is famous for. The Jambe Lhakhang, built the same time as Paro Kyichu, dates back to a time even before Sindhu Raja's reign in Bumthang. At the Kurje and Padma Sambhava Lhakhang, the bodily marks of the Guru remain to this day impressed on solid rock faces.

11th Day: Jakar to Thangbi (13 kms.)
This trek route takes you along the Chamkarchu, a river known to be very rich in trout, and if you are interested you have ample time for a cast or two. Camp is at Thangbi Lhakhang, a temple built by the first Karma Shamar in the thirteenth century. Overnight in camp.

12th Day: Thangbi to Ngang Lhakhang (11 kms.)
You enter "Swan Land" (Ngang Yul) with its centre, "Swan Temple" (Ngang Lhakhang). This part of the valley was at first inhabited only by swans who gave their name (*ngang*) to the place. The Lama Namkha Samdrup, having dreamt a vision of how to build a gompa, shot an arrow and at the spot where the arrow landed the Ngang Lhakhang was erected. Overnight in camp.

13th Day: Ngang to Lhakhang to Tahung Jangsa (13 kms.)
Climb gradually to Phephela Pass (3,353 m./11,000 ft.), the highest point on the trek route. Follow the trail until the pass takes you through one of the most beautiful forested areas of this region. Allow for many stops to enjoy the natural beauty of the surroundings. Camp at Tahung.

14th Day: Tahung Jangsa to Ugyenchoeling (10 kms.)
You now approach Tang Valley, and the palace of Ugyenchoeling. Built by the great saint Longchen Rabjampa in the fourteenth century and restored by Tongsa Penlop Tshokye Dorji in the nineteenth, this palace now shelters the descendants of the saint Dorji Lingpa (1346-1405). The rest of the day is leisure-time. Overnight in palace.

15th Day: Ugyenchoeling to Pangshing (10 kms.)
The trail you follow takes you along the Tang-chu, another trout-rich river. Along the banks of this river is Tang Rimochen Lhakhang, whose first foundation is ascribed to Guru Rimpoche and its second to the "treasure finder" Terton Pemalingpa. On the rock wall that rises perpendicularly behind the temple hang bee-hives whose honey can be collected only with the help of lowered ropes. On the rock wall at the back of the temple can be seen the footprints of the "Lotus Princess," daughter of King Thisongdetsan. She is said to have accompanied Guru Rimpoche on pilgrimage and died at the age of eight in Rimocher. Her body is believed to be enshrined in the rock with the most precious of hidden treasures. "The mystic keys to the future" are dedicated for those not yet born. Overnight in camp at Pangshing.

16th Day: Pangshing to Dechenpelrithang to Jakar (10 kms.)
This trail takes you through the birthplace of the famous
Terton Pemalingpa and Kunzangda, "the Monastery of
All Kind." The holy monastery, whose foundation is
attributed to Khandoma Yeshe Tshogyal (the most
famous mystic consort of Guru Rimpoche), is famous
for an anvil which bears the footprint of Pemalingpa.
Pemalingpa the saint, treasure-finder and incarnate of
Guru Rimpoche, was by profession a blacksmith. In
commemoration of the oath he took to give up his
profession before beginning his religious career, he
scaled his anvil with his own footprint.
Overnight in camp.

17th Day: Dechenpelrithang to Jakar (10 kms.)
Visit Membar Tsho. Overnight in camp.

18th Day: Jakar to Tongsa
In the morning visit Jakar Dzong, "Castle of the White
Bird," Lame Gompa (palace built by the first king Sir
Ugyen Wangchuk for his two nun sisters), and a
Bhutanese paper-processing plant. After lunch drive to
Tongsa. Overnight in guest house or camp.

19th Day: Tongsa to Shemgang (120 kms.)
Drive to Shemgang. En route pass the Jigme Wangchuk
Waterfall and visit Kuenga Rabten (winter palace of
His Majesty and Second King, Jigme Wangchuk).
Overnight in guest house or camp.

20th Day: Shemgang to Gaylegphug/Sharbhang (135 kms.)
After visiting the *dzong* of Shemgang, drive to
Gaylegphug. Overnight in guest house.

21st Day: Gaylegphug/Sarbhang to Siliguri
Drive to Siliguri. Overnight at Sinclairs Hotel.

Samtengang Trek

This is a short, easy-going cultural trek — takes 13 days.

1st Day: Bagdogra to Phuntsholing (175 kms.)

2nd Day: Phuntsholing to Paro (168 kms.)

3rd Day: Paro
You can spend a full day sightseeing in Paro.

4th Day: Paro
Excursion to the famous "Taktsang" (Tiger's Den),
3,000 m./9,840 ft.

5th Day: Paro to Thimphu (66 kms.)

6th Day: Thimphu to Khuruthang
Drive to Punakha and Wangdi Valley. Visit the Punakha
and Wangdiphodrang Dzongs. Camp at Khuruthang
(1,400 m./4,592 ft.).

7th Day: Khuruthang - Limukha (12 kms.)
The trek begins with a gradual climb through chirpine forests. A stop to visit the village of Dompala can be organised, depending on group choice. Overnight in camp at Limukha.

8th Day: Limukha to Chungsakha (14 kms.)
The trail today takes you through rhododendron and oak-forested areas. The famous Drukpa Kuenley Lhakhang can also be visited en route. Overnight in camp.

9th Day: Chungsakha to Samtengang (13 kms.)
The trail now takes you through the villages of the Sha Wangdi district. Camp at Samtengang at lakeside.

10th Day: Samtengang to Khelekha (15 kms.)
The trail now follows the old mule track to Gangte Gompa. Allowing for many stops to enjoy the scenery of the untainted villages of the Sha region, you camp at Khelekha for the night.

11th Day: Khelekha to Thimphu
Drive to Thimphu via Wangdiphodrang. After a late lunch at the Motithang/Bhutan Hotel you can spend the afternoon shopping at the Handicrafts Emporium and local shops. Overnight at Motithang/Bhutan Hotel.

12th Day: Thimphu to Phuntsholing
In the moring you can see the mask and folk dances of Bhutan. Drive to Phuntsholing. Lunch at Bunakha Jakhang. Overnight at Kharbandi Hotel.

13th Day: Phuntsholing to Bagdogra

Gangte Gompa/Gogona/Khotakha Trek

This trek, which takes 18 days, will be of special interest to botanists.

1st Day: Bagdogra to Phuntsholing (175 kms.)
From Bagdogra airport or Siliguri drive to Phuntsholing. The drive lasts approximately three hours before you enter Phuntsholing, the gateway to Bhutan. This small town is Bhutan's commercial centre and holds most of Bhutan's Commercial Organisations. Overnight at Kharbandi Hotel 4 kms. away from the town.

2nd Day: Phuntsholing to Paro (168 kms.)
The twisting road takes you high into the mountains to give a breathtaking view of Phuntsholing and the bordering plains of India. The scenery and vegetation changes. Lunch at Bunakha Jakhang, a three-hour drive from Phuntsholing. After a further two-and-a-half-hour

208

drive you reach Paro, one of Bhutan's most beautiful
valleys.

3rd Day: Paro
You can spend the day sightseeing in Paro.

4th Day: Paro
Excursion to the famous "Taktsang" (Tiger's Den) at
3,000 m./9,840 ft. This will no doubt be one of the
highlights of your stay in Bhutan.

5th Day: Paro to Thimphu (66 kms.)
Drive to Thimphu, en route visit the great Tashichho
Dzong. Overnight at Motithang or Bhutan Hotel.

6th Day: Thimphu to Khuruthang
Drive to Punakha and Wangdi Valley. Visit the *dzongs*
of Punakha and Wangdiphodrang. Camp at Khuruthang
(1,400 m./4,592 ft.).

7th Day: Khuruthang to Limukha (12 kms.)
The trek begins with a gradual climb through chirpine
forests. A stop to visit the village of Dompala can be
organised depending on group choice. Overnight in
camp at Limukha.

8th Day: Limukha to Chungsakha (14 kms.)
The trail is heavy with rhododendron and oak forests.
The famous Drukpa Kuenley Lhakhang can also be
visited en route. Overnight in camp.

9th Day: Chungsakha to Samtengang (13 kms.)
The trail now takes you through the villages of the Sha
Wangdi district. Camp at Samtengang at lakeside.

10th Day: Samtengang to Khelekha (15 kms.)
The trail now follows the old mule tract to Gangte
Gompa. Allow for many stops to enjoy the scenery of
the untainted villages of the Sha region. You camp at
Khelekha for the night.

11th Day: Khelekha to Gangte Gompa
The climb to Shasila Pass takes you through a forest rich
in rhododendrons and a variety of orchids. Offers several
chances for occasional glimpses of wild life.

12th Day: Gangte Gompa
Visit the temples of the gompa of Gangte, the seat of
the Nyingma Pelri sect, and surrounding villages.
Overnight in camp.

13th Day: Gangte Gompa to Gogona (17 kms.)
Cross Tselela Pass. Visit the gompa of Gogona.
Overnight in camp.

14th Day: Gogona to Khotakha (16 kms.)
Cross Shobjula Pass. Reaching camp visit the village
of Khotakha. Overnight in village house or camp.

15th Day: Khotakha to Wangdiphodrang to Lobesa/Khuruthang (18 kms.)
Cross Tashila Pass. The trail passes through the village of Ruibesa and Nizergang. Drive from Wangdiphodrang to Lobesa/Khuruthang. Overnight in camp.

16th Day: Lobesa to Thimphu
Drive to Thimphu. Stop at Dochula Pass for tea and if lucky, you might be able to get a view of the Himalayan ranges. After lunch at hotel you can spend a free afternoon in Thimphu. Overnight at Motithang or Bhutan Hotel.

17th Day: Thimphu to Phuntsholing
Drive to Phuntsholing. Lunch at Bunakha Jakhang. Overnight at Kharbandi or Druk Hotel.

18th Day: Phuntsholing to Bagdogra

Chomolhari Trek

This trek will take you 15 days.

1st Day: Bagdogra to Phuntsholing (175 kms.)

2nd Day: Phuntsholing to Paro (168 kms.)

3rd Day: Paro
You can spend the day sightseeing in Paro.

4th Day: Paro
Excursion to the famous "Taktsang" (Tiger's Den) at 3,000 m./9,840 ft.

5th Day: Paro to Shana (17 kms.)
Drive to Drugyel Dzong. Trek onwards to Shana (9,184 ft./2,800 m.) along "Pachu" Paro River. Takes about five to six hours. Overnight in camp.

6th Day: Shana to Soi Thangthanka (22 kms.)
Takes seven to eight hours. Continue to follow the Pachu through forests of pine, conifer and juniper. Overnight in camp at Thangthanka (11,545 ft./3,520 m.).

7th Day: Soi Thangthanka to Jangothang (Chomolhari Base Camp), (19 kms.). Takes five to six hours. Stop at Tangethang to see the winter homes of Yak herdsmen. You can get a close view of Mount Chomolhari and Jichu Dage from camp at Jangothang (13,251 ft./4,040 m.).

8th Day: Jangothang to Lingshi (19 kms.)
This would take five to six hours. Cross the Nyelela Pass (13,940 ft./4,250 m.) to reach Lingshi (13,612 ft./4,150 m.).

9th Day: Lingshi to Sho-du (22 kms.)
Takes seven to eight hours. Cross Yalila Pass (15,800 ft.). From here Mount Chomolhari, Tserim Gang and

Masang Gang can be seen. Overnight in camp. (Sho-du lies at an altitude of 13,000 ft.).

10th Day: Sho-du to Dolamkoincho (24 kms.)
Takes seven to eight hours. Follow the Thi-chu through forests of rhododendrons. En route pass the ruins of Barshong Dzong. Overnight in camp (11,900 ft.).

11th Day: Dolamkoincho to Thimphu (14 kms.)
This trek would take about four to five hours. Stop at Dodina to visit Chenri, the first monastery built by Shabdrung Ngawang Namgyal. Many monks from Thimphu who decide to lead a life of meditation start their practice here. Guests are requested to move in silence. Overnight at the Motithang or Bhutan Hotel.

12th Day: Sightseeing in Thimphu
In the morning you can visit the Handicrafts Emporium and Thimphu Memorial Chorten. After lunch at hotel visit the great Tashichho Dzong (Bhutan's administrative and religious centre). The rest of the day is leisure time. Overnight at hotel.

13th Day: Excursion to Punakha/Wangdi
A full day's excursion with packed lunch to Punakha and Wangdi Valley. Visit the Punakha and Wangdiphodrang Dzongs. On the way back stop at Dochula Jakhang. Overnight at Motithang/Bhutan Hotel.

14th Day: Thimphu to Phuntsholing
Mask and folk dances can be seen at Thimphu. Drive to Phuntsholing. Lunch at Bunakha Jakhang. Overnight at Kharbandi or Druk Hotel.

15th Day: Phuntsholing to Bagdogra

Lingshi/Laya/Lunana Snowman Trek

This is the longest alpine trek route of Bhutan covering a total distance of 365 kms. in 18 walking days (an average of 20 kms. a day). The trekker crosses 11 passes, of which three are over 5,000 m. Two trekking peaks for climbing can also be included. Although the trek is of alpine nature it can pass as a cultural one. The trek route passes through the villages of the mountain tribesmen of Lingshi, Laya and Lunana. You get an excellent opportunity to see "Yak herdsmen," as they are called by tourists, and their nature of living. Points of reference will be Paro, Thimphu, Phuntsholing and Punakha.

The trekker has a very high chance of seeking two rare animals: the "Blue Sheep" and *trakhin*. Flowers ranging from rhododendron (the national flower of Bhutan) to the blue poppy bloom in abundance.

1st Day: Bagdogra to Phuntsholing (175 kms.)

2nd Day: Phuntsholing to Paro (168 kms.)
3rd Day: Paro
4th Day: Taktsang Pelphug
           Drive to Satsam Chorten and trek to Taktsang and back.
           Lunch at Taktsang Jakhang.
5th Day: Paro to Shana (17 kms.)
           Drive to Drugyel Dzong and trek onwards to Shana
           (9,184 ft./2,800 m.) along "Pachu" Paro River. Takes
           about six hours.
6th Day: Shana to Soi Thangthanka (22 kms.)
           Continue along the "Pachu" Takes seven to eight hours.
7th Day: Soi Thangthanka to Jangothang (Chomolhari Base
           Camp), (19 kms.).
           Takes five to six hours. Stop at Tangethang to see winter
           homes of Yak herdsmen. Close view of Mount
           Chomolhari and Jichu Dage from camp (at Jangothang,
           13,251 ft./4,040 m.).
8th Day: Jangothang to Lingshi (19 kms.)
           Takes five to six hours. Cross the Nyelela Pass (13,940
           ft./4,250 m.) to Lingshi (13,612 ft./4,150 m.).
9th Day: Lingshi to Chebisa (14.5 kms.)
           Takes three to four hours. In the morning visit Lingshi
           Dzong. After arrival at Chebisa (12,628 ft./3,850 m.)
           guests can visit village homes.
10th Day: Chebisa to Shomuthang (17 kms.)
           Takes four and a half to five and a half hours. Cross
           Gobula Pass (14,268 ft./4,350 m.). Shomuthang is at
           13,612 ft./4,150 m.
11th Day: Shomuthang to Robluthang (14 kms.)
           Takes approximately five hours. Cross Jarila (15,088 ft./
           4,600 m.) and stop at Tsai Jathang to see *trakin*, if
           possible. Robluthang is at 14,530 ft./4,430 m.
12th Day: Robluthang to Laya (29.5 kms.)
           Takes seven to eight hours. Cross Shinjela Pass (16,072
           ft./4,900 m.); Laya is at 12,628 ft./3,850 m.
13th Day: Laya
           Rest day. Visit village homes and mix with local people.
           You can watch the villagers dance in the evening.
14th Day: Laya to Rodufu (19 kms.)
           Rodufu (13,645 ft./4,160 m.) takes six to seven hours.
15th Day: Rodufu to Tarina (30 kms.)
           Takes eight to nine hours. Cross Tsimola Pass (13,842 ft./
           4,220 m. and Gangla Karchung Pass (16,720 ft./5,100 m.)
           for Tarina (13,284 ft./4,050 m.).
16th Day: Tarina to Woche (15 kms.)
           Takes five hours. On arrival at camp visit a village house

of Woche (12,628 ft./3,850 m.). From here begins the area of Lunana.

17th Day: Woche to Lhedi (19 kms.)
Takes six to seven hours; cross Kechala Pass (14,924 ft./ 4,550 m.) and stop at Thega Village en route. Lhedi is 11,808 ft./3,600 m.

18th Day: Lhedi to Thaanza (19 kms.)
Takes five to six hours. En route visit Chozo Dzong. Thaanza is at 13,284 ft./4,050 m.

19th Day: Thaanza to Tso-Chena (18 kms.)
Takes six to seven hours: Cross Jazela Pass (16,564 ft./ 5,050 m.). Tso-Chena is at 15,744 ft./4,050 m.

20th Day: Tso-Chena to Jiche Dramo (14 kms.)
Takes four to five and a half hours. Cross Lojula Pass (16,203 ft./4,940 m.). Jiche Dramo is at 16,006 ft./ 4,880 m.

21st Day: Jiche Dramo to Tsonsothang (27 kms.)
Takes seven to eight hours. Cross Rinchennzoe Pass (16,859 ft./5,140 m.). Tsonsothang is at 13,842 ft./ 4,220 m.

22nd Day: Tsonsothang to Maorothang (30 kms.)
Takes eight to nine hours. Cross Tampela Pass (14,924 ft./4,550 m.). You can see the Umtso Lake in which religious treasures were found by Terton Pamalingpa. Maorothang is at 11,644 ft./3,550 m.

23rd Day: Maorothang to Nikachu Chazam (23 kms.)
Takes six to seven hours. Pass through the villages of Sephu. Camp at Rukubji.

24th Day: Rukubji Camp to Khuruthang
Early morning drive (by coach) to Khuruthang. Lunch at Wangdiphodrang. Visit Wangdiphodrang Dzong. Camp at Khuruthang.

25th Day: Khuruthang to Thimphu
After breakfast visit Punakha Dzong. Lunch at Khuruthang, then drive to Thimphu. En route visit Simtokha Dzong. Overnight at Motithang or Bhutan Hotel.

26th Day: Thimphu

27th Day: Thimphu to Phuntsholing
Stop for lunch at Bunakha Jakhang on the way to Phuntsholing. Overnight at Kharbandi.

28th Day: Phuntsholing to Bagdogra
Drive after breakfast to Bagdogra airport.

Climbing in Bhutan

For climbing peaks in Bhutan, mid-June to mid-September is the ideal period. According to local rules a group must consist of a minimum of six members. These are reasonably difficult treks and fairly difficult climbs, which demand stamina and physical fitness. Those without previous experience are advised not to undertake them. For the approach march the local government provides an emergency riding horse or yak for each group.

For major climbing expedition: tne government at present allows only one expedition. This is Jichu Dage (Tsheringang), which lies 7,000 m. A royalty of US S2,500 is charged for this peak and prior permission should be obtained from the Bhutanese government.

China

The Country and the People

The People's Republic of China is situated in the eastern part of Asia on the west coast of the Pacific Ocean. It covers an area of about 9.6 million sq. kms. and has land boundaries totalling over 20,000 kms. in length.

China is a unitary multi-national state with over 800 million people. Hans make up about 94 per cent of the total population, while the remaining 6 per cent are taken up by over 50 fraternal minorities including the Mongol, Hui Zang, Uygur, Miao, Yi Zhuang, Bouyei, Chaozian, Kazak and Dai. Most of the minority nationalities live in north-west, south-west and north-east China.

China's capital, Beijing, is situated in the north-western part of the North China Plain. It covers an area of 17,800 sq. kms. and has a population of over 7 million. It is the political, economic and cultural centre of China. Built in 937 A.D., it has an 800-year-old history, with many famous historical sites and scenic spots. Since the founding of the People's Republic of China in 1949, large-scale reconstruction has taken place in Beijing, which has been turned into an industrial city from a consumer one.

To the east of China's mainland lies the Bohai Sea, Yellow Sea and East China Sea, and to its south the South China Sea. While the Bohai is an inland sea of China, the Yellow Sea and the East and South China Seas are adjacent to the Pacific. Off the long and crooked coastline there are over 5,000 islands of varying sizes, and along it, many good ports.

China's terrain descends from west to east. The topography is varied and complicated, with mountains making up 33 per cent. Among the famous mountain ranges are the Himalayas, the Atlay, the Tianshan and the Kunlun. Mt. Qomolangma, 8,848 m. ASL, is the highest peak in the world and located on the China-Nepal border.

China has more than 370 large lakes. The principal freshwater lakes include the Poyang, Dongting, Hongze and Taibu Lakes. Among China's salt lakes the Quinghai is the largest.

China has a varied climate and covers the tropical temperate and high frigid zones. There is a big disparity in temperatures between the north and the south, with a difference of over 30 degrees between Gaungzhou and Harbin, for instance. The annual

THE CHINESE MAP OF EVEREST AREA

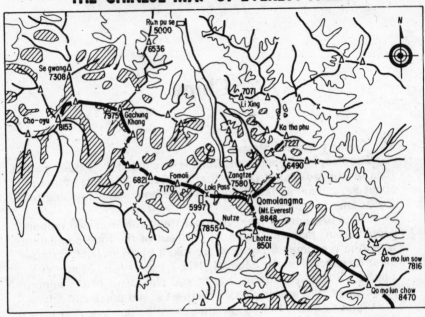

rainfall ranges from 1,500 mms. in the south-east to 50 mms. in the north-west.

China is rich in natural resources. There is an abundance of rice in the south, whereas the north and west produce wheat, millet and maize. Soyabeans, sorghum and wheat are plentiful in the north-east. Cotton is the principal industrial crop. Underground mineral resources include coal, iron, petroleum, copper, aluminium, tungsten, antimony, tin, manganese, lead, zinc and mercury.

China has a very long history. According to archaeological discoveries made in 1964 in Lantian Country (Shaanxi Province), primitive men lived and laboured along the Yellow River as far back as 600,000 years ago. China has a recorded history of nearly 4,000 years.

Visas

Foreigners wishing to travel to China must hold valid visas issued by the Chinese authorities.

Foreigners may apply for visas to China by themselves or through their travel agencies to any Chinese embassy or consulate in a foreign country. Those who are in Hong Kong may ask the China Travel Service (H. K.) Ltd. to apply for visas on their behalf.

Foreigners who have been approved to visit China may choose an itinerary prepared by *Luxingshe*. Travel permits required for the places to be visited can be obtained after the tourists have entered China by applying to the authorities concerned or asking the local

216

Luxingshe to do it for them.

Tibet Region of China

Tibet, covering over one million sq. kms., lies north of India, Nepal, Bhutan and Burma. It is often called the Roof of the World. Its wind-swept plateau is the highest in the world. Tibet had been closed to the outside world for many years, until 1921, when a British team was permitted to carry out the reconnaissance of Mount Everest.

Now a part of China, Tibet still follows a primitive way of life. The Tibetans are sometimes called the hermit people. Buddhist monks, called lamas, still wield considerable influence.

The legendary Potala Palace of Lhasa, the capital of Tibet, is a 1,000-room hilltop citadel. It is situated at a height of 11,850 ft., houses from 200 to 300 monks, and has numerous art treasures.

Several parts of Tibet have never been explored. The snowy Himalayas in the southern part rise higher than any other part of Tibet. This includes Mount Everest (29,028 ft.), which is known as Qomolangma, Goddess Mother of the Earth. The highways from main China to Tibet were built in 1954.

Large parts of Tibet are of rock sand and gravel. Tibet possesses hundreds of lakes but most of them have barren shores. Many have a large salt content. Some of the great rivers of Asia, which include the Indus, Brahmaputra, Mekong, Salween and Yangtze, rise in the mountains of Tibet.

Climatically, Tibet gets less than 10 inches of rainfall annually. The Himalayas shut out moisture-bearing winds from India. Blizzards and snowstorms are quite common. Violent winds sweep across Tibet throughout the year.

The exact population of Tibet is not known, but according to some estimates it is about two million. Most of the people live in southern Tibet, and earn their livelihood from farming.

The Tibetans belong to the Mongolian race, and their dialect has some semblance to the Burmese languages. The people are short and sturdy, and are used to tremendous physical effort. Polygamy, which had been widespread at one time, is very much on the decrease now. The country has nomads, farmers, town people, nobility and clergy. The nomads live in tents made of yak hair.

Tibetan homes have stone or brick walls with flat roofs. The ground floor is mostly used for animals. The rich drink yak milk, and the poor goat milk. The dress of both men and women consists of a long robe, with long sleeves and a high collar.

The Tibetans celebrate their New Year in early spring. The festivities continue for about three weeks, and the people enjoy dancing, singing, eating, drinking and praying.

217

Treks in Tibet and Other Regions of China

A visit to the rooftop of the world is today one of the most exciting experiences. The most popular of these is the visit to Lhasa, which captures all the magic and mystery of Tibet.

The Chinese have recently opened Tibet to foreign trekkers and mountaineers and the biggest draw is Qomolangma, Goddess Mother of The Earth, to the north of Mt. Everest. The parties visiting Tibet first fly to Beijing, and from there to Lhasa (11,850 ft.) after a visit to the legendary Potala Palace. Full of mystery, this place was almost unapproachable for centuries. But today one can reach Potala, the traditional seat of the Dalai Lama, in just a day from Beijing.

After Potala it is worth visiting Drepung, the world's largest monastery, and Jokhang, the holiest shrine in Tibet.

The group leaves Lhasa by bus and travels along the Yarlung Zangbo Valley to Xigase (12,400 ft.), visiting Tashilumpo, the traditional home of the Panchen Lama. The trek start from Kharta, the road-head, and takes about ten days, passing through Sao-La (16,500 ft.) and Kangshun Glacier (17,500 ft.)

Once on this trek it is worth taking a day's trip into the beautiful Kama Valley. On this trek you can enjoy the beautiful views of Chomo Lonzo (25,558 ft.). Loads are carried by yaks. While driving you can pass through Gyantse, which boasts of a Kumbum stupa, the largest in Tibet.

Mount Minya Konka (24,950 ft.): This is one of the most beautiful mountains in the world. It is located on the edge of the Tibetan Plateau, its base drained by the Tatu River, barely 3,000 ft. ASL.

The groups visiting this area fly from Beijing to Chengdu, capital of Sichuan Province, and then travel by bus for two days to reach Kanding, a small town in the Western Sichuan. From Kanding one can trek with pack horses through the Yulongshu Valley, crossing Tshunei Pass (15,200 ft.) to the gompa high up in the Konga Valley. The advance base camp at 17,000 ft. provides spectacular views.

Sacred Mountains of China: According to Taoist-Buddhist history there are nine sacred mountain areas, each representing a symbolic portion of the universe. On the most beautiful peaks in each region exquisite temples were built to house the reigning deity. Built in classical Chinese style, they had been closed for more than 50 years, before being reopened to tourists again. Trekking trails pass through tropical canyons and ancient stone and wood sculptures. These areas have several hidden sanctuaries which were used by mystics and kings in the past for refuge. You can go by train or bus to the Emei Shan Mountains of Sichuan Province, where an 8,000-ft. plateau dotted with temples provides spectacular views of the 25,000-ft. Minya Konka Range. While visiting the various peaks you can see Chengdu, Taian, Nanking and the archaeological treasures of Xian.

Trekking in the Siguniang: These are a spectacular group of granite peaks in the remote valleys of Sichuan Province. Comparatively unexplored, the most spectacular among them is Siguniana ("Four Sisters" Peak) which is 21,600 ft. high. It has never been climbed and is one of the most difficult peaks in the world.

From Beijing you can fly to Chengdu, capital of Sichuan, and drive up to Siguniang. En route you can stop to visit the Wolong Panda Reserve, established in 1960 to provide a sanctuary for the Giant Panda and other species, including golden-faced monkeys, wild yaks, snow leopards, *bharal,*sheep and several types of Himalayan pheasant. This is a very beautiful area which has inspired some of the finest Chinese landscape painting. Driving upto Palund Pass (14,500 ft.), you descend into an area which is very much like Tibet.

From Zelune (10,500 ft.) there is a six-day trek through breathtaking glaciers to the north face of Mt. Siguniang. It is also possible to take a one-week or two-week trek into the Siguniang area.

Mount Anyemaqen Trek: Mt Anyemaqen is located in the East Kunlun Range of the Qinghai Province. This range overlooks the Tibetan Plateau and is inhabited by Ngoloks — wild Tibetan nomads. The horsemen of this area present interesting sights as they ride through dusty and wild areas with rifles slung over their shoulders.

In this area you can trek around Mt Anyemaqen (20,600 ft.). This is one of the most sacred mountains in China. It is known that every year over 10,000 Tibetan Buddhists go around the mountain, on which, at a height of 16,000 ft., you can see some wild life, including snow leopards.

From Beijing you can fly to Lanzhou and then take a train to Xining, from where you can view the largest lake in China. It takes roughly 11 days from here to go around the mountain.

On this trek it is also interesting to visit the Huashi Xia Lake, which is the source of the Yellow River.

Bogda Ola Trekking: Tian Shan (Celestial Mountains) is a one-thousand-mile-long range extending to the western Soviet Turkestan. The highest mountain in this area is Mt Bogda Ola

(17,900 ft.), which was attempted in 1946 by Shipton and Tilman of England. It has several unexplored peaks around it.

To reach this area one can fly from Beijing to Urumqi and then drive to the road-head at Tian Schi. In the "heavenly lake" in this place you can see the image of Mt Bogda, which looks superb. From here one can go on a six-day trek to the base of Mt Bogda with pack horses. The actual walk to the base takes only two days but takes more if one leisurely explores nearby glaciers and climbs upto 14,000 ft. for better views. On this trek you can also see several Cossack tent camps and other nomadic settlements. You can also visit the world-famous archaeological excavations.

Trek to Kailash and Mansarovar

Kailash and Mansarovar are situated across the Himalayas in the Tibetan region of China. Closed for the past 20 years, these sacred places have been opened to a limited number of Hindu pilgrims annually, under a recent agreement between the Indian and the Chinese governments.

Simply referred to as Mt Kailash (6,740 m.) in the map, the Hindus worship the mountain as the abode of Lord Shiva and his consort Ganesa. South of Mt Kailash lies the Mansarovar, the highest body of fresh water in the world. Both Mt Kailash as well as Mansarovar have been places of pilgrimage since time immemorial. The route to these places is prescribed even in the Hindu scriptures. In 1949 Jawaharlal Nehru said: "I was full with regret that I would never reach Kailash and Mansarovar."

For decades inaccessibility to these natural shrines and the physical efforts involved in getting there deterred many pilgrims. In 1981, when the area was opened for the first time, several groups of Hindu pilgrims visited it.

The distance from New Delhi to Lipulekh is about 742 kms. Of this the first 642 kms., from New Delhi to Tawaghat, are motorable but the last 100 kms., from Tawaghat to Lipulekh, have to be trekked. Most groups take seven days to cover this distance, with the following stops:

Tawaghat	
Pangu	11 kms.
Sirkha	11 kms.
Gipti	18 kms.
Buddi	17 kms.
Gunji	14 kms.
Kalapani	14 kms.
Samchun	9 kms.
Lipulekh	5 kms.

The trek includes three steep ascents of about 4 kms. each — Sumri-Rungling, Buddi Shaylac and Sanchun-Lipulekh. These ascents are quite difficult and exhausting. From Lipulekh Pass (18,000 ft.) you step into the Tibetan region of China. The first halt beyond the pass is at Taklakot, a township at the confluence of three rivers and inhabited by Tibetan and Chinese, who live in separate locations. An interesting place to visit here is Climbing Gompa, a Buddhist monastery overlooking the township. You can do a fair amount of shopping at Taklakot at the Chinese shopping centre. From Taklakot you can go to the base camp at Mt Kailash, passing Rakshash Tal on the way. Many pilgrims do this 64-mile *parikrama*. It takes about two days to go around the lake. En route you see a number of gompas — Pauri-Ango-Chugun.

The pilgrims also do the 32-mile *parikrama* around Mt Kailash, which takes three days. This is comparatively more difficult than the *parikrama* of the Lake. Here you have to climb upto Dolmala Pass (18,600 ft.). You can trek back to Tawaghat in five days.

Rules and regulations: People who wish to undertake the pilgrimage to Kailash and Mansarovar have to apply to the Ministry of External Affairs (Government of India) at New Delhi, with full particulars. In view of the limited number of pilgrims allowed by the Chinese authorities and the large number of applicants the ministry usually makes a selection by a draw of lots from amongst applications received.

The physical arrangements for the trek upto Lipulekh Pass are made by the Uttar Pradesh State Government, which charges Rs 2,500 per head. This expense includes cost of transportation, boarding, lodging and porterage.

The expenses on the Chinese side come to about 300 US dollars per head. The total time of 12 days in Tibet is usually recommended for a proper visit to these places, and also the *parikrama*.

Mt Qomolangma (Mount Everest)

Mt Qomolangma, rising 8,848 m. ASL and located at 27° 59' 15" north latitude and 86° 55'39" east longitude, straddles the border between China and her friendly neighbour, the kingdom of Nepal, with the north side lying within China's Tibet Autonomous Region. As the main peak of the Himalaya Mountains, it is the highest in the world.

Mt Qomolangma soars above dozens of peaks of over 7,000 m. including Mt Lhotse (8,516 m.), Mt Makalu (8,470 m.), and Mt Qowowuyag (8,189 m.). Overlooking the snow-clad Himalaya massif like a colossal pyramid, its magnificent contour can be seen from Tingri, 100 kms. away.

Natural conditions are extremely trying in the Qomolangma area, particularly on the north side. There the climate is indescribably harsh, with a northwester raging through the long winter months, starting from October, to March the following year. In 1960 a high-altitude wind with a speed of over 90 m. per second was recorded. For the rest of the year the southeast monsoon prevails, causing frequent snowfalls and a low temperature of 30 or 40 degrees below zero.

Qomolangma is a glacial centre of the modern type; its slopes are covered with perennial snow and its valleys filled with massive glaciers. On the north side stretches the famous Rongbuk Glacier with its east, west and central branches. Between, 5,500 and 6,200 m. there lies a serac region with a hundred and one ice towers of various shapes and sizes, some jutting into the air in isolation, some linking up in a range, and some rising to a height of over a dozen metres. Glittering in the sun and casting their shadows on the icy surfaces of lakes and streams underneath, they present a fantastic wonderland scene.

To reach the top of Qomolangma from its northern slope, three different routes may be taken:

(a) The traditional route over the north-east ridge. This involves the crossing of two dangerous areas: the North Col and the "Second Step."

Linking Qomolangma with the 7,538 m. Zhangzi Peak to the north, the North Col stands in the way of the climber like a silver wall. Climbing up the East Rongbuk Glacier to 6,600 m., you reach the foot of the North Col whose icy slope rises to 7,050 m. — a vertical height of over 400 m. from top to foot, with a gradient averaging 50 degrees and in some parts reaching 70 degrees. Criss-crossed with numerous crevasses, overt or covert, and frequently harassed by ice and snow avalanches, the North Col area is considered a most difficult pass for a climber when scaling Qomolangma from the north-east ridge.

The "Second Step," lying between 8,680 and 8,700 m. on the north-east ridge, is a huge rocky cliff with a steep gradient of about 70 degrees over a stretch of 5 m. at the top. There a metal ladder was placed by Chinese mountaineers on their way to the summit of, Qomolangma in 1975. If it is still there, it will be a great boon for climbers.

(b) The route over the "North Wall." Running through the Central Rongbuk Glacier and extending nearly 2,600 m., from 6,200 m. to the summit, the route is largely featured by precipitous rocky cliffs.

(c) The route over the west ridge — also running through the Central Rongbuk Glacier. Starting from the Lho-La mountain pass (6,006 m.), it extends over ice and snow terrains all the way to 7,600 m., from where flights of rocky cliffs lead up to the summit. This is also a route never attempted before.

It was by the route over the north-east ridge that two successful ascents of Qomolangma were made by Chinese climbers: the first time by Wang Fuzhou, Gongbu and Qu Yinhua on May 25, 1960 and the second time by Panduo, Sodnam Norbu and seven others on May 27, 1975.

Trekking Regulations

Regulations for foreign mountaineering and tourist groups conducting expeditions to China are designed to promote international mountaineering activities with a view to increasing exchanges and enhancing friendship among the peoples.

These are:

Mountain Peaks Open to Foreigners:

Tibet: Mt Qomolangma (8,848.13 m.) and its sister peaks.
          Mt Xixabangma (8,012 m.) and its sister peaks.

Xinjiang: Mt Muztagata (7,546 m.).
          Mt Kongur (7,719 m.).
          Mt Kongur Tiubie (7,595 m.).
          Mt Bogda (5,445 m.) and its sister peaks.

Sichuan: Mt Gongga (7,556 m.) and its sister peaks.
          Mt Siguniang (6,250 m.) and its sister peaks.

Qinghai: Mt Anyemaqen (6,282 m.) and its sister peaks.

Application

1. All mountaineering or tourist groups coming to China shall submit their application to the Chinese Mountaineering Association (CMA). After an application has been approved, the visiting group and the CMA shall enter into negotiations and conclude a protocol, whereupon a permit for mountaineering tourism shall be issued by the CMA.

2. The visiting mountaineering or tourist group shall, within the time limit set in the protocol, send to the CMA a mountaineering or touring registration fee as well as its members' photos, biographical notes, passport numbers and names of places where their visas are issued.

3. The peaks to be climbed, the routes to be taken, the number of climbers, the date of entry into China and the time of commencement of the climb shall not be altered at will. Any alteration shall be made known to the CMA before the date as specified in the protocol and become valid after confirmation by the CMA.

4. In case it is necessary to conduct on-the-spot reconnaissance or scientific investigation along the route of the projected climb prior to the actual expedition, a plan shall be submitted in advance for examination and approval by the CMA. The specific provisions for scientific investigation are explained in detail on pp. 235 -234

5. The CMA may, when it deems it necessary, disqualify a mountaineering or tourist group or its member or members from expedition in China.
6. The CMA has the right to allow more than one mountaineering group to climb the same peak along different routes in the same season. If two mountaineering groups intend to climb the same peak along the same route in the same season, they shall enter into negotiation and reach an agreement between themselves before bringing up the matter to the CMA for approval.
7. Mountaineering or tourist groups visiting China shall make all the payments as stipulated in the *Provisions on the Collection of Charges from Foreign Mountaineering or Tourist Groups in China.*

Entry and Exit of Supplies and Equipment
1. All the supplies and equipment to be used by a mountaineering or tourist group visiting China shall be shipped to China within the time limit and to the destination as agreed upon in the protocol. A list of the categories, amount, weight, unit price and total price of the equipment and supplies to be brought to China, and another list of the type, power and number of the walkie-talkies to be brought to China with the permission of the CMA, shall be sent to the CMA one month before their arrival in China.
2. Before the exit of the supplies and equipment from China at the conclusion of the mountaineering expedition or tour, the mountaineering or tourist group shall submit to the CMA and the Chinese customs a list of the categories and amount of supplies and equipment consumed or lost in China. The list shall be checked and signed by a liaison officer of the CMA. The mountaineering or tourist group shall pay duties in accordance with the regulations of the Chinese customs if the supplies and equipment are to be made over or sold to a third party or individual.
3. A detailed list of the categories and amount of the equipment, fuel and food a visiting mountaineering or tourist group wants the CMA to purchase in China on its behalf shall be sent to the CMA within the time limit as agreed upon in the protocol.

Provision on Chinese Service Personnel
1. The liaison officer is a CMA representative working with the visiting mountaineering or touring group. All foreign mountaineering or tourist groups admitted to China shall

be accompanied by liaison officers on the way to and back from the mountains. The duties of the liaison officer are:

(a) to assist the visiting mountaineering or tourist group in solving problems related to its expedition;

(b) to supervise the fulfilment of the provisions incumbent on the visiting mountaineering or tourist group;

(c) to make reports to the CMA; and

(d) to arbitrate disputes between the visiting mountaineering or tourist group and the Chinese service personnel.

2. Maximum load (including equipment, food and fuel for personal use) allowed for each high altitude assistant climber is:

5,001 - 6,000 m.	20 kgs.
6,001 - 7,000 m.	17 kgs.
7,001 - 7,500 m.	14 kgs.

3. Usually no high altitude assistant climbers are available for climbing peaks below 8,000 m.

4. Maximum load (including equipment, food and fuel for personal use) allowed for each low-altitude (5,000 m. and under) local porter is 25 kgs.

5. The maximum loads allowed for draft animals of various kinds shall be determined by the altitude and topographical conditions of the peak to be climbed.

6. The distance to be covered in a march by the high altitude assistant climbers, low-altitude local porters and draft animals of various kinds shall be arranged properly so that they can have sufficient rest.

7. Apart from being prepared at all times to provide the Chinese personnel with oxygen in case of emergency when climbing at an altitude of 8,000 m. and above, the visiting mountaineering group shall ensure the supply of oxygen to the Chinese high-altitude assistant climbers for use at night at an altitude of 7,500 m. and above.

8. The mountaineering equipment and outfits needed by the liaison officers and other Chinese service personnel shall be lent or provided gratis by the visiting mountaineering or tourist group as stipulated by the CMA (see pp.235-237) These outfits and equipment shall be checked by a liaison officer before they are allowed to be brought into the mountains. Any donations the visiting group wishes to make shall be handled by the CMA.

9. The visiting mountaineering group shall include physician or other members with clinical experience who shall give the Chinese service personnel physical check-ups before the climb and free medical treatment in case of injury or

illness during the climb. Subsidies to those Chinese service personnel who have fallen ill or sustained injuries shall not be suspended, nor shall any of these personnel be dismissed, without the agreement of the liaison officer.

Other Matters

1. The visiting mountaineering or tourist group shall observe the laws and decrees promulgated by the Chinese government as well as regulations on the protection of cultural relics, animal and plant resources.
2. The visiting mountaineering or tourist group is requested to name an organization in its own country which is responsible for the group's affairs, and to name a representative in Beijing who shall be responsible for contacting the CMA.
3. All correspondence with the CMA shall be written in Chinese or English.
4. The names and heights of mountain peaks publicized by China shall be regarded as official.
5. All news or press interviews to be published during the stay of the visiting group in China shall be made known to the CMA in advance. News about the results of the climb shall be issued by the CMA. The CMA shall be promptly informed of any accident occurring during the climb, and may release news about them as circumstances require.
6. Should the national flag of the country to which the visiting group belongs be displayed during the climb or on the top of the peak, the national flag of the People's Republic of China of similar make shall be displayed at the same time. No mementos of any kind shall be placed along the route of the climb or on the top of the peak.
7. No transceivers, arms or amunition shall be allowed into Chinese territory.
8. Nothing detrimental to the relations between China and her neighbouring countries shall be done when the foreign visitors move round a peak on the border.
9. Social morality as well as the national customs and culture of the local people shall be respected.
10. Mountain areas shall be kept clean. All the refuse and other waste material left in the base camp and in camps at different altitudes as well as along the march shall be cleared away or buried.
11. Copies of all the photos, films and video tapes on mountaineering or tourist activities in China shall be supplied to CMA free of charge.
12. Two copies of each publication of the mountaineering or

226

tourist activities in China shall be supplied to the CMA free of charge.
13. At the end of the climb a verbal or written report on it shall be made to the CMA. This shall be followed by formal written report to be submitted to the CMA within one year.
At the end of the climb the visiting group and its members shall each receive a certificate from the CMA. Any visiting mountaineering or tourist group violating the above regulations are liable to be fined or disqualified for mountaineering or tourist activities in China for a number of years, or as the CMA see fit. The CMA is vested with the right to interpret and revise these regulations.

Registration fees: Special registration fees of 15,000 yuan shall be charged for the first ascents of the following virgin peaks above 7,500 m. by foreign mountaineering groups:

Mt Zhangzi (7,538 m.).

Mt Molamenqing (7,703 m.).

Mt Kongur (7,719 m.).

A special registration fee of 10,000 yuan shall be charged for the first ascent of any of the following isolated peaks or the highest peak in a mountain area:

Mt Kangpengqin (7,281 m.).

Mt Xifeng (7,070 m.).

The highest peak of Mt Siguniang (6,250 m.).

Mt Zhongshan (6,886 m.).

Mt Jiazi (6,540 m.).

The highest peak of Mt Bogda (5,445 m.).

The special registration fee for climbing any nameless peak in Anyemaqen, Bogda and Siguniang mountain areas shall amount to double the ordinary registration fee.

(1) Anyemaqen mountain area, Qinghai.

No 2 Peak (6,268 m.).

No 3 Peak (6,090 m.).

No 4 Peak (6,070 m.).

No 5 Peak (5,966 m.).

No 6 Peak (5,869 m.).

No 7 Peak (5,722 m.).

No 8 Peak (5,722 m.).

No 9 Peak (5,611 m.).

(2) Bogda mountain area, Xinjiang.

No 2 Peak (5,362 m.).

No 3 Peak (5,288 m.).

No 4 Peak (5,287 m.).

No 5 Peak (5,213 m.).

No 6 Peak (5,180 m.).

No 7 Peak (5,149 m.).

No 8 Peak (4,613 m.).
(3)   Siguniang mountain area, Sichuan.
No 2 Peak (5,664 m.).
No 3 Peak (5,454 m.).
No 4 Peak (5,386 m.).
Those paying the special registration fee shall be exempted from the ordinary registration fee.

Collection of Charges: There are several provisions on the collection of charges from foreign mountaineering or tourist groups in China.
1. Foreign mountaineering or tourist groups visiting China shall cover all their own expenses in this country.
2. The expense budget of the visiting mountaineering or tourist group is subject to examination and approval by the Chinese Mountaineering Association (CMA).
3. After being given permission to come to China, the visiting mountaineering or tourist group shall pay a registration fee to the CMA within the time limit fixed in the protocol. Failure to do so shall be considered an automatic withdrawal of the application for visiting China. In the case of a foreign mountaineering or tourist group failing to come to China for reasons of its own after the signing of the protocol, it shall be charged a registration fee provided it notifies the CMA of the matter within the time limit set in the protocol, but shall be fined an equivalent of over one-fifth of its expense budget provided it notifies the CMA after the aforesaid time limit. However, it shall be exempt from such a fine provided it can recommend another group to come to China in its place with the permission of the CMA.
4. The visiting mountaineering or tourist group shall remit to the Banking Department, Head Office, Bank of China (Beijing), to the credit of the account of CMA, one-fifth of its expense budget within the time limit set in the protocol and the remaining four-fifths before entering the mountain. The CMA will balance accounts with the visiting group at the end of its visit.
    A photocopy of the money order shall be sent to the CMA for future reference. Any debts owed by a visiting mountaineering or tourist group shall be cleared with interest within the fixed time.
5. Registration fees for various destinations:
    Mt Qomolangma   4,000 yuan (for each group).
    Peaks of 8,000 m. and above 3,200 yuan (for each group).
    Peaks of 7,000 m. and above 2,400 yuan (for each group).

Peaks of 6,000 m. and above 1,600 yuan (for each group). The above rates apply to groups each with a maximum of 20 members. For larger groups each extra member shall be charged a registration fee of 80 yuan.

For peaks below 6,000 m. each climber or tourist shall be charged 80 yuan. A special registration fee shall be charged for the first ascent of any virgin peak newly opened in China.

6. Subsidies rates (in yuan per person per day)

	Mountaineering	Touring
Liaison officer	32	26
Interpreter	32	26
High altitude assistant	29	—
Service personnel in camp	26	23
Low altitude porter	16	16
Driver of yak, horse or camel	16	16

7. Travelling fees needed by Chinese personnel for coming to join the expedition or tour and returning home after its conclusion (in yuan per person):

High altitude assistant	40
Service personnel in camp	40
Low-altitude porter	20
Yak driver	20
Horse driver	20
Camel driver	20

The above-mentioned Chinese personnel shall report their arrival within the time limit fixed in the protocol.

8. Those who stay in expensive hotels or special-grade rooms in such cities as Beijing, Guangzhou and Shanghai shall be charged additional fees for accommodation. Those living in their own camps around Lhasa with the permission of the local government in Tibet shall be charged an overall amount of 50 yuan per person per day for the issuance of permits and for sanitation, sightseeing tickets, visa arrangement and booking of air tickets for leaving Tibet. Those who have paid the expenses for food, lodging and intra-city commuting will be exempt from additional charges for such services as the booking of air tickets, visa arrangement and transportation between the lodging place and the airport (provided the luggage to be transported does not exceed 20 kgs. in weight) For the transportation of the excess luggage and goods (including the hiring of vehicles, transporting and safekeeping up to three days), a service fee amounting to 10 per cent of the transportation cost shall be charged.

For sight-seeing tours to outer suburbs, vehicles shall be

FOOD, LODGING AND INTRA-CITY COMMUTING EXPENSES
(IN YUAN PER PERSON PER DAY FOR DIFFERENT GROUPS)

	Single person	Group of 2-14	Group of 15 and more	Economy class	
Beijing	130	90	65	50	including intra-city commuting
Shanghai	"	"	"	"	"
Guangzhou	"	"	"	"	"
Chengdu	"	"	"	"	"
Xining	"	"	"	"	"
Urumqi	"	"	"	"	"
Kashi	"	"	"	"	"
Lhasa	280	240	210	180	excluding intra-city commuting
Xigaze	150	120	100	90	"
Xegar	90	60	50	45	"
Yaan	"	"	"	"	"
Kangding	"	"	"	"	"
Luding	"	"	"	"	"
Baoan	"	"	"	"	"
Yulin	"	"	"	"	"
Tianchi	"	"	"	"	"
Kuerle	"	"	"	"	"
Akesu	"	"	"	"	"
Kuche	"	"	"	"	"
Dawu	"	"	"	"	"
Qiabuqia	"	"	"	"	"
Rilong	"	"	"	"	"
Wenquan	"	"	"	"	"

hired at local rates.

Foreign visitors shall cover their own expenses for laundry, medical care, post and communications service, beverage, etc., as well as for hiring vehicles not provided by the CMA.

For things left in safekeeping, a service fee shall be charged at 1 fen per kg. per day within a month and at half this rate for the days exceeding one month.

Those who cover their own food and lodging expenses and fares in Beijing shall be charged 20 yuan per person per day for such services as the organization of talks, the supply of interpreters and the arrangement of visas.

9 Food expenses (per person per day) in the mountains:

Liaison officers, interpreters, administrative personnel, and high altitude assistants: 22 yuan.

Service personnel in camp: 17 yuan.

Drivers of yaks, horses or camels and porters working at altitudes below 5,000 m.: 5 yuan.

Drivers and porters working at altitudes above 5,000 m.: 17 yuan.

The CMA shall supply food (and also cooking utensils and fuel) to the Chinese personnel at the above rates. The visiting mountaineering or tourist group shall supply cooking tents, gasoline stoves and pressure cookers for use in the base camp and shall cover the expenses for the transportation of food, cooking utensils and fuel.

10. Transport fees:

Vehicle type (yuan/kms.).	Tibet and Sichuan	Xinjiang, Qinghai (yuan/day) (yuan/kms.)	Parking fee
First-class jeep (5-seat)	2.50	2.20	64
Second-class jeep (7-seat)	2.40	1.92	64
Third-class jeep (4-seat)	2.20	1.76	64
First-class minibus	5.50	4.40	180
Second-class minibus	4.40	3.20	120
Truck	4.80	3.36	160
First-class coach	7.00	5.60	200
Second-class coach	6.40	5.12	200

(Transport fee for trucks running on the Qinghai-Tibet line is 3.36 yuan per kms. Capacity of each truck running on this line and in Tibet is 2.5-3 tons and that in other areas is 3-3.5 tons. Volume of each truck is 11 cubic m.)

For empty vehicles on return trips, transport fees shall be charged at half the above rates. Transport fees for vehicles on duty in the base camp shall be charged according to mileage. No parking fee shall be charged, but the foreign mountaineering or tourist group shall provide the driver with subsidies and pay his food expenses and insurance fee, and shall lend him or provide him with necessary work-clothes. The road-maintenance fee for motor vehicles running on the highway between Xegar or Tingri and Rongbu Temple is 2,000 yuan for each truck and 500 yuan for each jeep. No more than 10,000 yuan shall be charged for each trip made by a visiting group.

11. Fees for hiring yaks, horses and camels: Yaks and horses can be hired at 32 yuan and camels at 40 yuan per head per day. For yaks working at altitudes above 5,000 m. the rate is 40 yuan per head per day. After the arrival of a hired animal, payment shall be charged for it at half the above rates pending its actual employment.

    Upon the arrival of a hired animal, a journey fee equivalent to one day's hire shall be charged. The same amount shall be charged upon its departure. The death of a hired animal shall be compensated for according to local regulations.

12. Insurance against deaths and injuries and medical expenses: The visiting mountaineering or tourist group shall insure with the People's Insurance Company of China against deaths and injuries and medical expenses for the liaison officer and other Chinese service personnel. The insurance against deaths and injuries shall be 25,000 yuan for each liaison officer or service personnel, and 15,000 yuan for each low-altitude porter or yak, horse or camel driver. The medical expenses for all the above-mentioned personnel shall be 5,000 yuan per head.

    The premium rate varies with altitude and service:

Altitude and service	Insurance time	Premium rate for insurance against deaths and injuries (per cent)	Premium rate for medical insurance (per cent)
6,000 m. and above	3 months	2	1
Below 6,000 m.	3 months	1	1
Porters and draft animal drivers	3 months	1	1
Touring	2 months	0.6	1

In case no insurance against personal accidents and medical expenses has been arranged for some reason or other, Chinese liaison officers and service personnel who lose their lives or are injured, disabled or taken ill during expeditions or tours shall be compensated by the visiting mountaineering or tourist group with sums otherwise insured. The CMA undertakes to arrange insurances for the visiting mountaineering or tourist group.

13. Among the supplies and equipment which the visiting mountaineering or tourist group must bring to China, those which have to be handled with special care (e.g., cine-cameras, cameras, wrist watches, communications apparatus, mountaineering equipment and clothes) shall, for the time being, be duty-free and let in after registration, while in the case of those for consumption (e.g., fuel, food, films and medicine) the Customs Administration of the People's Republic of China shall charge the visiting mountaineering or tourist group import duties amounting to 10 per cent of their total worth.

14. The costs for post and telecommunications facilities, food, fuel and mountaineering equipment that need to be arranged by the CMA for the visitors shall be determined through negotiation between both parties.

15. The expenses incurred by the visiting mountaineering or tourist group and the Chinese liaison officer and other service personnel working with it in travelling by air or rail in China shall be charged as stipulated by the departments concerned.

16. The visiting mountaineering or tourist group shall pay the CMA a photographing fee for taking cinema films and making video-tapes during its journey into the mountains or in the course of its expedition. When these films or video tapes are sold or are shown in a third country, the CMA shall take 10 per cent of the total selling price or of the total fees collected from the showing of films or tapes. The photographing fee shall be paid at the following rates (in yuan):

Qomolangma	25,000
Xixabangma	20,000
Kongur	17,000
Molamenqing	17,000
Zhangzi	15,000
Kongur Tiubie	15,000
West Peak of Mt Xixabangma	10,000
Anyemaqen	10,000
Siguniang	7,000
Jiazi	7,000
Sister peak of Mt Siguniang	5,000
Gongga	15,000

Muztagata	15,000
Kangpengqin	10,000
Bogda	7,000
Zhongshan	7,000
Sister peak of Bogda	5,000
Sister peak of Anyemaqen	5,000

17. The CMA undertakes to arrange the activities of foreign mountaineering or tourist groups in China. It shall charge an overall service fee equivalent to 5 per cent of the visiting group's total expenditure in China.

18. The "yuan" as referred to in these provisions is the monetary unit to the Chinese *Renminbi*.

Scientific survey: The following are some of the regulations concerning scientific surveys by foreigners in their mountaineering expeditions or tours in China:

1. Without the permission of the Chinese Mountaineering Association (CMA), no mountaineering or tourist groups or individuals from abroad shall make systematic observation or collect specimens of the living things (including animals, plants, insects and micro-organisms), paleoorganisms, rocks, minerals, ice and snow lying in their way.

2. The following rules shall be observed regarding the specimens and samples collected by foreign mountaineering or tourist groups or individuals with the permission of the CMA:

The CMA shall be supplied with a list of the collected specimens and samples, which states clearly the names of the collectors, locations of the collection and their altitudes, and the quantities and serial numbers of the specimens and samples as well as the results of their field identification.

Any new or special categories discovered among the collected specimens and samples shall be reported to the CMA. These shall be studied, and the results of the studies published, jointly with the Chinese scientific research units concerned.

All the original model specimens of the new or special categories collected shall be sent back to China, so that the CMA can forward them to related scientific research units for preservation, while the other model specimens may be allocated through consultation.

Two sets of analytical duplicates of the collected specimens and samples (animals, plants, rocks, minerals, ice, snow, paleoorganisms, water samples, etc.) shall be given to the CMA gratis after their indoor analyses are completed.

3. A copy of each film, telefilm or photograph related to the

.scientific survey shall be given to the CMA gratis.
4. No books, periodicals or articles on the scientific survey shall be published without the permission of the CMA.
5. All matters relevant to scientific surveys conducted on virgin peaks in China with the consent of the CMA shall-be discussed separately.
6. The liaison officers appointed by the CMA to work with the foreign mountaineering or tourist groups are authorized to supervise the execution of these regulations.
7. In the event of violation of the aforesaid regulations, all the specimens, samples and data shall be confiscated. Serious cases may result in disqualification of the violator(s) from mountaineering or touring in China.

Outfits: Regulations on the provision of outfits by foreign mountaineering or tourist groups to Chinese personnel are:
1. High-altitude assistant climbers—outfits to be lent to each person:
   an eiderdown sleeping bag
   a suit of eiderdown clothes
   an ice axe
   a pair of crampons
   a karabiner
   a safety belt
   a damp-proof mattress
   a tent (for collective use)
   Outfits to be provided gratis to each person:
   a suit of nylon wind-proof clothes
   a pair of trousers
   a suit of woollen sweater and pants
   a suit of sports jacket and pants
   a woollen cap
   a pair of climbing shoes
   a pair of cold-proof boots
   a pair of gaiters
   two pairs of woollen socks
   two pairs of cotton socks
   a pair of cold-proof gloves
   a pair of woollen gloves
   a pair of sunglasses
   a pair of snow glasses
   a water bottle
   a flashlight
   a rucksack or its rack
   a duffle bag
   Note: A raincoat should be lent to each person climbing in rainy seasons.

2. Liaison officers and base camp personnel — outfits to be lent to each person:

  an eiderdown sleeping bag
  a suit of eiderdown clothes
  a damp-proof mattress
  a tent (for collective use)
  Outfits to be provided gratis to each person:
  a nylon wind-proof jacket
  a pair of trousers
  a suit of woollen sweater and pants
  a suit of sports jacket and pants
  a cap
  a pair of climbing shoes
  two pairs of socks
  a pair of gloves
  a pair of sunglasses
  a water bottle
  a rucksack or a duffle bag
  a flashlight
  Note: (a) The amount of outfits needed by liaison
              officers and base camp personnel working at
              altitudes above the base camp shall be decided
              by both sides through negotiation.
         (b) Shoes should be cold-proof when climbing in
              winter.
         (c) In rainy seasons, a raincoat should be lent to
              each person in addition.

3. Liaison officers and Chinese service personnel working with a tourist group — outfits to be lent to each person:
  a sleeping bag
  a suit of cold-proof clothes
  a damp-proof mattress
  a tent (for collective use)
  Outfits to be provided gratis to each person:
  a hood
  a pair of climbing shoes
  a pair of socks
  a pair of gloves
  a pair of sunglasses
  a rucksack
  a stick

  Note: (a) On winter tours shoes must be cold-proof.
         (b) In rainy seasons, a raincoat should be lent to
              each person in addition.

236

(c) For tours lasting less than three days in the mountains only a sleeping bag, a suit of cold-proof clothes, a damp-proof mattress and a tent for collective use shall be lent to the Chinese personnel.

4. Low altitude porters and drivers of yaks, horses and camels — outfits to be lent to each person:

a sleeping bag

a tent for collective use

Outfits to be provided gratis to each person:

a pair of cold-proof shoes

a pair of socks

a pair of gloves

Note: If the porters or draft animal drivers work at altitudes above the snowline, or if they join an expedition or tour in winter, they shall each be lent a suit of eiderdown clothes and be supplied gratis with a pair of down gloves and a pair of sunglasses in addition.

Afghanistan

The Country and the People

Bordering Russia, China, Pakistan and Iran the Democratic Republic of Afghanistan is a developing nation in south-western Asia. It is a land of great mountains, scorching deserts, fertile valleys and rolling plains.

Afghanistan is amongst the poorest nations in the world, and about three-fourths of its people are farmers, using old-fashioned methods and tools. Nomads make up about a sixth of the population. They roam the grasslands with their herds of livestock.

The mountain valleys of eastern Afghanistan and the grasslands of north-western Afghanistan are the main areas of habitation. Kabul, the capital and largest city, lies in the eastern part of the country.

The entire population of about seventeen million people is Muslim and Islam binds them together. They consist of 20 ethnic groups and several tribes, each group having a distinct language and culture — which has been found to hinder the country from developing into a unified state.

Afghanistan has disturbed history. There have been invasions by Persians, Greeks, Arabs and Mongols. The country has faced bitter struggles for power within — from revolts to political assassinations. At present the highest organ of state power is the Revolutionary Council, which controls all state and government activities.

The largest ethnic groups in the country are the Pushtuns (or Pathans) and Tajiks. Together they make up about 70 per cent of the population. Most Pushtuns live in the south-eastern part near the border with Pakistan. They are the most powerful group in the country and hold vital positions in the government. Their language is Pashto. The majority of Tajiks live in central and western Afghanistan. Many of them live in the cities and towns and are merchants or craftworkers. They speak Dari, which, along with Pushto, is the official language.

The majority of Afghans live in the rural areas. People live in homes made of stone or sun-dried mud bricks. Most of the nomads live in dome-shaped felt tents.

The Afghans serve flat loaves of bread at every meal. They

also enjoy mutton and rice. Popular desserts include cheese, nuts and fresh or dried fruit. Tea is their favourite drink.

Afghans enjoy rugged sports and games. Almost all men hunt, and many of them use the famous Afghan hounds as hunting dogs. Men of the northern plains play *buzkashi*. In this game, hundreds of horsemen try to grab a dead calf and carry it across a goal.

About two-thirds of Afghanistan consists of the towering Hindu Kush range with peaks rising over 25,000 ft. (7,620 m.) along the Pakistan border. Most Afghans live in the high, narrow valleys of the Hindu Kush.

Afghanistan's most famous transportation route is the Khyber Pass, near the Afghanistan-Pakistan border, which has been an important trade route for centuries.

Kabul: Kabul, the capital, is a fast-growing city where modern buildings are springing up, besides bazaars, which have not changed since the city was founded. It lies within a ring of mountains sparkling with white snow in the winter sun, emerald green in the spring, and scorched to a greyish brown in summer.

The rugged mountain ridges crowded by old strongholds and fortification reach down to the city, through which the Kabul River flows. Founded by Babur, Kabul was beautified by architects from as far away as Buchara.

Weather: Afghanistan is a country of contrasts. Winters are cold, wet and muddy and summers are hot, dry and dusty. Even day and night temperatures vary greatly. At noon there is oppressive heat but after sunset it is cold and at night there is often frost. The magnificent mountain regions, the scenic beauty of green valleys, wild streams, willows and poplars alternate with desert, dust, wasteland and stifling winds.

Hindu Kush: Situated in the central highlands of Aghanistan the Hindu Kush were called the Caucasus by historians during the time of Alexander the Great. The name Kush, which means death was probably given to the mountains because of their dangerous passes. The mountains are a westward continuation of the Pamirs.

For 500 miles (800 kms.) the Hindu Kush form a great watershed, or water divide, between the Indus and Amu Darya Rivers. They are part of the boundary between eastern Afghanistan and north-western Pakistan. The highest peak in the range is Tirich Mir (25,230 ft. or 7,690 m.).

Trekking and Climbing in Afghanistan

The formidable Hindu Kush mountains, and the vast expanse of the Turkestan plains have preserved Afghanistan's raw, natural beauty. There are vast trekking areas in the country. The numerous trails take people to the remotest rural areas.

Some of the usual trekking trails in Afghanistan have been:

(a)   Bamiyan to Savghan to Bande Amir
(b)   Bamiyan to Ajar Valley to Bande Amir
(c)   Panjsher to Mirsamir to Panjsher
(d)   Panjsher to Anjoman to Jurm
(e)   Pansher to Anjoman to Zebak

Most of these areas lie in the west and north of Kabul. Afghanistan is hard country. The mountains of the Hindu Kush are mostly very arid and cultivation only occurs where snow-fed streams irrigate little fields that cling to the edges of the valleys. By these fields are found small settlements of farmers. Their main crops are barley, peas and mulberries, in addition to goats and sheep which are kept on the high scrub up to 4,500 m.

Trekking is therefore hard. There are no shops and rarely any food to be bought or exchanged. The riches of the country are the dignified hospitality of the people, and the precious stones which lie around to be picked out by a quick eye.

One ambitious trek is the 14-day Badak-Shan one crossing Hindu Kush from north-east and south-west, which allows the traveller to get a feel of many parts of the country. This trek is only one of many which can be made.

The local tourist organisations offer support and assistance in getting permits to various areas, and they also provide guides and porters as well as pack animals.

For mountaineers the Hindu Kush range has more than 200 peaks which exceed 6,000 m. The highest mountains of the Hindu Kush are Tirich Mir, Noshaq, Istor-o-Nal and Saraghrar. Close to the Hindu Kush there is the well-known Pamir plateau and the Wakhan corridor. The weather conditions in Afghanistan are comparatively more favourable than those in other parts of the Himalayas.

Prior to 1945 there was little climbing activity in Afghanistan. It was only in the sixties that mountaineering expeditions in greater numbers turned their attention towards the Hindu Kush. The first climb was on Istor-o-Nal by a Spanish party in 1969.

One of the better known points is the Koh-e-Baba Range, on which the highest peak, Shah Fuladi (5,135 m.) was attempted in 1971 by a two-man Japanese team.

Also worthy of note is the Jurm Valley which is bounded with major features on three sides: the Pegish Valley in the east, Urgunt-e-Bala in the west and the Kotgaz Glacier in the south. This was first visited by an Italian expedition in 1972. Though a small deserted valley, it changes character dramatically at about 3,000 m., when Kohe Staza and Kohe Urgunt (7,028 m.) come into view.

The mountains of northern Afghanistan, situated north of the Ishkashim-Zebak depression and next to the Wardudj-Kokcha

Valley, belong from the geological and geomorphological points of view to the Pamir, with which they were formed. Geographically they are separated from the Pamirs by the narrow valley of the Ab-e-Panja or Oxus, which here forms the frontier between Afghanistan and the USSR.

The mountains of Badak-Shan in this big bend of Ab-e-Panja do not form distinct chains; there is rather a complex tangle of mountain knots crossed by deep valleys of rivers and streams, often difficult to cross. The most outstanding one of them is the valley of Darya-i-Snewa, over a hundred distinctly separate regions. First lies the region of the western upland at an average height of about 3,000 m. ASL, devoid of a real alpine character; in this region the higher Darya-i-Shewa dale can also be included, forming practically a separate geomorphological unit. The second is the region of the mountains of Safed Khers (South) and of the Afghan Darwaz (north). The third is the region of the Shewa mountains and the fourth the region of the Lal (Wal) mountains. The last three regions have a distinctly alpine character and cover, in all, about 1,200 sq. kms. In this area, which is equal to roughly one-twentieth of the area of the Alps, rise several hundred peaks over 4,000 m. in altitude, and among them more than 200 peaks over 4,500 m. and more than 20 peaks over 5,000 m.

Both from the alpinistic and scientific points of view this region is almost completely virgin. Only in the surroundings of Lake Shewa (Shignon) have some small scientific expeditions, mostly geographical and geological ones, operated — the Italians in 1937 and 1951, the French in 1959, the Swedish geologist K. Lindberg in 1959 and 1960 and the Japanese in 1960 and 1972. In 1970 a five-member Polish expedition from Warsaw arrived in the region of Lake Shewa and its members climbed six 4,000 m. peaks here.

You can fly from Faizabad by the local airline to the airfield of Bawaz (about 1,650 m.). From there you have to take donkeys from the village of Radoj and proceed along the Gaway Darrah, Kaj Darrah and Rast Damoh Rivers. In 1975 a Polish expedition climbed 15 peaks, among them five over 5,000 m. and eight over 4,500 m. They crossed five large passes and several minor ones.

Badak-Shan Trek

1st Day:	Faizabad to Jurm
	Barak Road, moving east to Ishkashim and Wakhan.
2nd Day:	Jurm to Hazrat-E-Said
	This distance will have to be covered by truck.
3rd Day:	Robat Ebala
	Arrange donkeys at Hazrat-E-Said. Move on through the

241

BADAK-SHAN TREK

REFERENCES

Motorable Roads	——————
Trekking Route	– – – – –
Town	○
Pass	⊥
Peak	🏔

Faizabad

To Ishkashim →

Barak

Jurm
16 km

Hazrat-E-Said
60 km

Robat E Bala
90 km

5880 m

5646 m

Sarisang
100 km

5637 m

5841 m

5862 m

Wisti
135 km

Skazer
115 km

4500 m
Anjuman Pass
150 km

To Panjshir Valley

684

4500 m

Shahri Munjan
115 km

To Nuristan

5669 m

6060 m

immense gorge ahead. The Hindu Kush mountains tower directly on the right and left. Spend the night in the deserted village of Robat Ebala.

4th Day: First Lake
Very hot and dry. You will pass Asia's only lapis lazuli mine at mid-day. Souvenir-hunting is discouraged (but the stones here are very fine) Cover 20 kms. to reach camp at First Lake.

5th Day: Second Lake
Road branches to Munjan, from where you have to trek over many passes to reach Nurishtan. Move on towards Kon-e-Bandavar, and reach the small village of Shazer (10 kms. altogether). Camp for the night.

6th Day: Wisti
Continue up Anjuman River, in semi-desert hills to Wisti (20 kms. altogether).

7th Day: Towards Anjuman Pass
Past last village settlements and Aylaqs. Past camps of nomadic Kuchis. Camp by out-filled lakes below Anjuman Pass (4,500 m.).

8th to You can climb local peaks around Anjuman Pass.
9th Days: Koh-e-Separ (5,260 m.), explore the approach to the north-east ridge. Mirsamir (6,060 m.) can be reached from Point, 5,669 m.

10th Day: Anjuman Pass
This is rest day.

11th Day: Across Anjuman Pass
A well-used pass, it shows much evidence of nomadic crossings. (Takes 15 kms. altogether.)

12th Day: Parian
Continue down Panjsher Valley to Parian. From here starts the direct route to Mirsamir. (Takes 15 kms. altogether.)

13th Day: Parian to Dasht-e-Rewat
The track passes through narrow gorges and frequently crosses the ice-cold Panjsher River. It is extremely hot at mid-day, semi-desert hills with intervals of green stream-fed fields.

14th Day: Kabul
Take a truck or bus back to Kabul.

Frontier Restrictions

As this publication goes to press, the Government of India has declared Nanda Devi Sanctuary in India a National Park and banned all entry into it until further orders. The Valley of Flowers has also been declared a National Park and entry into it will now been regulated. As restrictions on the entry of foreigners into the frontier areas in the Himalayan states undergo change from time to time it is desirable that the latest situation from the Missions of concerned countries in your area be ascertained before concrete travel arrangements are made.